John Bull and the Bear

John Bull and the Bear

British Public Opinion, Foreign
Policy and the Soviet Union
1941–1945

P.M.H. Bell

Edward Arnold
A division of Hodder & Stoughton
LONDON NEW YORK MELBOURNE AUCKLAND

© 1990 P. M. H. Bell

First published in Great Britain 1990

Distributed in the USA by Routledge, Chapman and Hall, Inc.
29 West 35th Street, New York, NY 10001

British Library Cataloguing in Publication Data
Bell, P. M. H. (Philip Michael Hett) *1930–*
    John Bull and the Bear: British public opinion, foreign policy and
    the Soviet Union 1941–1945.
    1. Soviet Union. Foreign relations with Great Britain,
    history   2. Great Britain. Foreign relations with Soviet Union,
    history
    I. Title
    327.41047

    ISBN 0–340–53307–2

Typeset in 10/11 pt Symposia by Colset Private Limited, Singapore
Printed and bound in Great Britain for Edward Arnold, a division of
Hodder and Stoughton Limited, Mill Road, Dunton Green,
Sevenoaks, Kent TN13 2YA

Contents

List of Illustrations

Preface and acknowledgements

'Of making many books there is no end', and an author has some duty to explain why he is adding to the existing pile of paper. The main reason for writing this book lies in the double fascination of its subject: first, the general aspect of the links between public opinion and foreign policy, which have concerned both historians and politicians since at least the time of Canning; and second, the particular nature of British relations with the Soviet Union during the Second World War. The first of these issues provides the frame of reference for this study. What is public opinion? How far is it concerned with questions of foreign policy? Are politicians serious when they say that they cannot do this or that because public opinion would not stand for it, or they must do the other because public opinion demands it? These are questions of wide and continuing significance in British political life. The conditions of wartime offer favourable circumstances for their examination, because the evidence is notably extensive in quantity and rich in quality. The second issue supplies the focus without which the enquiry would be dissipated over too vast and ill-defined an area. It also involves matters which have retained their interest over the half-century which has passed since the Second World War: how was the Soviet Union presented to the British people, and what was the reaction of British opinion to the great events on the eastern front? Behind both issues lie deeper questions still, concerning the role and influence of censorship and propaganda, and the capacity of governments to guide or even to mould public opinion.

These preoccupations have determined the shape of the book. The first chapter deals with general questions: the role of public opinion in wartime Britain, the methods of censorship and propaganda which were brought to bear upon it, and how we can define and assess public opinion. Chapters 2 and 3 provide a panoramic view of British public opinion and the Soviet Union, including both government policy on the guidance of opinion and the reactions of opinion itself. Chapters 4 and 5 then narrow the focus by concentrating on two case studies (the revelations about the mass graves at Katyn in 1943, and the Warsaw Rising in 1944) which enable us to follow in detail, and often day by day, the interaction between public opinion and foreign policy, and to examine closely the effects (or lack of them) of censorship and propaganda. Chapter 6 draws the story to an end by looking at the debate on Yalta, and offering some reflections on the study as a whole.

In writing this book I have incurred many obligations, and I am glad to have this opportunity to thank those who have helped in its completion. The Trustees of the Nuffield Foundation provided a generous research grant which enabled me to do the archival research on which the first part of the book is based. The British Academy and the University of Liverpool gave further grants which greatly assisted the work on the case studies. To these various institutions I am most grateful. Like all researchers, I have been much assisted by the staff of the various archives where I have worked. These are listed in the Bibliography, but I would like to make special mention of the BBC Written Archive at Caversham Park, where the keepers provide not so much a service as another pair of eyes for the historian.

My friends David Dutton, John Gooch and Ralph White subjected a draft to scrutiny which was at once keen, tactful and invaluable. Not for the first time, I am greatly in their debt. As always, my greatest debt is to my wife, who has borne with this project for rather a long time, and has done much to advise, to encourage and to sustain.

Department of History,   P. M. H. BELL
University of Liverpool   February 1990

Illustrations

The publishers are grateful to the Cartoon Study Centre, University of Kent at Canterbury for supplying prints of cartoons from its archive and to the following for permission to reproduce illustrations on the pages indicated: The Trustees of the Imperial War Museum, London (pp. 54, 55, 75, 89, 92, 111); Express Newspapers (p. 33); *Punch* (pp. 49, 82); Solo Syndication (pp. 78, 123, 134).

1

Government and Public Opinion in Wartime

In war opinion is nine points in ten.
(Swift)

Swift's aphorism has a fine, resounding ring to it, and its force appeared to be acknowledged by the actions of all the belligerent powers during the Second World War. All possessed Ministries of Information or Propaganda. All sought to stimulate or confirm the will to fight of their own people, while striving with equal zeal to subvert the morale of their opponents. All acknowledged at different times that the war would be total in its character, yet all were conscious of the difficulty of maintaining total effort among their peoples, whose day-to-day preoccupations were the problems of their own lives, not those of the state.

This book is about one aspect of public opinion in wartime: British public opinion and foreign policy in relation to the Soviet Union during the Second World War. This was a subject of burning interest at the time, when the Soviet Union attracted intense admiration for its military efforts and keen speculation (not to say dispute) as to its political and social system. It is a subject which still commands interest, both in itself and because it focuses attention on the nature of British opinion and its interaction with foreign policy, and even sometimes with strategy. But before we come to the main theme of the book, a number of preliminary questions must be examined, for without them no precise discussion can begin.

First, how did the British government envisage public opinion? Why was it thought to be important, and how could it be assessed, controlled and guided? Second, what was this public opinion which was so much talked about: what forms did it take, and did it exist in an independent form or was it merely the subject of manipulation and control? These questions will require explanation of government censorship and propaganda, which are central topics in any study of public opinion in wartime, and also involve a definition of public opinion itself – an elusive, even a slippery concept. They are also questions which tend to generate more assertion than argument, more heat than light. But the material exists for explanation, which may be set out under two main headings: the position of government in relation to public opinion (the view from above); and next a discussion of public opinion itself (the view from below). In both cases, we must look at the broader issues of public opinion in wartime as well as the narrower ones involving foreign policy and the Soviet Union. An outline map is a necessary introduction to the close survey of our central subject.

Government and public opinion

The British government, like others, was convinced that public opinion was of great, and possibly crucial, importance in wartime. From the First World War there had descended a powerful and widely accepted belief that British propaganda contributed substantially to the defeat of Germany in 1918, by sapping civilian morale and undermining confidence in the Hohenzollern regime.[1] The inter-war years reinforced this belief in the power of propaganda. A German campaign of publicity against the alleged injustices of the Versailles peace settlement had made deep inroads into British public sentiment, and weakened the will to sustain the terms imposed on Germany. The three totalitarian regimes of the 1920s and 1930s, Communist Russia, Fascist Italy and Nazi Germany, made constant use of propaganda both at home and abroad, and claimed that it was one of the keys to their success. Even among their opponents, these claims carried conviction. A somewhat reluctant British government began, even in peacetime, to undertake propaganda in foreign countries – though it preferred to use the word 'publicity' to describe its operations.[2] If war were to break out again, it was taken for granted that government would have to conduct propaganda and control information; and in 1935 preparations were begun for the creation of a Ministry of Information in the event of war.[3]

When war began in 1939, these long-standing assumptions were powerfully reinforced by the government's concern with two aspects of the conflict as it affected the British people: administration and morale.

As the war went on, the people of these islands were subjected to a greater degree of administration than ever before in their history. Everyone had an identity card, a ration book and clothing coupons. A black-out was imposed every night. Regulations of many kinds, and sometimes of infinite complexity, controlled (or at any rate sought to control) most aspects of daily life. There was conscription for the armed forces, and direction

---

[1] Campbell Stuart, *Secrets of Crewe House: The Story of a Famous Campaign* (London, 1920) did much to propagate this view. Michael Balfour, *Propaganda in war 1939–1945* (London, 1979), pp. 3–10, demonstrates its weaknesses.

[2] Philip M. Taylor, *The Projection of Britain: British Overseas Publicity and Propaganda, 1919–1939* (Cambridge, 1981). See, e.g., p. 292: '"Propaganda" remained a dirty word which left an unpleasant taste in the mouths of English gentlemen.'

[3] *Ibid.*, pp. 260–92; and Ian McLaine, *Ministry of Morale: Home Front Morale and the Ministry of Information in World War II* (London, 1979), p. 12.

of labour for the civilian workforce. These vast and cumbrous systems of control were manned by a multitude of civil servants, who often lived in hotels in safe seaside resorts and were not much loved. The apparatus was clumsy, and its working was bound to generate friction and discontent. This was recognized by the administrators themselves, who knew that their elaborate arrangements would work better, and in some cases would only work at all, with the co-operation of the people concerned. It was believed, usually correctly, that if people understood what was required of them and why, and if those requirements were seen to be necessary and fair, then most regulations would be accepted. But if administrators fell short on any of these points, there was likely to be trouble. Public opinion, therefore, was vitally important in this heavily administered society; and it was closely linked with questions of morale.

Morale was a difficult concept to define, but it represented something of vital importance. Stephen Taylor, who for much of the war was head of the Home Intelligence Division in the Ministry of Information, held that morale was a state of conduct or behaviour, to be judged by what people did rather than what they said. Good morale was conduct indicating that people were willing to carry on the war and to meet its costs, which were of many kinds. Such conduct, Taylor argued, was mainly affected by material factors – food, warmth, work, rest, sleep, a secure home base and the safety of dependants. There were also mental factors, though these were less important: belief in the necessity and justice of the war, confidence in victory and in the ability of government to achieve it, a sense of fairness in the way that sacrifices were demanded from the population.[4] It was true that the sacrifices being demanded were much smaller in terms of military casualties than in the 1914–18 war; but the government was profoundly conscious that this was the second time round, and the British Army in the Second World War was acutely anxious to keep casualties to a minimum. In any case, the cost was still high, and much of it (in terms of bombing, loss of life and property, rationing and other restrictions, and general disruption) was borne by the civilian population as much as by the armed forces – indeed, in the British Isles there was no great distinction between the two in terms of casualties or discomfort.[5] The price of the war was heavy, and it was quite possible that people would become unwilling to pay it. There was a widespread belief that this was what happened in France in 1940: that division, doubt, apathy and pessimism, with a dash of treachery and Fifth Column activity, had so rotted the foundations of the French state that it was ready to fall over at a push from the German Army. Between the wars, it was the creed of many advocates of air power that civilian morale could be shattered by bombing, so that countries would surrender rather than endure air bombardment for long. At some points during the German attacks on

4 Memorandum by Taylor, 'Home morale and public opinion', 1 Oct. 1941, INF 1/292, Home Intelligence Report 52, Appendix.

5 Michael Howard, 'Total war in the twentieth century: Participation and Consensus in the Second World War', in Brian Bond and Ian Roy, eds., *War and Society: A Yearbook of Military History* (London, 1975), p. 223. Out of a total of some 360,000 British war dead, one in four was a civilian.

British cities during the winter of 1940–41 it seemed that morale might be in danger of breaking under the strain, though in fact it did not do so.[6]

The British government kept an eye on German morale, in so far as it could. In September 1942 the War Cabinet received a paper which held that German civilian morale had been profoundly shaken during the winter of 1941–42. The symptoms which it adduced were: apathy and scepticism about war news; an increase in rumours and a tendency to believe them; a revival of subversive literature; an increased appetite for foreign propaganda; and a revival of religion, indicating a declining faith in Nazi ideology.[7] In some stages of the war, much of this list could have been applied to Britain: what could happen to the enemy could happen at home. The government could not possibly afford to neglect morale on the home front.

These were internal issues. Public opinion was also significant in terms of foreign policy. War represented the irruption of foreign affairs into everyone's life, and meant that public opinion was much more concerned with external events and the doings of overseas countries than would normally be the case. It is doubtless true that a large proportion of the population continued to be preoccupied with their private lives, affected by the war only in so far as it brought air-raids, or a change of job, or the call-up of a member of the family. But despite such natural concerns, most people were also affected by the conflict in its wider aspects, either because events were so dramatic, like the fall of France in 1940 or the battle of Stalingrad in 1942–43, or so pervasive, like the presence in Britain of large numbers of foreign troops. The war brought a heightened consciousness of the world outside these shores, and foreign policy made an unusually direct impact upon public opinion.

The reverse was also true. In the circumstances of war, public opinion impinged to an unusual extent on foreign policy. It made itself felt in a wide variety of ways, sometimes simply by the public discussion of some event or issue in the press, which could rapidly create an international incident, arouse suspicion between governments, or foment ill-will between peoples. Press reporting and comment could also help to improve relations with another state by warm and favourable treatment of its affairs and leaders – as was usually the case in the presentation of Roosevelt and Stalin in the British press during the war. Either way, the aspect of public opinion which was represented by the press's handling of foreign affairs was of constant, and often nervous, concern to the government.

There were other, deeper and more all-pervading ways in which public opinion was seen to impinge upon the whole conduct of foreign policy. In principle the British government recognized that foreign policy and public opinion must be kept in broad alignment, because otherwise foreign policy would lose an essential support. In 1937 Anthony Eden, then Foreign Secretary, told the Imperial Conference that if Britain were to announce her

---

[6] McLaine, chapter 4, 'Air Raids and Morale'; cf. Tom Harrisson, *Living through the Blitz* (London, 1978), sections on Southampton, Plymouth, and Morale Questions.

[7] CAB 66/29, WP(42)432, 26 Sept. 1942, memorandum by Eden, 'Morale in Germany'.

readiness to fight for Czechoslovakia or Austria, this would be to venture 'far beyond where the people of this country were prepared to go. *There could be no greater danger than for the Government to declare themselves in favour of a policy which did not command the general support of public opinion at home'.*[8] This principle was of crucial importance in the context of war: to go to war, to sustain a prolonged struggle, and to secure a firm and satisfactory peace, the government needed the widest possible support from people, press and Parliament. This was the fundamental influence of public opinion on foreign policy.

Such support had to be long-term. This was seen as one of the crucial lessons of recent history. In April 1943 a War Cabinet paper on the future of Germany argued that the peace settlement of 1919 had failed largely because it had rapidly ceased to command public support. When the current war was won, it would be necessary to impose some measure of dismemberment upon Germany (dismemberment, a fiercer word than partition, was the language of the day); but this would have to command the continuing support of British opinion. For this, the ground would need to be carefully prepared, not least in moral terms. 'If the British and American public could accept the fact that dismemberment was in the interest of Germany as well as of the rest of Europe, the moral force would not be lacking to maintain such a settlement.'[9] The same point was made in public discussion. The historian David Thomson argued in September 1944 that a vital element in peace-making was the climate of opinion which prevailed about the settlement. The experience of the inter-war period showed that when public opinion became disenchanted with parts of a peace treaty, even those sections which needed to be upheld were abandoned.[10] At about the same time, R.B. McCallum's widely read and influential book on *Public Opinion and the Last Peace* emphasized the same reasoning about the repudiation of the 1919 settlement by the British public, and the disastrous consequences thereof. The experience appealed to was recent, and the argument weighty. Public opinion had been crucial to the fate of the last peace, and would be so again for the next.

In matters relating to the peace settlement and the fate of Germany, public opinion would have to be guided by government. Otherwise – as had happened in 1918 and 1919 – it would probably take a dangerous course. In June 1942 Eden warned the War Cabinet that public opinion was showing an increasing interest in the question of war criminals and their punishment. The experience of the previous war, he maintained, showed that there was serious danger of public opinion 'getting out of hand' on this matter unless the government gave a firm lead. The Law Officers were instructed to prepare a paper, and the War Cabinet worked out a policy on this difficult and controversial question.[11]

These discussions looked ahead to the peace. While the war was still in

8 Quoted in Corelli Barnett, *The Collapse of British Power* (London, 1972), pp. 465–6. Italics not in the original.
9 CAB 66 35, WP(43)144, 8 April 1943, memorandum by Lord Selborne.
10 David Thomson, 'The Public and Peace', *Spectator*, 22 Sept. 1944, pp. 259–60.
11 CAB 66/25, WP(42)264, 22 June 1942, and CAB 66/29, WP(42)445, 5 Oct. 1942, memoranda by Eden.

progress, public opinion offered more immediate, and sometimes dangerous, possibilities. It could be mobilized to try to force the government's hand, against its better judgement, as in the agitation for a 'Second Front Now' in 1942. Parts of the press, the newsreels and political leaders like Lord Beaverbrook and Sir Stafford Cripps took the lead in this campaign. Ivan Maisky, the Soviet Ambassador in London, exploited the widespread public sympathy and admiration for Soviet resistance against the Germans to stimulate the movement; and in the climate of the time he was sometimes able to appear on-stage and address public meetings in a way not normally open to an ambassador.[12] In the event, the government and Chiefs of Staff followed their own cautious course, and a cross-Channel invasion was postponed until June 1944; but the 'Second Front' agitation and Maisky's role in it bear witness to the use of public opinion to try to influence policy and strategy.

Similarly, but in the opposite direction, the British government considered using public opinion to influence Soviet policy and actions. Clark Kerr, the ambassador in the USSR from 1942 to the end of the war, sometimes argued that Stalin was susceptible to British opinion, and that his policy on Poland might be softened by the threat of public debate and displeasure. Churchill tried to make use of this threat during the Warsaw Rising, when he tried to impress the Soviets with the danger of alienating British public opinion by their refusal to allow help to be sent to the desperate defenders of the Polish capital.[13] Unhappily there is no sign that Stalin was impressed; but in April 1945 Sir Alexander Cadogan, the experienced and highly professional Permanent Under-Secretary at the Foreign Office, was still referring to the possibility of confronting Stalin with a 'showdown' on the Yalta agreements by means of a statement to the House of Commons.[14]

In relations with the United States, the presence in the United Kingdom of large numbers of American troops was bound to affect British public opinion, with potential consequences which the government contemplated with both anxiety and hope. No country can be expected to welcome unreservedly the presence of a vast foreign army, no matter how necessary it may be. The points of friction and friendship between American servicemen and the British people have left long memories, and have been vividly described.[15] In the background lay a colour problem which caused the War Cabinet serious anxiety, lest the British public might offend American susceptibilities by being too friendly towards negro troops.[16] The government was convinced that the long-term future of Anglo-American relations might well be decided by American public opinion, which would itself be

[12] Ivan Maisky, *Memoirs of a Soviet Ambassador: The War, 1939–43* (London, 1967), gives a lively though partial account of its author's activities.

[13] W.S. Churchill, *The Second World War*, vol. VI, *Triumph and Tragedy* (London, 1954), pp. 125–6. See the detailed discussion in Chapter 5, below.

[14] Minute by Cadogan, 4 April 1945, in Graham Ross, ed., *The Foreign Office and the Kremlin* (Cambridge, 1984), p. 203.

[15] Norman Longmate, *The GIs, The Americans in Britain 1942–1945* (London, 1975).

[16] David Reynolds, 'The Churchill Government and the Black American Troops in Britain during World War II', *Transactions of the Royal Historical Society*, 5th series, 35(1985), pp. 113–33.

influenced by the experience of the US Army in Britain. Before the first troops arrived, the Chiefs of Staff gave their formal opinion that: 'Untold harm may result if relations between the American soldiers and the local inhabitants go awry, and they recommended 'carefully designed publicity' to influence the attitude of the public.[17] This advice was followed. The Ministry of Information set up a special division for liaison with the American forces, and undertook a large-scale operation to smooth the path of their relations with the British people.[18] Similarly, though in a wider context, the BBC made a deliberate attempt to promote Anglo-American understanding and so lay a sure foundation for future peace.[19] It is plain that the government believed that public opinion would play a vital role in the development of Anglo-American relations.

The pressure of public opinion was also felt in the whole working of British diplomacy in the Grand Alliance. For much of 1941, 1942 and 1943 the strength of pro-Soviet feeling, especially in the press, was such as to inhibit any public expression of doubt about Soviet policies, intentions or virtues, and any politician who dared to break that taboo found shot and shell flying round his head. There was also strong public pressure to draw the Soviet Union more closely into the process of Anglo-American consultation, and there was public disappointment at Stalin's absence from the conferences at Casablanca and Quebec in January and August 1943. By the time the Foreign Ministers of the three great allies met in Moscow in October 1943, and the 'Big Three' at Teheran in November, the pressure of public expectation was such as to make a convincing show of success a necessity. For Eden and Churchill to come home with any sign of failure would have been seen as a calamity, for which they would probably have been held responsible. The same was true of the Yalta conference in February 1945. Big conferences had to be seen to succeed, and this constant and powerful impulse did much to produce a profound element of make-believe, even among the participants, which influenced negotiations between the great allies.[20] After a summit meeting, neither Churchill nor Roosevelt dared go home and express reservations, and still less failure. In this sense, the conduct of British foreign policy at the highest level was under heavy pressure from public opinion.

The British government therefore had good reason to believe that public opinion was important in the whole conduct of the war, and notably in terms of administration, morale and foreign affairs. In these circumstances, the government had to undertake three tasks: to assess the state of public

17 CAB 66/25, WP(42)257, 16 June 1942.
18 McLaine, pp. 263–5. Bracken, the Minister of Information, stated that this task was imposed upon the Ministry by the government rather than being conceived within the Ministry itself. See also the reports by Regional Information Officers in 1945, INF 1/297, which concentrated heavily on this aspect of their activities – a further indication of their importance.
19 Asa Briggs, *History of Broadcasting in the United Kingdom*, vol. III, *The War of Words* (London, 1970), p. 413.
20 The idea of the importance of make-believe in the summit conferences is taken from Lord Strang, 'Foreign Policy in Wartime', in David Dilks, ed., *Retreat from Power*, vol. II (London, 1981), pp. 66–100.

opinion, to impose negative control over it through censorship, and to exercise positive influence on it through propaganda.

For these purposes there was brought into being, as soon as war was declared, the Ministry of Information.[21] The functions of this body were to control censorship and propaganda, to act as a channel for information between government departments and the press and radio, and to collect intelligence about public opinion and morale. It made a bad start, with a series of ineffective Ministers of Information and almost inextricable confusion about its functions. It was a target for much ridicule (Evelyn Waugh's *Put Out More Flags* included a painfully funny caricature of its early days), and almost as much abuse, especially from the press. Duff Cooper, the third Minister of Information, wrote a plaintive memorandum for the War Cabinet in June 1941, shortly before he left the Ministry:

> Owing to initial mistakes, many of them pre-natal, the Ministry has never enjoyed the full confidence of the public. Once a Department has incurred ridicule it has great difficulty in regaining its status. I do not think that the Ministry has lost ground in the last year, but it has a great deal of ground to make up, and unless it is given the authority which it demands there is danger of it ceasing to be an object of ridicule in order to become only one of pity.[22]

Yet in fact 1941 was the year in which the Ministry of Information turned the corner. In July Duff Cooper resigned, and was replaced by Brendan Bracken, who for the first time made a success of the job, establishing good relations with the press and exploiting his close personal relations with Churchill at appropriate moments. With his new Director-General, Cyril (later Lord) Radcliffe, Bracken set up a stable and effective regime which lasted until the end of the war. For almost the whole of the period covered by this book, the Ministry of Information was a serious and efficient department, with an important job to do.

In order to influence public opinion, it was important to know what that opinion was. During the war, the government had at its disposal several different means of assessing public opinion. For some types of opinion, the normal channels of communication, familiar in peacetime, remained open. Parliament continued to be the focus of much political opinion, through debates, questions, and a host of informal contacts. Pressure groups still operated in the corridors of power. The newspapers were there to be read, and at the head of the government Churchill was an avid reader. In the midst of all his work it remained his custom to see the newspapers twice each day, once about midnight and once over breakfast, when he skimmed expertly through at least nine daily papers.[23] He was on friendly terms with several newspaper owners and editors, and for much of the time the War Cabinet included a notable newspaper-man in Lord Beaverbrook. Churchill was occasionally furious with the *Daily Mirror*, and in January 1945 he attacked

---

[21] McLaine, *Ministry of Morale*, provides an excellent account of the origins and working of the Ministry of Information.

[22] CAB 66/17, WP(41)139, memo. by Duff Cooper, 24 June 1941.

[23] Martin Gilbert, *Finest Hour: Winston S. Churchill 1939–1941* (London, 1983), p. 894.

The Times in the House of Commons over its attitude to British actions in Greece. There was no lack of contact between government and press, mostly friendly, sometimes prickly, occasionally hostile.

These links with political opinion and the press were personal, informal and long established. Means of assessing opinion among the people as a whole were newer and in many ways more systematic. Public opinion polling had begun life in the United States, and the Gallup Poll organization extended its operations to Britain in 1938, as the British Institute of Public Opinion (BIPO). It continued to conduct polls throughout the war, using a quota sampling system with a normal sample of about 2,000 interviews, which was calculated to have a margin of uncertainty within 4 per cent in either direction. Its findings were regularly communicated to the Ministry of Information, and sometimes it undertook special enquiries commissioned by the Ministry. Gallup Poll findings presented some difficulties, both in the reliability of their sampling methods and in the interpretation of their results. There could be glaring errors (soon after the war, the polls' failure to predict correctly the outcome of the Truman-Dewey Presidential election in the United States was a damaging *gaffe*); and since the Second World War the methods of enquiry have been greatly developed and refined. Those who conducted the polls during the war were well aware that they were on much safer ground when dealing with matters of fact (for example, how many people owned a wireless set, or read a newspaper) than on questions involving attitudes or opinions. In 'attitude polling,' the framing of questions could easily affect the responses (through questions which strongly invited a particular answer), or create problems by ambiguous or obscure phrasing. When answers were received to 'attitude' questions, they then had to be forced into categories in order to produce tabulated results. Moreover, those questioned might often give answers simply because they had been asked rather than because they held any firm view on the matter involved. This meant that a poll was a poor indicator of the strength with which an opinion was held, or the depth of feeling on a particular issue. In the early years of polling in this country, such reservations were widely current, and the polls were far from being accorded the interest and respect which they command today. But despite these drawbacks, the Gallup Poll provided quantitative information about the population and its views which was not available in other ways, and the Ministry of Information made considerable use of its services.[24]

The Ministry could also call on the services of the BBC Audience Research Department, which conducted two types of survey. One was the Continuous Survey of Listening, carried out from autumn 1939 onwards to estimate the size of audiences for different programmes, based on a sample of 800

---

[24] A full collection of BIPO results is available at the Gallup Poll offices in London. I am grateful to Gallup Poll for permission to examine this material, and to Mr Robert Wybrow for his help during my visit. Most of the results were published at the time in the *News Chronicle*, and later in Hadley Cantril, ed., *Public Opinion, 1935–1946* (Princeton, 1951). For the size of the sample, see Cantril, p. viii, and Hilton to Waterfield, 6 Oct. 1939, INF 1/261. For an excellent description of various polling methods, see Charles W. Roll and Albert H. Cantril, *Polls: Their Use and Misuse in Politics* (Cabin John, Maryland, 1980), pp. 65–93.

interviews each day, covering the whole population. The continuity of this survey was particularly valuable, producing a reliable record of the audiences for regular programmes like the news or the weekly 'American Commentary'. The second kind of material came from the BBC's Honorary Local Correspondents, who were used to sound opinion about broadcasting matters. These correspondents were in no sense a representative sample of the population as a whole, being self-selected by their keen interest in broadcasting and subject to what was called 'volunteer bias'; but they produced valuable reports on confidence in the news and attitudes towards the USA and the Soviet Union.[25]

Another outside body which was used by the Ministry of Information at the beginning of the war, and whose reports were always made available to it, was Mass-Observation. This organization, set up in 1937 by Tom Harrisson and Charles Madge, has made a powerful impression on later accounts of British life during the war.[26] In October 1939 Richard Crossman, then an official in the Ministry of Information, commented that Mass-Observation's strength lay in its imaginative approach, and its weakness in subjectivity and a tendency to turn a hint into an assertion of fact.[27] This judgement was well-founded. The organization used two small groups of specialists in Bolton and Fulham (disguised as 'Worktown' and 'Metrop' in its publications), and otherwise relied on a body of volunteer observers, making reports and keeping diaries in their spare time. A large proportion of this body was recruited in 1937 by means of an appeal in the *New Statesman*. Mass-Observation's own description in 1948 of its volunteers was as follows: 'a middle-class group, self-selected both in its desire to discuss its personal feelings and its capacity to express them. It is more than usually interested in social problems and inclined to the Left in its political outlook.'[28] The findings of the panel naturally reflected its composition, and should be regarded as more akin to the BBC's volunteer correspondents' reports than to those of Gallup or the Survey of Listening. On the other hand, Mass-Observation prided itself on its qualitative and imaginative approach, which helped it to get through to private opinions, which people might be reluctant to express to a pollster, and also to assess the intensity with which feelings were held. This gave its material a distinctive flavour, enhanced by the fact that many of the wartime reports were written by Tom Harrisson himself, and were marked by his views. The qualities of Mass-Observation probably just about outweighed its defects, and it certainly provided a useful addition to other methods of assessing opinion.[29]

[25] Robert Silvey, *Who's Listening? The Story of BBC Audience Research* (London, 1974) gives a fascinating account of BBC audience research, by the man who devised it. See especially pp. 28–31, 77–100, 103–4, 110–17. The reports themselves are in the BBC Written Archives at Caversham Park, Reading.

[26] See especially Angus Calder, *The People's War: Britain 1939–1945* (London, 1971). In the preface to this second edition of his book the author defends his view that the Mass-Observation papers provide the richest available source for the social history of the period.

[27] INF 1/261, memorandum by Crossman, 26 Oct. 1939.

[28] For the *New Statesman* appeal, which produced 450 observers, Mass-Observation Archive (University of Sussex), FR 2479; the quotation is from FR 3015, July 1948.

[29] Tom Harrisson, 'What is Public Opinion?', *Political Quarterly*, vol. XI, 1940, is a valuable discussion of his views.

As well as using outside bodies, the Ministry of Information developed, from the end of 1939, its own Home Intelligence service. In the crisis of 1940, when the fall of France and the danger of invasion raised an alarm about the state of morale, the Home Intelligence division produced daily reports on public reaction to events, dealing with morale, rumours and the effects of broadcasts by ministers. These reports were hastily improvised, and relied heavily on assessments telephoned by Regional Information Officers, with no means of checking their reliability.[30] At the end of September 1940 daily reports were abandoned in favour of a more careful and systematic weekly Home Intelligence report, the first of which was produced on 9 October, starting a series which continued unbroken until the end of 1944.

Under the guidance of the head of Home Intelligence, Stephen Taylor, the system of preparing these reports was furnished with checks to filter out items for which there was insufficient evidence. The range of sources was wide: Regional Information Officers, with their staffs and contacts; postal censorship reports, which were made on mail going abroad; police reports; and material from outside bodies, including voluntary organizations, the BBC, and the British Institute of Public Opinion. The whole process of compilation was compressed into 48 hours, which precluded collaboration between Regional Officers even if they had wished to attempt it. The Regional reports were checked against one another and against central sources at the Ministry of Information.

These weekly Home Intelligence reports provided a careful and sensitive method of assessing public opinion. They covered the whole country, and their continuity gave them particular authority. It is true that their results could not be expressed statistically, and they made no claim to produce quantitative assessments in the manner of the Gallup Polls; but they were able to register the range, and to a considerable degree the intensity, of views expressed up and down the country. They were invaluable to government departments in picking up information about small but vital matters (for example, the availability of torch batteries). They could also observe public reactions on issues which were too sensitive for public opinion polls to tackle. There was no Gallup Poll on questions raised by the discovery of the mass graves at Katyn in April 1943, but people talked about them, and Home Intelligence noted their comments. Those who used the reports came to trust them and to act upon them. During the worst months of the war, in 1942, when the War Cabinet was anxious about the state of home opinion and morale, a monthly digest of the reports was presented to Cabinet by the Minister of Information. The main weakness of the reports, as their compilers recognized, lay in their imposition of order on often confused or obscure opinions so as to produce a smoothly written result, with categories and points neatly docketed. But despite this drawback, the Home Intelligence reports had a range, balance and continuity which gave them great authority as a means of assessing public opinion.[31]

30 These daily reports (18 May–27 Sept. 1940) are in INF 1/264.
31 The making of the Home Intelligence reports is detailed in INF 1/290, Report on the work of the HI Division, and in INF 1/292, Appendix to HI Report 79, 'How the Weekly Report is

The combined resources of these various methods of monitoring public opinion provided large quantities of information, with ample opportunity to check one source against another. The government thus had access to a detailed and finely nuanced picture of the opinions which it sought to influence. In exercising that influence, the government's principal instrument in a negative sense was censorship. This is a word with a wide range of meanings and often emotional connotations. Much censorship is informal: the constraints imposed by a generally accepted climate of opinion, in which certain things simply cannot be said. Often – perhaps always – a form of self-censorship is operated by editors, sensitive to the requirements of some outside influence. These forms of control were powerfully at work in wartime Britain. However, the centre of the stage was held by legal censorship: the prohibition by law of the publication of certain items. The working of this legal censorship involved some difficulties and obscurities, but its main lines may be simply set out, and form a vital background to a study of public opinion and foreign policy.

Defence Regulations were the basic instruments of censorship. No. 3 forbade the obtaining, recording, communicating or publishing of 'information which might be useful to an enemy', and was the basis of security censorship. Even on security matters, pre-publication censorship was voluntary, in that government had no power to prohibit publication. British newspapers did not appear with blank spaces where items had been cut out by the censor's scissors. What the press censor exercised, however, was the power to *authorize* publication, which protected a publisher from prosecution under the Defence Regulations. Under this combination of the stick of possible prosecution and the carrot of immunity, vast quantities of material were in practice submitted to the censorship authorities; but it remained perfectly possible for a publisher or editor to take a chance and omit to send an item to the censors, and on occasion this was done. The necessity for security censorship was generally accepted, and newspaper editors were normally anxious to co-operate with government in imposing it. After a troubled start in the first months of the war, the system worked fairly smoothly.[32]

Censorship of opinion in the press presented greater problems. In October 1939 Defence Regulation 39B laid down that:

> No person shall endeavour by means of any false statement, false document or false report to influence public opinion in a manner likely to be prejudicial to the defence of the realm or the efficient prosecution of the war.

Made'. INF 1/291 includes comments by the Report's recipients, September 1943. I am very grateful to the late Lord Taylor of Harlow for a long and enlightening conversation on his work as head of Home Intelligence. Cf. Balfour, *Propaganda in War*, pp. 72–80.

[32] INF 1/190 contains material on censorship matters. George P. Thomson, *Blue Pencil Admiral. The Inside Story of the Press Censorship* (London, 1947) is both enlightening and entertaining. Balfour, *Propaganda in War*, pp. 59–60, and McLaine, pp. 35–41, include good accounts of the early problems. There is a valuable general discussion in Philip Taylor, 'Censorship in Britain in the Second World War: An Overview', in *Too Mighty to be Free: Censorship and the Press in Britain and the Netherlands* (Zutphen, 1988), pp. 157–77.

A valid defence could be made by showing that there was reasonable cause to believe that a statement was true. In May 1940 a further Regulation (2D) provided that if the Home Secretary was convinced that there was in any newspaper 'a systematic publication of matter which is in his opinion calculated to foment opposition to the prosecution' of the war, he could make it an offence to print, publish or distribute that newspaper. This regulation was used in January 1941 to suppress the *Daily Worker*, the newspaper of the Communist Party.[33] (This was the period when the German-Soviet agreements were in operation). In autumn 1941 the War Cabinet considered introducing a new regulation to prevent the publication of matter 'likely to react unfavourably on this country's relations with foreign powers'. A committee made up of the Foreign Secretary, Home Secretary and Minister of Information reported that most newspapers were co-operative on such matters, though some (the *Daily Mirror* was a case in point) believed that they understood the national interest better than the government did. The committee was opposed to attempting censorship of opinion at the request of sensitive foreign governments, and it also wanted to preserve a useful cover. Under the existing system, the Foreign Office could always reply to complaints by explaining that it had no power to interfere with the expression of opinion, but the proposed regulation would change this: 'the indiscretions of a controlled press are much more embarrassing than those of a free press'. It was far from clear that newspaper articles were doing lasting damage to relations with other countries, and the committee recommended no change.[34] The War Cabinet agreed, and no new regulation was introduced.

There, as far as law went, censorship of the press ended. Occasionally, as in May 1940 and March 1942 (both times of acute crisis) the adoption of a more rigorous political censorship was discussed, but not pursued. However, Defence Regulations on censorship were supplemented by the long-standing system of Defence Notices (D Notices). The Ministry of Information described their purpose as to indicate 'the kind of matter the publication of which without Censorship authority is likely to prove dangerous to the national security'. In some cases, a notice stated that no information might be published without submission to the censorship, which meant that all such references would be stopped by the censor. In wartime, D Notices were numerous. A list in October 1942 ran numerically from D1 (Broadcasting) to D95 (Interruption of traffic as result of an air raid), and alphabetically from Access to beaches (D42) to Workers, factory, presence of (D84). Most were concerned with military, economic and financial matters. On foreign policy, D Notices laid down that no information should be published about special missions to or from foreign states, negotiations with neutral states, or measures to bring economic pressure upon the enemy. In addition, an 'Observation' attached to the list of D Notices ran thus:

there are matters which, unwisely treated, may be of disservice to this

---

[33] CAB 66/12, WP(40)402, 8 Oct. 1940, sets out the relevant regulations; CAB 66/19, WP(41)268, 12 Nov. 1941, reviewed the position.
[34] CAB 66/19, WP(41)269, 12 Nov. 1941.

country, because discussion of them may alienate those whom we would make our friends or provide material for our enemies to make use of to estrange us. Advice on the treatment of such matters may be obtained by submission to Censorship or consultation with the Foreign News Department at the Ministry. Examples are:- (i) matters prejudicial to the good relations between ourselves and any neutral or allied country; (ii) the likelihood of any neutral entering the war for or against us.

The vague but emphatic warning on 'matters prejudicial to good relations' with allies or neutrals applied throughout the war.[35]

D Notices were, strictly speaking, for guidance only; but since they indicated what would not be acceptable to the censorship they were in most cases an effective form of control in advance of publication. They were willingly accepted by almost the whole press on grounds of patriotic wartime duty. The same process was taken further by the 'Guidance Memoranda' which the Ministry of Information began to issue in 1941, ostensibly 'to provide Editors with background information or guidance on incoming material, thus enabling them to form their own judgement on the use they make of such material.' These appear to have been mainly concerned with military matters, but some dealt with questions of foreign policy.[36]

Press messages going abroad for publication in overseas newspapers were subject to a separate system of censorship. Until March 1942 this was confined to information likely to be of military use to the enemy, but it was then extended to include 'any Press message calculated to create ill-feeling between the United Nations, or between them and a neutral country.'[37] ('United Nations' was at the time in common use as another term for 'the Allies'.) Censorship of cables for overseas newspapers could affect the British press, which often reported material published abroad – for example, a news item could be sent from Britain, published in the United States, and then be repeated in the British press.

Beyond this structure of formal censorship and guidance, there was much scope for pressure, complaint and uncertainty. The range of informal censorship was wide, but so on the other hand was the measure of freedom which the press continued to enjoy – guidance could be ignored as well as accepted.

The rules for censoring broadcasting were more rigorous than those applied to the press, largely because anything put out on the radio was gone beyond recall, and could be heard by anyone within range. In theory, BBC news editors, like newspaper editors, were not compelled by law to submit items for advance censorship, but in practice all broadcasts were subject to

---

[35] BBC Written Archives, R61 (Censorship) includes three consolidated lists of D Notices, dated respectively Nov. 1939, Oct. 1942, and 1945. For the history of the D Notice system, see Colin Seymour-Ure, *The Press, Politics and the Public* (London, 1968), pp. 154–8.

[36] BBC Written Archives, R61, includes the phrase quoted, and also a large number of Guidance Memoranda. Cf. Francis Williams, *Nothing So Strange: An Autobiography* (London, 1970), pp. 185–6, where the author describes the introduction of these memoranda; Thomson, *Blue Pencil Admiral*, pp. 29–30.

[37] Statement by Bracken, House of Commons, 26 March 1942, *HC Deb.*, 5th series, 378, cols. 2156–60; CAB 66/23, WP(42)124, 17 March 1942.

security censorship, both by the submission of scripts in advance and by switch censors, who sat with a cut-off switch to push in case of need. When, in the nature of the broadcast, there was no script (e.g. improvisation in a variety programme), the general ideas had to be submitted in advance to the BBC censor. A set of rules governing these matters was drawn up just before the war began, and revised in May 1941. The basic principle was emphasized by the use of capital letters:

THE ATTENTION OF ALL STAFF IS DRAWN TO THE ABSOLUTE AND INVARIABLE NECESSITY OF SEEING THAT EVERY WORD BROADCAST IS CONSIDERED IN ADVANCE FROM THE POINT OF VIEW OF SECURITY CENSORSHIP.

Moreover, unlike the press, the BBC was also subject to continuous policy censorship. Anything even remotely likely to cause political problems was referred by the BBC censorship to the Ministry of Information. This occurred, for example, in February 1941 with a series of talks on Lord Chatham, Edmund Burke and Disraeli. In June 1941 a BBC official explained that while the security censor might pass jokes derogatory to Serbs or Greeks, these would not be allowed on policy grounds. The position was clearly summed up by another official in July 1940: 'the BBC can use *no* material that has not been passed for publication.' Occasional statements by Ministers of Information claiming or implying a degree of control looser than this were simply misleading.[38]

Newsreel films were subject to a similarly strict system of advance censorship. In its fully developed state, from July 1941, this involved censors in viewing all material proposed for inclusion in newsreels; the submission of proposed commentaries to the censor; and a final viewing by the censors of the finished film.[39]

Censorship was primarily a matter of security, but it could be used to influence public opinion in a negative sense by keeping certain matters out of the public eye. The positive arm of government in relation to public opinion was propaganda. Like censorship, this was a word which tended to generate emotion and covered a wide range of meaning. The word itself was distrusted in both the Ministry of Information and the BBC, where the Director of Talks wondered in October 1939 whether his Department could 'properly be required to do propaganda, in the sense of perverting the truth in order to maintain national morale and the will to war.[40] Despite such doubts, propagandists knew they had work to do, both at home and abroad.

Home propaganda took three main forms. The first was propaganda of

---

38 BBC Written Archives, R61, Censorship: MOI memo. on Broadcasting Censorship, Secret Paper No. 50 (undated, but datable to just before the war); memo. by Nicholls, 1 May 1941, including the sentence in capitals; memo. by Nicholls, 30 June 1941, on security and policy censorship; memo. by Gilliam, 3 Feb. 1941; memo. by ASNE to Director (Secretariat), 22 July 1940. Balfour, *Propaganda in War*, pp. 84–85, prints various statements by Duff Cooper and Brendan Bracken which were in varying degrees misleading.

39 N. Pronay, 'The News Media at War', in N. Pronay and D.W. Spring, eds., *Propaganda, Politics and Film 1918–1945* (London, 1982), p. 193.

40 BBC Written Archives, Talks Policy 2A, Maconachie to Nicholls, 12 Oct. 1939.

action: carry your gas-mask, turn pans into planes, make tanks for Russia. Such exhortations met with varying success. A 'tanks for Russia' week in September 1941 caught the mood of the day and went well. Gas-masks, on the other hand, became a lost cause: as the war went on, people simply ceased to carry them, however much they were urged to do so. Secondly there was indirect or consolidating propaganda, designed to maintain a climate of opinion in which support for the war was kept up even when events provided little stimulus, or (as in much of 1942) were downright depressing. In this process the general tone of press, broadcasting and films was more important than specific items. Thirdly, propaganda (which in this case could properly be called publicity) was used to explain government actions to the public, and to seek their co-operation in the various activities of wartime administration. In March 1943 the Director-General of the BBC estimated that each week some 180 separate broadcasts in the Home Service were devoted to aspects of government publicity.[41] The press too was full of government advertisements, notices and 'inspired' news items.

Foreign propaganda was directed towards allied, neutral, enemy or enemy-occupied states. In the last two cases it took on the nature of subversion, a notion which attained unexpected importance in the dark days of 1940. After the fall of France, even if one assumed that Britain could somehow survive, there was no clear idea of how the war could actually be won. Among various speculative ideas, subversion by a mixture of propaganda and clandestine guerrilla action seemed hopeful. The Special Operations Executive (SOE) was set up in 1940, and the Political Warfare Executive (PWE) in August 1941, after long and complicated struggles between government departments.[42] PWE controlled propaganda to enemy and enemy-occupied countries, with the objectives of sapping enemy morale, rallying the peoples of occupied Europe against the invader, and inciting resistance, strikes and in the long run insurrection. Its main instrument was broadcasting, and the European Service of the BBC was placed under its control. Frank Newsome, the head of the European Service for most of the war, threw himself whole-heartedly into propaganda activities. In a special directive (23 September 1941) he stressed that 'Modern, total war is fundamentally and essentially political. That is, "political warfare" is not a branch of war: it *is* war.' In waging war, truth was useful but not sacrosanct:

> All output must bear the stamp of authenticity and authority and must not be in danger of being *exposed* as otherwise (whether in fact it is or is not authentic and authoritative). . . .
> In short, if we depart from accuracy and the truth we must do so not accidentally and carelessly but deliberately and systematically either because we know we shall not be found out or because it is considered essential to risk being found out for very special reasons.[43]

[41] CAB 66/34, WP(43)90, 2 March 1943.
[42] M.R.D. Foot, *SOE: An Outline History of the Special Operations Executive 1940–46* (London, 1984); Charles Cruickshank, *The Fourth Arm: Psychological Warfare 1938–1945* (London, 1977).
[43] BBC Written Archives, OS 137E, Special Directive by Newsome, 23 Sept. 1941.

For the most part, however, honesty was the best policy, on grounds of expediency as much as integrity. As Newsome wrote a few weeks later: 'It goes without saying, I think, that we must, above all, be *honest*, with ourselves and therefore with our listeners. Phoney arguments should no more be broadcast than phoney news. . . . Hell knows no fury like a sucker taken in by a confidence trick when he discovers his mistake.'[44] Newsome was also well aware of how to write a news item in such a way as to incorporate comment and interpretation without appearing to depart from a plain narrative of events.[45]

The BBC was well aware that overseas audiences listened to its Home Service, and home listeners to its overseas broadcasts – they called it eavesdropping, and commissioned surveys to ascertain its extent in December 1941 and April 1944. The official BBC policy was 'to tell the same truth to everyone', and while this hardly squared with Newsome's pugnacious propaganda directives it was certainly the case that any serious discrepancies soon came home to roost. German radio made a practice of quoting different BBC services against one another whenever it could.[46] Anything broadcast anywhere in the world was likely to be known across the globe in minutes rather than hours. Propaganda to Europe, therefore, even though it was a part of political warfare and ostensibly different from home broadcasting, could not in practice be separated from it.

The British government thus had at its disposal varied, sensitive and effective means of assessing the state of public opinion. It also possessed instruments for influencing public opinion by means of censorship and propaganda which were in appearance formidable. It is time to leave the government view and turn to public opinion itself.

Public opinion

It is no easy matter to define public opinion, and in relation to Britain during the war we must recognize that we are dealing with a number of different kinds of opinion. The traditional focus of political opinion was Parliament. It is true that during the Second World War Parliamentary opinion was muted by wartime conditions, and by the existence of a coalition government which ruled the country from May 1940 to May 1945, almost eliminating formal opposition. But despite this, no reader of *Hansard* or of the ministerial files which accumulated round Parliamentary questions (whether asked or merely threatened) would discount the continuing significance of Parliamentary opinion. At one end of the scale the House of Commons could focus opinion in great debates, one of which, on 7 and 8 May 1940, brought down the government headed by Neville Chamberlain, despite its apparently secure majority. This was exceptional, but what had happened once might happen again. On 1 and 2 July 1942, after six months of calamitous defeats in the Far East and North Africa, Churchill faced a vote of censure which

44 *Ibid.*, Special Directive by Newsome, 9 Dec. 1941.
45 *Ibid.*, directive on 'Presentation of News', undated but probably May 1941.
46 Briggs, vol. III, p. 179 for the quotation, and generally pp. 179–80, 490.

appeared to pose a serious challenge, though in the event the government retained an overwhelming majority in the vote which ended the debate.[47] In quite a different way, a member of either House could bring some pressure to bear on the government by proposing to put down a question on some subject where publicity would not be welcome. At all times Parliament remained a forum for the airing of views, the raising of questions, and the staging of debates; and it was often the best means by which the expression of opinion could achieve practical results.

Secondly, and often closely connected with Parliamentary opinion, there was (borrowing Sir Lewis Namier's phrase) 'the political nation': the activists of various kinds who worked in the constituencies for the political parties, who ran trade unions, whether at the centre or in the branches, and who formed pressure groups or subcribed to political book clubs. Despite the demands of the war effort, there were still many who were willing to canvass at by-elections, attend meetings, and write letters to MPs or the press. Indeed, some aspects of wartime affairs (for example, post-war planning, which sometimes amounted to building the New Jerusalem) gave a fresh impulse to this kind of activity. The significance of this kind of opinion was always considerable, and could on occasion be vital. As recently as 1935 a combination of opinion in Conservative constituency parties and the League of Nations Union had created a furore over the Hoare-Laval Pact and done much to bring down the Foreign Secretary, to the profound embarrassment of Baldwin's government.[48] During the war, a number of new organizations (for example, the Anglo-Soviet Friendship societies) worked hard to keep foreign policy in the forefront of the mind of the 'political nation'.

Next came the mass media of the day: press, radio and cinema. What the papers said, what was broadcast on the wireless, and what appeared on the screen made up an important element in public opinion, with an ambiguous role half-way between reflecting and forming other opinions. These three forms of communication reached an enormous public. When Gallup enquired about reading a morning newspaper in January 1941, 70 per cent of its sample replied that they read one regularly, 13 per cent occasionally, and only 17 per cent not at all.[49] Within these general figures, individual papers varied widely in their readership and circulation. In 1943 *The Times* had a circulation of 158,000, and the *Daily Mirror* one of over two million.[50] (Most copies were shared by a household, so the number of readers exceeded the figure for circulation by a considerable extent.) The great diversity of the press gave the public a far wider range of choice than either radio or cinema, and allowed the expression of almost every shade of opinion. In reaching the vast mass of the population, however, radio was more successful than any single newspaper. In 1939 there were about nine million licensed wireless sets in the United Kingdom. In January 1942 Gallup asked its sample 'Is there a wireless set in your home?' and 90 per cent answered Yes. The high points

[47] The government majority was 475–25, though there were 27 abstentions.
[48] Daniel Waley, *British Public Opinion and the Abyssinian War* (London, 1975).
[49] Gallup Archives, BIPO Survey 75, Jan. 1941.
[50] Ministry of Information, *The Press in Wartime* (Feb. 1944); William Armstrong, ed., *With Malice Toward None. A War Diary by Cecil H. King* (London, 1970), p. 5.

in the daily listening pattern were the news bulletins at 6 p.m. and 9 p.m., which were normally heard by between 30 and 50 per cent of the adult civilian population. On certain occasions, for example when Churchill was speaking on the news, the figure rose to over 60 per cent; and on the day of the Normandy landings (6 June 1944) the figure for the 9 p.m. news was 80 per cent.[51] Cinema attendances also reached extraordinary figures. In 1940 the average weekly admissions to all cinemas in Great Britain were over 21 million – these, of course, included many who went to the cinema more than once in the week, but however qualified the figure remains formidable.[52] Audiences saw a highly selective mixture of news, entertainment and propaganda in the newsreels, which formed a part of every cinema programme. Feature films, while mainly entertainment, also included a good deal of propaganda.

Press, radio and cinema put those who controlled their output in contact with the vast majority of the British people, including a large proportion of the armed forces, because between 1940 and 1944 large numbers of servicemen were based in Britain. It is an open question how far these mass media formed or reflected the opinions of their audiences. Radio and cinema were under very close government control, and certainly attempted the role of opinion-formers. The press remained more ambiguous. John Freeman, who edited the *New Statesman* in the 1960s, wrote that under his predecessor Kingsley Martin that journal had 'played a crucial role in shaping the thought of a generation.' If Martin's *New Statesman* had not existed, he claimed, then public opinion on anti-fascism, war aims, the welfare state, and anti-imperialism would have been very different.[53] There may well be truth in this: it was more than merely a *bon mot* that readers of the *New Statesman* waited each week for the paper to tell them what they thought. However, the same journal's historian took a different view: 'It is a mistake to see an editor as a creator of opinion; he is, if he is good at his job, a man who finds terms to express an opinion already there but inarticulate.'[54] Philip Zec, the brilliant cartoonist for the *Daily Mirror*, said that the normal practice of the *Mirror's* editorial team was to ask 'What's going to interest people today?', and so catch the mood of their readers. But sometimes they would say to their readers: 'This is something you *ought* to be thinking about, whether you know it yet or not.'[55]

It is safe to say that press, radio and cinema often provided prominent subjects for people to talk about, and focused the attention of their audiences on particular issues. On the other hand, it was perfectly possible for people to feel strongly about some matters even when editors did not think them newsworthy, and equally possible for the mass media to be intensely

51 Silvey, pp. 120–1. These very high figures were a wartime phenomenon: when the war in Europe ended, there was an immediate drop. 'It was as though the curtain had rung down and the audience – or half of them – had promptly left the hall.'

52 For the size and nature of cinema audiences in the 1930s and 1940s, see A. Aldgate, *Cinema and History: British Newsreels and the Spanish Civil War* (London, 1979), chapter 3.

53 Edward Hyams, *The New Statesman* (London, 1963), introduction by John Freeman, p. x.

54 *Ibid.*, p. 179.

55 Interview with the late Philip Zec, 2 August 1978.

preoccupied with questions which left the public at large quite unmoved. (The American Presidential election of 1944 furnished an example of intensive press and other coverage of an event which aroused little public interest.)[56]

This leads us to a fourth kind of public opinion, often described as public opinion *tout court*, or mass opinion. The latter term is misleading, since the accumulation of individual opinions does not form an undifferentiated mass, and when opinions are opposed to one another they do not cancel one another out but persist side by side.[57] 'General opinion' may be a better term. Whatever label we use, this type of opinion is not easy to ascertain, even by the carefully developed methods of public opinion polling. It is difficult to cross the gap between publicly expressed opinion (what a man will say to a stranger) and private opinion (what he really thinks, but may prefer not to reveal to an interviewer or pollster).[58] Even if ascertained, it is hard to assess how deeply held or how fixed such opinions may be. There are some views – though not many – for which a man will go to the scaffold, and others which he will change without a qualm. General opinion was an assemblage of innumerable individual opinions, often obscure but sometimes remarkably clear.

These were the different shapes assumed by public opinion. For an enquiry into public opinion and foreign policy in wartime, we must ask how we can find out about public opinion, how far that opinion was interested in foreign affairs, and whether public opinion existed in its own right or was merely the creation of propaganda and manipulation.

As to the first two of these questions, the answers are already apparent. The amount of information available at the time about the state of public opinion provides ample evidence for the historian, with useful opportunities to check one source against another.[59] In time of war, the obvious importance of foreign affairs prevailed even over the traditional British indifference to events outside these shores. The British people found themselves being bombed by the Germans, and rubbing shoulders with the Americans; while at long range they were deeply impressed by the deeds of the Soviet army. It was not a time to pretend that the outside world did not exist, or did not matter even if it did.

The third question is more difficult. There are many who, impressed by the instruments of government censorship and propaganda and taking a low view of peoples' independence and good sense, would say that public opinion was largely moulded by outside pressures. This is very doubtful. It was certainly not the view of those who practised propaganda upon the British people. The files of the Ministry of Information and the BBC alike reveal a

[56] See INF 1/290, Report on the work of the Home Intelligence Division, 1939–44, not dated or signed, but in fact by Stephen Taylor.

[57] See the discussion by Taylor, 'Home Morale and Public Opinion', 1 Oct. 1941, INF 1/292, HI Report 52, Appendix.

[58] This distinction between public and private opinion was made repeatedly by Tom Harrisson, the founder of Mass-Observation. See, e.g., his article 'What is Public Opinion?', *Political Quarterly*, XI, 1940.

[59] See pp. 8–11, above.

distrust of propaganda and a sceptical view of its likely effects. A Ministry of Information paper of November 1941 reviewed the obstacles in the path of propaganda campaigns, notably the ineffectiveness of propagandists and the reluctance of the British people to be propagandized. Its conclusion was that if results were really important the only certain method was legislative or administrative action accompanied by explanation. If this was not going to be done, then 'On the principle of not badgering the public, there is a good case for dropping the campaign altogether.'[60] The level of resistance to propaganda was thought to be high. A.P. Ryan, who was appointed by the Ministry of Information as Home Adviser to the BBC in March 1941, held strong views on this. 'The State can require the BBC to broadcast, or to abstain from broadcasting, anything it likes. What it cannot do is to require listeners in this country or abroad either to listen to or to believe the BBC.' He explained forcibly that the audience could always go elsewhere, or simply switch off.[61] Ryan wrote to Bracken, the Minister of Information, on 20 October 1941: 'The wireless audience is a hanging judge of a speaker. If they don't like him when he starts, he is not aware of it, and cannot recover himself. He just gets switched off.' Talks in the news period must be kept to five minutes and to subjects of outstanding importance, otherwise they stood no chance of being listened to. 'Indeed, they stand worse than no chance: they positively annoy listeners, which is good neither for the speaker nor, in the long run, for the BBC.' Only Churchill and Beaverbrook were exceptions to the rule that 'longer than five minutes in the News is a flop.'[62]

This is not the language of men who believed that they controlled instruments which could mould public opinion according to their will. They were, on the contrary, acutely conscious of the limitations of their influence. There is much evidence that they were right. The effects of censorship and propaganda, though considerable, fell far short of total control – to which, indeed, no-one seems even to have aspired. Censorship, with its complete hold over the BBC and with the zealous co-operation of most newspaper editors, was generally effective on security matters. The secrecy surrounding the place and date of the Normandy landings in 1944 was tight, and that which protected the 'Ultra' decodings and most other secret intelligence matters appears to have been absolute. On political matters, the potentially contentious issue of returning Soviet prisoners of war to the USSR in 1944 and 1945 was very largely kept out of the public eye. But in some cases even security matters could not be kept secret (the nature of the V-2 rocket attack was one example), and despite the severe wording of the D Notice 'observation' on 'matters prejudicial to good relations' with allies, it proved impossible to keep such issues out of the newspapers. Such a category of news and comment was too vast and amorphous, and interested too many people, for a policy of suppression, or even appeals to patriotism, to be effective. There were indeed times when no attempt at a censorship 'stop' had any serious chance of success, because a story being broadcast by the transmitters

60 INF 1/292, memo. attached to HI Report No. 58, 12 Nov. 1941.
61 BBC Written Archives, 830/37, Ryan to Monckton, 4 June 1941.
62 *Ibid.*, Ryan to Bracken, 20 Oct. 1941, and attached memo.

of half the world could not be excluded from the receivers of the other half – though an efficient jamming system could do something.

Propaganda too was limited in its effects, and was at its strongest when it reinforced what people already wished to believe. Otherwise, men would hold the views which they wished to hold, disregarding all information or exhortation to the contrary. One example of this was the way in which people clung to their own ideas as to how long the war would last, irrespective of what government might say through all its means of publicity.[63] Throughout the war there was a strong tendency to give credence to rumour, quite independently of the regular sources of news and sometimes in defiance of them. Lord Haw-Haw, the English-language broadcaster on Radio Hamburg, was repeatedly credited with mentioning a particular town or factory in his talks, yet whenever these stories could be checked against the BBC monitoring reports of the actual broadcasts, no such mention could be traced. For example, there were rumours in Wells that Haw-Haw had predicted the imminent bombing of the cathedral; and others from Bedfordshire of threats to St Albans, Bedford and Harpenden, supported by the story (perhaps the commonest of all forms of rumour) that the German broadcaster knew that the St Albans town hall clock was three minutes fast. These stories were duly investigated, and those who reported them were assured that Radio Hamburg had never mentioned any of the places named. But such rumours sprang repeatedly into existence by a sort of spontaneous combustion, and spread in defiance of both government injunctions not to listen to German radio and, more surprisingly, of the actual content of the transmissions. Exactly the same thing happened in France during the winter of 1939–40, when circumstantial stories circulated about German broadcasts which were alleged to refer to the British forces in Le Havre, which were not borne out by the texts of the broadcasts themselves. In Britain, these stories diminished in number as the war went on, but even the later years produced a substantial file in the Ministry of Information archives.[64]

Almost certainly the greatest single influence on peoples' views was, quite naturally, personal experience and contact. To minimize air-raid damage when thousands of people could see it with their own eyes merely diminished respect for the news, whether in the press or on the radio, and aroused distrust of it in other respects. Stories about the events of Dunkirk, and the apparent failure of the Royal Air Force to protect the troops on the beaches, spread from soldiers on leave, in the teeth of government attempts to promote its own version of these events. Polish troops stationed in Scotland gave their own accounts of the Soviet Union to those with whom they came into contact, and their views made headway in the face of powerful propaganda on behalf of the Soviets.[65]

---

[63] See INF 1/261. In December 1939 only 13 per cent of those questioned in a BIPO survey accepted the government's estimate that the war would last three years or more. Everyone else thought it would be shorter.

[64] INF 1/265. Cf. J-L. Crémieux-Brilhac, 'L'opinion publique française, l'Angleterre et la guerre, septembre 1939-juin 1940', in Comité d'Histoire de la 2e. Guerre Mondiale, *Français et Britanniques dans la Drôle de Guerre* (Paris, 1979), pp. 34–7.

[65] On the importance of personal experience, see Taylor's memorandum, 1 Oct. 1941, INF 1/292, HI Report 52, Appendix.

This view of the essential autonomy of public opinion is supported by research on public opinion in wartime Germany, where the weight of censorship and propaganda was markedly greater than in Britain. There too a combination of rumour and personal experience – for example, the stories of men on leave from the eastern front – built up a network of news and opinion quite independent of the official propaganda machine. Though outwardly ubiquitous and all-powerful, Nazi propaganda was in fact subject to severe limitations in its influence.[66] As in Germany, so in Britain: despite all the external influences brought to bear upon it, public opinion retained a substantial degree of autonomy.

Government, public opinion and foreign policy

Government believed that public opinion was of vital importance in the conduct of the war, and adopted various means of assessing and influencing that opinion. At the same time, public opinion, in its various forms, retained a considerable measure of independence. This book examines the interaction between government and public opinion in the domain of foreign policy. As we have seen, the British government held that public opinion was often significant, and could on occasion be crucial, in foreign affairs; and in wartime public opinion itself was more than usually concerned with matters of foreign policy.

Within the wide range of British foreign policy, the book concentrates on one specific (though very large) subject: British relations with the Soviet Union. By common consent, all elements of British public opinion during the Second World War were concerned with this matter; and equally the British government was keenly interested in, and sometimes worried about, public opinion relating to the Soviet Union. Broad questions relating to public opinion and foreign policy were thus brought into sharp focus.

These questions may be examined in two ways. First we need to establish the main outlines of how the government saw the problem, and what it wanted public opinion to be in relation to the USSR; and also the principal developments in public opinion itself. For this purpose there will be two general chapters dealing with public opinion and Anglo-Soviet relations in the whole wartime period. Secondly, we must try to probe more deeply at specific points and analyse the precise interaction between policy and opinion. This demands a day-by-day scrutiny of government policy on censorship, propaganda and guidance of opinion, with an equally detailed examination of the evolution of public opinion about the subject under discussion, and an assessment of the interplay between the two forces. To this end there will be two detailed case studies, one on the affair of the Katyn graves in 1943, and the other on the Warsaw rising in 1944.

Throughout the book, we shall be asking three main questions. First, what

---

[66] See Ian Kershaw, *Popular Opinion and Political Dissent in the Third Reich: Bavaria 1933–1945* (Oxford, 1983), p. 378, where the author concludes that 'beneath the monolithic uniformity of the Third Reich's propaganda image' an independent popular opinion continued to exist in Germany.

policy did government adopt towards public opinion and the Soviet Union: what did it want public opinion to be, and what role did it expect that opinion to play in relations with the USSR? Second, how did public opinion in fact develop: how far did it conform to government guidance, and how far did it maintain a will and shape of its own? Third, how much interaction was there between policy and opinion: how far was public opinion used as an instrument of policy, and (in the other direction) how far did public opinion have significant effects on policy?

2

'A Favourable Reference to the Devil': British Opinion and the Soviet Union, 1941

He [Churchill] replied that he had only one single purpose – the destruction of Hitler – and his life was much simplified thereby. If Hitler invaded Hell he would at least make a favourable reference to the Devil!

(Colville Diary, 21 June 1941)[1]

In the early hours of 22 June 1941 German forces invaded the Soviet Union. Operation BARBAROSSA was under way, opening the greatest land campaign of the Second World War. This extraordinary event, which was to prove decisive for the whole course of the war, posed problems of all kinds for the British government. It was clear that for British to win the war against Germany, in which she had fought almost alone since the fall of France in June 1940, the aid of a great ally was essential. British eyes (and especially Churchill's) had turned longingly towards the United States, whence much verbal encouragement and some modest material support had been forthcoming. But in the event Britain's first major new ally took the unexpected, and in many ways difficult, form of the Soviet Union. The Soviet Union in the 1920s and 1930s was the centre of world communism, and commanded the allegiance of Communist Parties everywhere. British governments regarded communism as a dangerous ideology, the Communist Party of Great Britain as a subversive organization, and the USSR as an unfriendly power, with which their relations (when they existed at all) had never been more than tepid. Public attitudes towards the Soviet Union varied from the most fervent admiration to the deepest abhorrence.

What the British government would say, and what its people might think, about the Soviet Union was, in the early morning of 22 June 1941, an

---

1 John Colville, *The Fringes of Power: Downing Street Diaries 1939–1955* (London, 1985), p. 404.

unknown quantity. To understand some of the difficulties involved, we must look back briefly over events since the Bolshevik revolution of 1917.

Before BARBAROSSA: the background, 1917–June 1941

Relations between the British government and the Bolsheviks who seized power in Russia in November 1917 got off to a very bad start. This was partly because the two were self-proclaimed ideological enemies, and even more because the Bolsheviks took Russia out of the war against Germany, leaving the Allies to face a German onslaught in France in spring 1918. Then Allied forces, with the British prominent and almost ubiquitous, intervened against the Bolsheviks in the civil strife which followed the revolution in Russia. Churchill, as Minister of War in Lloyd George's government from 1918 to 1921, was among the most ardent advocates of military action to overthrow the Bolsheviks – something which was still remembered in 1941.

In 1924 diplomatic relations between the British and Soviet governments were opened, only to be broken off in 1927 amidst British accusations of Soviet espionage and subversion. They were restored in 1929, but were little more than formal, generating no warmth. The Soviet Union joined the League of Nations in 1934, and made a treaty of alliance with France in 1935, both steps towards becoming a more normal power supporting the European *status quo*. But then, between 1936 and 1938, came the great purges in the USSR, shaking the confidence of any reasonable onlooker. If the accusations levelled against those put on public trial were even half true, then the Soviet state was riddled with treachery and intrigue. If they were not true, then Stalin was slaughtering his opponents by means which were ruthless, theatrical and barbaric. Either way, the Soviet regime was in disarray and its officer corps decimated, and Soviet influence in Europe was gravely weakened. It was not surprising that during the Czechoslovakian crisis of 1938 Britain kept the Soviet Union at arm's length. The Soviet government was not invited to the Munich conference, and would indeed have been unwelcome to any of the participants.

Yet when European war seemed imminent in 1939, an Anglo–Franco–Soviet alliance seemed the only measure likely to deter Germany from her course of aggression. But negotiations for such an alliance failed, and the British government was much criticized for its clumsy and dilatory conduct of the talks. These criticisms were well-founded and yet basically irrelevant, because no amount of speed or skill could have removed the fundamental obstacle to success, which lay in the substance of the negotiation. Stalin's price for an alliance was the acceptance of a Soviet sphere of influence in eastern Europe, which at that point the British were unwilling to concede. The Germans, however, were willing to pay the price without demur, and on 23 August 1939 the Nazi–Soviet Pact was signed, leading straight to war and the partition of Poland between Germany and the Soviet Union. This first Ribbentrop–Molotov Pact was followed by other agreements, political and economic. For nearly two years the Soviet Union provided resources for the German war effort, as well as giving help in smaller ways, for example sending an ice-breaker to lead a German commerce-raider through Soviet Arctic waters to the Pacific. At the same time the Soviet occupation of eastern Poland raised a territorial dispute which was to dog British foreign policy for most of the Second World War.

In late 1939 and 1940 the Soviet Union extended its grip on northern and eastern Europe. It fought the Winter War against Finland (November 1939–March 1940) to enforce claims for bases and territorial expansion. It imposed garrisons upon, and in July 1940 annexed, the Baltic states of Estonia, Latvia and Lithuania. In July 1940 it also annexed Bessarabia and northern Moldavia from Rumania. These events involved friction with Britain, though not as much as might have been expected. The Winter War evoked keen popular admiration for the gallant Finns, and revulsion against the bullying Soviets. The British government gave small amounts of material help to the Finns, under cloak of secrecy, and came near to sending an expeditionary force to intervene in the war and seize the Swedish iron ore mines *en route*. This plan, if carried out, would have brought British troops into direct conflict with the Red Army. At much the same time, the British and French were contemplating an air attack on the Soviet oil-wells at Baku from bases in Syria, in the sanguine hope of cutting off oil supplies to Germany from that source.[2] These plans were disclosed in detail to the Soviet government when the Germans captured French papers in summer 1940. In practice, British policy was more prudent than these far-fetched schemes seemed to indicate, and even during the phoney war the British government recognized the advantages of avoiding conflict with the Soviet government, despite the Nazi–Soviet Pact and the Winter War.

When France fell in June 1940, Britain at once saw powerful reasons to improve relations with the Soviet Union, and so pose a diplomatic threat, however shadowy, to Germany. Sir Stafford Cripps, a brilliant though wayward Left-wing politician, and an amateur in diplomacy, was sent as Ambassador to Moscow, where he tried earnestly to develop contacts with Soviet leaders, but with little success. For six months of his mission Cripps did not even have an interview with Molotov, the Foreign Minister, never mind with Stalin. In April 1941 Cripps deliberately obstructed an attempt by Churchill to convey to Stalin a warning of a German attack on the Soviet Union, based on the Enigma decrypts. The Prime Minister was furious, but it seems unlikely that even personal and immediate delivery of the message to Stalin would have had any effect.[3] In June, on the eve of the attack, Stalin chose to ignore not only British warnings, but those of his own agents and the overwhelming evidence of German troop concentrations. It is reasonable to think that he distrusted the British, who might well have been trying to embroil him in conflict with Germany. The arrival of Rudolf Hess in Scotland on 10 May 1941, after his extraordinary flight from Germany, fed

[2] Martin Kitchen, *British Policy Towards the Soviet Union during the Second World War* (London, 1986), p. 21; Nikolai Tolstoy, *Stalin's Secret War* (London, 1981), pp. 163–7; Ronald C. Cooke and Roy Conyers Nesbit, *Target: Hitler's Oil* (London, 1985), pp. 21–51.

[3] See Gabriel Gorodetsky, *Stafford Cripps' Mission to Moscow, 1940–42* (Cambridge, 1984) for a favourable account of Cripps' period as Ambassador to the USSR.

Soviet suspicions of British intentions, and was to continue to do so for years to come.

When the German blow fell on the USSR on 22 June 1941, there had been no sign of improvement in Anglo–Soviet relations over the previous twelve months. Shortly before the German attack was launched, a meeting in the British Foreign Office offered the opinion that in the event of such an attack 'There would probably be strong pressure in some circles to treat Russia as an ally. This should be resisted.'[4] It is easy to see how this conclusion was arrived at. The record of the recent past provided little basis for an Anglo–Soviet alliance, and ample evidence of friction on substantial issues: a conflict of ideologies, the question of Soviet territorial claims in eastern Europe (especially against Poland), and the shadow of the German–Soviet treaties. It is true that necessity knows no law; but could these legacies of the past be simply eliminated or forgotten?

When we turn from relations between governments to the state of public opinion in relation to the Soviet Union, the position appears even more difficult. Ever since the Bolshevik Revolution, articulate opinion had been deeply and sharply divided.

There was a strongly pro-Soviet section of opinion, led by Communists and fellow-travellers, and particularly prominent among writers and intellectuals. Substantial anthologies of praise for the Bolshevik revolution and the Soviet experiment could be compiled.[5] This tide ran particularly fiercely in the 1930s, when the attractions of Communist Russia were highlighted amid the gloom of the great depression, which was itself seen as the proof of the decay of capitalism. Equally, in the late 1930s, it appeared that only the Soviet Union and the Communist International were prepared to fight fascism, notably in the Spanish Civil War. The appeal of the Popular Front against fascism acted powerfully upon those who feared Hitler and Mussolini, and could see no sign that other governments were willing or able to oppose them. In Britain, opposition to Chamberlain and appeasement led many towards sympathy with the Soviet Union. All this produced a heightened admiration for the great light in the east and the supreme socialist experiment. In 1935 Sidney and Beatrice Webb published a massive book, *Soviet Communism: A New Civilisation?*, and in later editions they removed the question mark from the title. They declared that 'the term dictatorship is surely a misnomer for this untiring corporate inspiration, evocation and formulation of a General Will among so huge a population'. They asked boldly 'Is Stalin a dictator?' and answered lamely 'We do not think that the Party is governed by the will of a single person; or that Stalin is the sort of person to claim or desire such a position.'[6] For many people, however, Stalin exercised a magnetic attraction. H.G. Wells wrote of him in 1934: 'I have never met a man more candid, fair and honest.'[7] Julian Huxley wrote in

---

[4] Quoted in Kitchen, p. 53.

[5] See especially David Caute, *The Fellow–Travellers* (London, 1973) – a most illuminating book, where many such remarks may be found. See also Neal Wood, *Communism and British Intellectuals* (London, 1959); F.S. Northedge and Audrey Wells, *Britain and Soviet Communism: The Impact of a Revolution* (London, 1982), especially Chapter 7, pp. 158–70.

[6] Sidney and Beatrice Webb, *Soviet Communism: A New Civilization?* (London, 1935), pp. 430–2.

[7] Quoted in Adam B. Ulam, *Stalin* (London, 1974), p. 359.

1932: '. . . one is told that Stalin himself sometimes comes down to the Moscow goods sidings to help'. The Five Year Plans shone like beacons amidst a chaotic world economy; piles of statistics demonstrated their success in terms of production, while photographs of smiling workers on collective farms showed their human face. Bernard Shaw (who visited Russia and lodged comfortably at the Hotel Metropole in Moscow) proclaimed that 'The success of the Five Year Plan is the only hope of the World.'[8] Similar ideas were propagated in many of the volumes issued by the Left Book Club, which came into existence in 1936. Up to 1939, the Club published 15 books dealing with the Soviet Union, all of them sympathetic and in some cases hagiographical. The maximum membership of the Left Book Club has been put at about 57,000, with some 1,500 organized study groups; so such ideas had a considerable as well as a receptive audience among the 'political nation'.[9]

The red tide thus ran strongly. But it was far from carrying all before it, even on the Left. The leadership of the Labour Party, while maintaining that the Soviets should be allowed to get on with their experiment in their own country, showed no wish for it to be extended to Britain. Attempts by the Communist Party to become affiliated to the Labour Party were steadily and successfully resisted. The idea of a Popular Front in alliance with the Communists was rejected, and in 1939 Cripps was expelled from the Labour Party for advocating such a Front. Walter Citrine and Ernest Bevin, heavyweights among the trade union leaders in the 1930s, were resolute opponents of Communism and Comintern – as Bevin declared in 1935, 'The philosophy of the Red International cannot mix with our form of democracy.'[10] On the political Right, the Conservative Party and press were strongly anti-communist, and for the most part anti-Soviet. Lord Rothermere's *Daily Mail* was particularly fierce in its anti-Bolshevism; and Churchill in the 1920s continued his militant stance of the intervention years. In a speech in September 1924 he proclaimed that: 'Judged by every standard which history has applied to Governments, the Soviet Government of Russia is one of the worst tyrannies that has ever existed in the world.'[11] Many other expressions of Right-wing hostility to communism and the Soviet Union could be quoted: for example, Neville Chamberlain's correspondence with his sisters gives occasional glimpses of his deep distrust of the USSR. To those who have been called the 'fellow-travellers of the Right', Nazi Germany appeared as a powerful bulwark against the threat from Communist Russia.[12] There is nothing strange or reprehensible about

8 Quotations from Caute, pp. 65, 66.

9 Sheila Hodges, *Gollancz: The Story of a Publishing House, 1928–1978* (London, 1978), pp. 126–41; John Lewis, *The Left Book Club: An Historical Record* (London, 1970), pp. 12–14, 107–11. Lewis – himself a communist – put up an unconvincing defence against the charge of extensive communist influence in the Club, which Hodges accepts as being perfectly true.

10 For the Labour Party and the Soviet Union generally, see Bill Jones, *The Russia Complex: The British Labour Party and the Soviet Union* (Manchester, 1977). Bevin's remark is quoted in Alan Bullock, *Ernest Bevin*, vol. I (London, 1960), p. 559.

11 Speech in Edinburgh, 25 Sept. 1924, quoted in Martin Gilbert, *Winston S. Churchill*, vol. 5 (London, 1976), p. 48.

12 Richard Griffiths, *Fellow Travellers of the Right: British Enthusiasts for Nazi Germany, 1933–39* (Oxford, 1983).

this. Bolshevism, after all, was the self-proclaimed enemy of much that Conservatives stood for, and their opposition to it was rational as well as emotional. The same was true of opposition to Communism and the Soviet Union within the Christian churches, and especially among Roman Catholics. The Soviet government had declared war on religion in its own country, and its materialist philosophy was hostile to all religion. Of course, there were occasional admirers of communism in the churches, but for one Red Dean (Hewlett Johnson, Dean of Canterbury) there were many zealous opponents of communist theory and practice.

By 1938 and 1939, there were those who were willing to abate a part of their hostility to the Soviet Union on grounds of power politics and the need for an alliance against Germany. Bevin and Churchill, from their widely different political standpoints, both came to take this view; but it was not easy for many to follow them. Frederick Voigt, then a foreign correspondent with the *Manchester Guardian*, and a cool, independent-minded observer, put the problem thus in March 1939:

> We ought, I think, to be critical about Russia. We need her and it isn't the time for polemics against her. But we must not, in my opinion, refer to her as a democracy – she is more tyrannically governed than even Germany is. The number of people done to death in Germany runs into thousands – in Russia into tens of thousands. Altogether, the terror in Russia is such that persons living even under the Nazi terror could hardly conceive of such a thing. But we cannot afford to be particular about our allies, though we must, I think, always remain particular about our friends.[13]

Voigt needed to add a couple of noughts to his figures for the victims of Soviet terror, but in principle he stated the problem clearly enough. It was to recur several times during the next few years.

The opinion of the political nation was thus very sharply divided in the 1930s; and it was not clear how far some were willing to suppress a deep-rooted antipathy to the Soviet regime on grounds of power politics and national interest. To what extent did popular opinion share these divisions and doubts in relation to the Soviet Union? A partial answer to this question can be provided from Gallup Poll enquires made between December 1938 and June 1939, with the usual reservation that the responses cannot reveal the depth or conviction of the views expressed.

From December 1938 to March 1939 three questions were put by Gallup to samples of the population.

December 1938. If there were a war between Germany and Russia, which side would you rather see win?
Germany 10.35%   Russia 58.65%   No Opinion 31%
January 1939. If you HAD to choose between Communism and Fascism, which would you choose?
Fascism 21   Communism 63   No Opinion 16

---

[13] Voigt to Crozier (editor of the *Manchester Guardian*), 21 March 1939, quoted in F.R. Gannon, *The British Press and Germany, 1936–1939* (Oxford, 1971), p. 24.

March 1939. Would you like to see Great Britain and Soviet Russia being more friendly to each other?
Yes 84   No 7   No Opinion 9[14]

The value of these results is not great. The first two questions were hypothetical, and the contingencies invoked were somewhat distant from everyday life, so the answers were presumably speculative – even when respondents were told they HAD to choose between Fascism and Communism, 16 per cent declined to do so. The third question was likely to produce a 'Yes' answer, because only the very curmudgeonly would oppose being 'more friendly', even to distant foreigners – there is a general presumption in favour of friendliness, especially at no cost to oneself. All that emerged was a trend of opinion broadly favourable to the Soviet Union (or Russia) as against Germany, and a preference for Communism against Fascism when confronted with a hypothetical choice.

The next two questions posed by Gallup about the Soviet Union were much more precise, and closely related to actual events – the negotiations for an alliance in 1939.

April 1939. Are you in favour of a military alliance between Great Britain, France and Russia?
Yes 87   No 7   No Opinion 6
June 1939. Are you in favour of a military alliance between Great Britain, France and Russia?
Yes 84   No 9   No Opinion 7[15]

These results show an overwhelming majority in favour of a military alliance, with no significant change between April and June. Popular opinion on this apparently straightforward question was clear-cut, and overrode the divisions of articulate opinion and the sort of anxieties expressed by Voigt. That the issue of a military alliance was separated in peoples' minds from likes and dislikes was shown by another question put in June 1939. This was a 'write-in' question, in two parts: 'Which foreign country do you prefer?' and 'Which is the foreign country you like least?' The results showed the USSR a poor third in the list of 'preferred' countries, after the USA and France; and fourth in the list of dislikes, after Germany, Japan and Italy.[16] It

---

14 Gallup Archive, BIPO Surveys 53, 54, 56. The results of No. 53 (Dec. 1938) were presented in a form which eliminated the 31% expressing no opinion, and those in favour of a German or a Russian victory were then presented as 15% and 85% respectively of the remaining 69%. In the text, these figures have been adjusted to give the actual proportions of the sample giving the three answers – hence the decimals, which do not usually appear in Gallup results. Paul Addison, *The Road to 1945* (London, Quartet Books, 1977), p. 140, quotes the figures for Dec. 1938 and Jan. 1939 omitting the Don't Knows, and presenting the other responses as though they were proportions of the total sample, which is misleading. For the problems involved in polling methods, see above, p. 9.
15 Gallup Archive, BIPO Surveys 57, 60.
16 Gallup Archive, BIPO Survey 60. The detailed results were:

Prefer		Like least	
USA	33	Germany	54

is true that the question asked for no grounds for preference or dislike, but despite this it was precise in form, and two points emerge clearly: that the Soviet Union was by no means either a popular favourite or an obvious villain; and that this question of preferences was quite distinct in respondents' minds from the practical question of a military alliance. It would be a mistake to attach too much importance to one Gallup Poll, but on this showing the debate about the shining virtues or the double-dyed iniquity of the Soviet Union seems to have left the British public largely indifferent. But faced with a straightforward question about an alliance, the same public produced a commonsense answer.

All this was before the Nazi–Soviet Pact, the Soviet attack on Poland, and the Winter War against Finland. In face of these events, some Communists and fellow-travellers renounced their support for the Soviet Union, though others still held firm. The Webbs found each Soviet attack on a small neighbour an act of self-defence; Hewlett Johnson thought the attack on Finland lacking in Christian qualities but based on a sound strategic conception.[17] But the Left-wing *Tribune* denounced the invasion of Finland, and in March 1940 the leadership of the Labour Party issued a public statement condemning both the foreign policy and the domestic system of the Soviet Union, and attacking their apologists in Britain.

> The Red Czar is now the executor of the traditional imperialism of Czarist Russia. Stalin's men in Great Britain use the freedom which they enjoy to defend War and Tyranny, a war of conquest by an alien and powerful despot against a small outpost of republican democracy. . . . Stalin's apologists defend the Russian war against Finland because they believe or seem to believe that the Soviet system is superior to any other, that it ought to be shared by everybody, and may justly be imposed by force or cunning upon States which are 'weak from a military point of view' and have no powerful allies. . . . They defend tyranny, either because they do not know, or those who know refuse to tell, that Fascism and Bolshevism have identical political systems. . . . Even now, these emissaries of a foreign despotism refuse to see through the disguise of the Red Czar, who has used a new social and political system to invent a new kind of slavery for the Russian people.[18]

France	22	Japan	11
USSR	12	Italy	9
Scandinavia	3	USSR	5
Germany	3	France	1
Switzerland	2	Spain	1
Denmark	1	Others	2
Holland	1	No Opinion	17
Belgium	1		
Others	3		
No Opinion	19		

[17] See the description of reactions in Caute, pp. 185–92.

[18] 'The Russian–Finnish War. A Statement of Facts', by the British Labour Party (March 1940), in C.R. Attlee, Arthur Greenwood and others, *Labour's Aims in War and Peace* (London, 1940). The statement, pp. 50–74; the above quotation, pp. 73–4.

The Bear as enemy: Finland 1939

This broadside bore the signatures of Attlee and Greenwood, leader and deputy-leader of the Labour Party, who in May 1940 were to join Churchill's War Cabinet.

With the German offensive in the west and the fall of France, public discussion (and condemnation) of the Soviet Union diminished markedly. There were more urgent things to think about, and the formation of the coalition meant that the leaders of the Labour Party, like those of the Conservatives, were restricted by the constraints of high office and by considerations of *realpolitik*. However, it remained the fact that the last concentrated expression of articulate opinion about the Soviet Union before BARBAROSSA was at the time of the Winter War, and with very few exceptions it was highly unfavourable.

Popular opinion about the Soviet Union in the period after the Nazi-Soviet Pact may again be partly followed through the Gallup Polls. In the autumn of 1939, Gallup put the following questions about Russia:

September 1939. Do you think that Russia's recent actions have helped or hindered Germany in making war against us?
Helped 31   Hindered 29   Both 13   Neither 8   Don't Know 19
October 1939. Should a British Cabinet Minister be sent to Moscow now to discuss our future relations with Russia?
Yes 47   No 34   Don't Know 19
November 1939. If Finland, or Sweden, Norway or Denmark becomes

involved in war with Russia, should Great Britain give them military assistance?
Yes 42   No 38   Don't Know 18
  Do you think that Russia intends to give Germany such help as will enable Germany to defeat Britain and France?
Yes 14   No 68   Don't Know 18[19]

These questions revealed marked variations and uncertainties in opinion. The wide range of answers to the September question reflects an understandable bewilderment, and interpretation is obscured by uncertainty as to whether the poll was taken before or after the Soviet attack on Poland. However, the fact that 29 per cent of respondents thought that Russia had hindered Germany in making war on Britain showed that a substantial minority was willing to put a favourable gloss on Soviet actions. The answers to the second November question emphasize this, showing 68 per cent reluctant to believe that Russia actually wished to bring about an Allied defeat. The question, at that time hypothetical, about helping Scandinavian states against Russia, showed a very even division of opinion; and on the whole the answers show no clear-cut hostile response to the Nazi–Soviet Pact.

  The Soviet attack on Finland (30 November 1939) and the subsequent war produced a distinct shift in popular opinion.

December 1939. Which do you think is the more dangerous to us, Soviet Russia or Nazi Germany?
Soviet Russia 24   Nazi Germany 57   Don't Know 19
March 1940. Would you like to see our Government trying to establish friendly relations with Russia?
Yes 41   No 47   Don't Know 12
  Do you think that one day we shall have to fight Russia?
Yes 41   No 30   Don't Know 29[20]

The answers to the questions in March 1940 show the effects of the Winter War, with the high figure of 41 per cent of respondents expecting to have to fight Russia one day. It is striking to compare the answers in March 1939 and March 1940 to similar questions about establishing friendly relations with Russia. An 84 per cent 'Yes' in March 1939 fell a year later to 41, while a mere 7 per cent 'No' rose to 47 – a sharp change in opinion; though in the circumstances of the Finnish War, and the almost unanimous denunciation of the Soviet Union in the press, it is remarkable that 41 per cent remained in favour of improving relations with Russia.

  At that point Gallup ceased to ask questions about Russia until April 1941, when the issue of friendly relations was given another airing.

April 1941. Would you like to see Great Britain and Soviet Russia being more friendly to each other?
Yes 70   No 13   Don't Know 17

---

[19] Gallup Archive, BIPO Surveys 62, 63, 64. That for September (No. 62) was not published.
[20] Gallup Archive, BIPO Surveys 65, 68.

The question was less precise in its wording than that of March 1940, but even allowing for this difference there had been another large-scale change in opinion, this time back in favour of better relations with the Soviet Union. On this occasion, a valuable analysis of spontaneous comments, as noted by interviewers, is also available:

> 44% of spontaneous comments were on the lines of: would help us; better with us than against us; Russia is powerful.
>
> 19% were on the lines of: our own fault it hasn't happened before; Russia is go-ahead, progressive, socialist.
>
> 18% were antipathetic to Russia: don't trust them; no truck with Communism.
>
> 19% were non-committal.[21]

The first and largest category of comment showed a plain concern with self-interest, and in the prospect of Russia as a strong support. The second and third groups, of roughly equal strength, indicated respectively ideological sympathy with and hostility to the Soviet Union.

So, under the impact of the Nazi–Soviet Pact and the Winter War, popular opinion was at first confused and uncertain, and then (by March 1940) to a considerable extent unfavourable to the Soviet Union, though still with a substantial element wanting friendlier relations. By April 1941 opinion had swung back again, with a large majority in favour of friendly relations with the Soviet Union, more for reasons of self-interest than out of sympathy for the Communist system. At this stage, as in 1939 when the question of a military alliance with Russia was put, popular opinion appears to have been in large part detached from the ideological concerns of the 'political nation', and also a good deal more sympathetic to the USSR than was the government. From the opinions revealed by Gallup between 1939 and April 1941, there was no reason to think that an alliance with the Soviet Union would be difficult for the British people to accept, provided that it brought solid help to Britain. It would be particularly welcome to a minority, and unwelcome to another minority, on ideological grounds; but in a desperate war against a powerful enemy it is not surprising that the majority took the view that Soviet help would be welcome.

BARBAROSSA: first reactions

When the German assault on the Soviet Union was launched, the Ministry of Information had no publicity policy to meet the situation, though its bureaucracy was rather nervously wondering what to do. There was no Russian section in existence, and on 17 June it was the Home Planning Committee which asked the Policy Committee for guidance. Harold Nicolson (Parliamentary Undersecretary in the Ministry) prepared a paper which began: 'Although it seems improbable that Russia will become involved in war with Germany, yet should such an event occur we shall be

---

21 Gallup Archive, BIPO Survey 77; INF 1/292, HI Report 38, which gives the analysis of spontaneous comment. Home Intelligence received a fuller version of the results than that which is retained in the Gallup Archive.

faced with a grave publicity problem both at home and abroad.' The question would at once be asked whether Britain regarded the USSR as an ally or not, and symbolic occasions would be seized on: should the Soviet Ambassador (Maisky) be admitted to the meetings at St James's Palace (where representatives of the Allied governments conferred from time to time with the Foreign Secretary), and should the 'Internationale' be played in the programme of 'National Anthems of the Allies', broadcast on the BBC every Sunday evening?[22]

The Policy Committee met to discuss the question on 19 June. Nicolson pointed out that the public would require to be told at an early stage what the government intended to do in the event of a German attack on Russia. 'More would be required than a mere indication that such a development would not be altogether to the advantage of this country. It was understood that the Foreign Office took the view that it would, in fact, be a disaster, and that an indication of this view should be given.' From the Foreign Office, Oliver Harvey (Eden's Private Secretary) reported the view that in the event of war Britain would help in any way possible, but would leave any question of an alliance to Russian initiative, and Peterson said that posts abroad had already been informed that, at the outset at least, 'Russia should not be regarded as an ally'. There were a number of references to likely problems in the United States, where the prospect of intervention on Britain's side might be damaged by an alliance with Russia – a Ministry of Information official thought that American opinion would take the line that the rival German and Russian gangsters had fallen out. The Director–General, Radcliffe, concluded that the real questions were not those of publicity but of government policy, and until that was decided little could be done.[23] But at that stage the War Cabinet offered little guidance. The question was raised in the War Cabinet on 19 June as to what line should be taken on publicity, but Churchill's only comment was that 'Germany should be represented as an insatiable tyrant, that had attacked Russia in order to obtain material for carrying on the war.'[24] This contained much truth, but would not stretch very far as a propaganda policy. In fact, there could be no propaganda line until government policy was clear; which at that stage it was not.

The first news of the German attack was broadcast to the British people in the BBC bulletin at 7 a.m. on Sunday, 22 June:

> A proclamation by Hitler, read by Goebbels over the German wireless, an hour and a half ago, announced that Germany, helped by Finland in the north and Rumania in the south, was marching on Russia this morning.

The news item added that Hitler had made a bitter denunciation of Russia, in which he repeatedly linked Britain with Russia as 'working to the same end'. That was all. The bulletin passed straight on to say that two enemy aircraft had been shot down over Britain during the night, and so to other matters.

---

[22] INF 1/849, memorandum by Nicolson, 17 June 1941, 'Possible War between Germany and the USSR'. Nicolson actually referred by mistake to the 'Red Flag', not the 'Internationale', as the national anthem of the Soviet Union.

[23] BBC Written Archives, 830/42, MOI Policy Committee, 19 June 1941.

[24] CAB 65/18, WM (41) 61st Conclusions, 19 June 1941.

The 9 a.m. news provided more detail on Hitler's statement, including his declaration that German forces were called on to save the civilized world from the dangers of Bolshevism. It also stated that nothing had yet been reported from Moscow, where the radio was broadcasting its normal programmes. At 1 p.m. a broadcast by Molotov two hours earlier was reported: he condemned the German attack, said that Russia had conscientiously observed the pact with Germany, and recalled the fate of Napoleon. This bulletin also offered the first comment on the news: that Hitler had turned a great power into an enemy, in a calculated step towards world supremacy.[25]

It is hard to imagine any great event being presented more prosaically. The world might hold its breath, but the BBC moved calmly on to the day's communiqué from the Air Ministry. This was, however, only the preliminary to a *coup de théâtre*. The news bulletin at 1 p.m. announced that the Prime Minister was to broadcast after the nine-o'clock news. This speech, one of the most dramatic and decisive in Churchill's long career, was delivered without consulting the War Cabinet and without even Eden seeing the complete text. The Prime Minister declared that 'The Nazi regime is indistinguishable from the worst features of Communism', and he resolutely refused to unsay anything he had said about Communism in twenty-five years of consistent hostility. 'But all this fades away before the spectacle which is now unfolding. The past, with its crimes, its follies, and its tragedies, flashes away. I see the Russian soldiers standing on the threshold of their native land, guarding the fields which their fathers have tilled from time immemorial.' (This was a vivid word picture, but unfortunately conceived, since much of the land involved had only recently been part of Poland and the Baltic States.) Churchill then went on to declare the British decision.

> We have but one aim and one single, irrevocable purpose. We are resolved to destroy Hitler and every vestige of the Nazi regime. From this nothing will turn us – nothing. We will never parley, we will never negotiate with Hitler or any of his gang. . . . Any man or state who fights on against Nazidom will have our aid. Any man or state who marches with Hitler is our foe. That is our policy and that is our declaration. It follows therefore that we shall give whatever help we can to Russia and the Russian people. We shall appeal to all our friends and allies in every part of the world to take the same course and pursue it, as we shall, faithfully and steadfastly to the end.

The German invasion of Russia, he said, was only a prelude to an assault on Britain, and then on America. 'The Russian danger is therefore our danger, and the danger of the United States, just as the cause of any Russian fighting for his hearth and home is the cause of free men and free peoples in every quarter of the globe.'[26]

The delivery of the speech was powerful and its impact immense. Yet in

---

25 Texts of news bulletins, BBC Written Archives.
26 Churchill, *Second World War*, vol. III, pp. 331–3.

some respects it was notably cautious. Churchill nowhere used the word 'ally' in relation to the Soviet Union, and his offer of help was carefully qualified – 'we shall give whatever help we can'. The question of British policy towards the Soviet Union was only partially resolved, and the next few days were to show that problems of publicity remained acute. The past, despite Churchill's hopeful words, had not flashed away, nor could ideology be simply brushed aside. Both very soon cropped up in a series of questions, sometimes minor but always difficult.

Broadcasting to the Empire at once provided illustrations of the ideological problem, from each end of the political spectrum. On the one hand, what was to be said in broadcasts to South Africa, where there was much sympathy for Nazi Germany among the Afrikaners? The Afrikaans news editor at the BBC wrote on 23 June: 'Hitler's attack on Russia places the Afrikaans Section in the stickiest spot it has yet been in. We have taken every advantage of the Afrikaner's hatred for Bolshevism to bring Germany into disrepute. We have now to make an entire *volte face*.'[27] But on the other hand an official in the Empire Division of the Ministry of Information pointed out that Left-wing opinion in Australia and New Zealand would be watching keenly for signs that the British government was lukewarm towards the USSR, or might harbour a 'secret desire to see Communism crushed even at the cost of extending the power of Hitler'.[28] One difficulty here was that there was little chance of holding these two publics apart, because South African radio often picked up and relayed broadcasts by the Pacific service.

A combination of ideological and territorial questions was raised in the unlikely context of a schools broadcast. The BBC invited Andrew Rothstein, who was both Press Attaché at the Soviet Embassy and London representative for the Soviet news agency Tass, to give a talk on Russia in a current affairs programme for schools, and then rejected his script on the ground that it was not objective. Maisky quickly complained to Eden, who took the matter up with Duff Cooper. The script described life in the 'Western Soviet Republics', including the territories annexed by the USSR in 1939 and 1940. Its tone is fairly represented by the following: 'It was only last year that the Lithuanian peasants decided to do without landlords any longer, and joined the Soviet Union.' There was a glowing account of collective farms in Belorussia, and a passing reference to 'the rubbish that has sometimes been talked about famine in the Soviet Union'. It was an object lesson in what could go wrong. Rothstein's script raised sensitive issues in crass language, and the rapid involvement of Maisky, Eden and Duff Cooper showed how an apparently unimportant proposal could draw in senior ministers.[29]

Another question, this time involving the Prime Minister himself, was that which Nicolson had raised earlier: whether the 'Internationale' should be played on the radio among the national anthems of the allies, broadcast after the 9 p.m. news on Sundays. Churchill was resolutely opposed to this,

[27] BBC Written Archives, Talks: Russia I, Myatt to DDES, 23 June 1941.

[28] INF 1/913, Harlow to DG, 1 July 1941.

[29] FO 371/29466, N3207/3/38, Eden to Bagallay, 26 June 1941, and attached minutes; INF 1/913, Eden to Cooper, 28 June, and Cooper to Eden, 28 June. Copies of the script are in both files.

showing that there was a limit to the ideological magnanimity displayed in his broadcast of 22 June. Various strategems were attempted. Duff Cooper tried to persuade Maisky that the 'Internationale' could not properly be described as a national anthem, and it would be better to use part of the '1812' Overture; but without success. Questions were put down in Parliament about the absence of the 'Internationale' from the Sunday evening programme; the press joined in; and the whole furore assumed a somewhat farcical appearance. But neither Eden nor Duff Cooper could move the Prime Minister from his position, and in mid-July the BBC had to take the programme off and replace it with one in which each ally had a separate turn, with its own music and 'national airs' (not anthems) being played.[30]

These matters were small, and in the case of the 'Internationale' even absurd, but they were not trivial. They were symbolic of a deep and genuine difficulty, and each episode revealed the government's nervousness about the effect of such matters on opinion at home and abroad, and also upon foreign policy. Harold Nicolson, who had foreseen some of these issues, did not exaggerate when he wrote on 28 June: 'No problems could be so difficult or dangerous as the many problems set to a propaganda ministry by this strange issue.'[31] What exactly were these problems, and why did they appear so dangerous?

First, it was widely expected, by the military staffs, by ministers, and by the press that the Soviet Union would be quickly defeated.[32] There was therefore a danger that the British people would feel a sense of relief, with the lifting of the tension of air attack and the peril of invasion, only to find their hopes dashed by yet another German victory. The last state of British morale would then be worse than the first. There was thus much concern to urge the public not to slacken the war effort, but to use the time offered by the German attack on the Soviet Union to the greatest possible advantage. Second, there was another side to this. If events went the other way, and the Soviets pulled off a miracle and held out against the Germans, then another danger would arise in the growth of public admiration for a government and a system which could win such a victory. Admiration for military success was likely to lead to sympathy for Communism. Third, there were the dangers arising from the reactions of overseas opinion. Strongly anti-Communist elements, notably in the Catholic church and in large sections of American

30 McLaine, p. 197; Briggs, vol. III, pp. 389–91; INF 1/849, Policy Committee, 3 July 1941 and 22 Jan. 1942, when Churchill finally relented on broadcasting the 'Internationale', after Eden had been repeatedly greeted with 'God Save the King' in Moscow. The programme of national anthems had been a popular one, and its audience was at once halved when it was changed.

31 INF 1/913, Nicolson to Radcliffe, 28 June 1941.

32 The expectations of the staffs and ministers are well known, but the point about the press may be worth elaborating. On 21 June the Left-wing New Statesman wrote that the Russian plains were ideal for the Panzers, that the Red Air Force was out of date, and Russian staff work would be inferior to German. On 23 June the Daily Express, later to be strongly pro-Soviet, wrote that after twenty years of Communism 'the best Russian factories are still only about half as efficient as the ordinary factories of Britain or America'. In the Daily Mail (23 June) Ward Price urged his readers to forget about Napoleon – Hitler's armies were mechanized. The News Chronicle, again to be highly favourable to the USSR, wrote on 25 June 'If a miracle happened, and the Red Army were able to prolong its defence into the autumn. . . .'

opinion, might be alienated by too open a pro-Soviet line in British propaganda. On the other hand – though this was a less weighty consideration – Left-wing opinion might be offended by inadequate enthusiasm for the Soviet Union.

These dangers could not be avoided by silence. The events on the eastern front were vast and cataclysmic, and comment on them was inescapable. Moreover, propaganda had become an accepted part of policy. This was true in general terms, so that, for example, the European, American and Empire services of the BBC had to work to some broad line of policy. It was also particularly true of policy in relation to the Soviet Union. Despite Churchill's brave words, there was very little that the British could immediately *do* to help the Soviet Union, so it became all the more incumbent on them to *say* something. For these reasons, the dangers had to be faced, and a policy for publicity and propaganda devised. In practice, such a policy emerged in piecemeal fashion, over a period of some six months.

Devising a propaganda policy, June–December 1941

The Ministry of Information began its search for a policy by the useful, if bureaucratic, step of bringing a Russian Section into being within its organization. At the end of June Harold Nicolson hoped that it would not take too long to do this, fearing a Parliamentary question on the subject – 'The House of Commons would not be satisfied, I feel, merely to be told that it was all very difficult.' However, the procedures proved somewhat lengthy, and it was not until 30 September that H.P. Smollett was appointed as head of the new section, whose brief comprised British propaganda to Russia (which was acknowledged to stand little chance), and publicity for the Anglo–Soviet alliance in Britain, including liaison with the BBC and the Soviet Embassy, and the vetting of speakers' notes for public meetings.[33]

While the Ministry of Information was reorganizing itself, the BBC had to face immediate questions as to what to broadcast about the Soviet Union. In the early days, efforts were limited to an occasional short talk: for example, five minutes after the 6 p.m. news on 26 June to introduce Marshal Timoshenko, one of the Red Army commanders, and later a household name. On 3 July it was decided that some systematic projection of Russia on the Home Service was desirable; but the BBC bureaucracy was unsure what line to take. Despite the recent *contretemps* about the schools broadcast, Rothstein at the Soviet Embassy was approached for suggestions. This time he proposed historical subjects: Pugachev's serf rebellion, the Decembrists and Narodniks, the struggle of national minorities for autonomy in Tsarist Russia and their present status. The BBC Controller (Home), Sir Richard Maconachie, was sceptical, thinking that even this list might veer too far towards praise of the Soviet system. He thought it would be inadvisable to

---

[33] INF 1/913, Nicolson to Radcliffe, 28 June 1941. For the formation of the Russian section, see INF 1/147. For its scope, Smollett to Aynsley, 13 Oct. 1941.

'sell' Russian political history in any form, 'partly because we do not want, I think, to glorify revolution, and partly because the autonomy of the various Soviet Republics is mostly, so far as my information goes, bogus.' His conclusion is interesting, if only because within a short space of time it was to prove wide of the mark:

> I think if we became suddenly appreciative of the Russian system and way of life, we might easily provoke cynical and hostile reactions from our audience. . . . The British public, I think, is very suspicious – and rightly so – of clumsy *volte-faces* of this kind.

His positive proposals were extremely cautious: talks on Russian culture, and perhaps a series on Russian 'types', as drawn by writers. (Guy Burgess, the Soviet agent who was then in the Talks Department at the BBC, added the sardonic comment: 'Let's have a talk on the Great Mogul.')[34]

Maconachie's wariness was shared by the BBC Talks Department, where it was agreed that enthusiasm about the Soviet regime would be unwelcome, partly because it would be an absurd *volte-face*, and partly because it would dismay many listeners. But it would be equally mistaken to concentrate on Russia before 1917. 'Ostentatious *ancien régime* would be as ridiculous as ostentatious revolution', as the Director of Talks remarked. The compromise proposed was for talks on geography ('of a simple facts type' was the hopeful prescription), on the peoples and history of the USSR, and on cultural and scientific subjects.[35] How any of these subjects was to be tackled without taking up some stance towards the Soviet regime was not made clear.

On 12 July a joint Anglo–Soviet declaration of mutual assistance, renouncing any separate peace negotiations, was signed. Presumably impelled by this development, the Foreign Office put pressure on the BBC to be more positive about the Soviet Union. On 11 July the BBC was instructed to provide in its news bulletins a full and continuous summary of the Russian military communiqués, uninterrupted by the rival German version of events as the Foreign Office claimed had been its practice so far.[36] (The actual effect of this is not clear: the most frequent pattern for news bulletins throughout July was to put RAF operations first, the Russian communiqué second, and the German account third.[37]) On 12 July the Director of Talks at the BBC told his Department: 'We have been asked to reflect Russia in our programmes, particularly in the coming week. Will World Goes By, At Home Today, etc, do what they can. . . . The matter is urgent and has got to be done.'[38] Guy Burgess responded to this directive with a string of suggestions: something on *War and Peace* (noting that the hunting scene was

---

34 BBC Written Archives, Talks: Russia I, and especially Maconachie to Barnes, 6 July 1941.
35 *Ibid.*, Barnes to Maconachie, 9 July 1941.
36 INF 1/913, memorandum by Nicolson, 12 July 1941.
37 BBC Written Archives, news bulletins for July 1941. It seems likely that the FO instruction was issued on the basis of particular bulletins rather than the whole series. There is no noticeable variation in BBC presentation after 11 July.
38 BBC Written Archives, Talks Policy 3, memo. by Barnes, 12 July 1941. 'The World Goes By' and 'At Home Today' were regular, magazine-type programmes of short talks.

Lenin's favourite passage), and long talks about economic planning, federa-
tion, foreign policy ('carefully handled') and agrarian policy. The actual
proposals made to the Foreign Office, without whose approval nothing
could be done, were more innocuous than this – indeed, ostentatiously
ancien régime. Eight programmes for 16–18 July were to comprise music
and readings from Lermontov, Gogol, Tolstoy and Chekhov.[39] These
doubtless gave pleasure to listeners devoted to the Russian classics, but had
little bearing on the titanic struggle on the eastern front and not much appeal
to the great British public, now apparently eager for information about the
Soviet Union. There were, it is true, occasional news talks about military
affairs, of an optimistic kind – one was about Soviet air attacks on oil
refineries in Rumania. But a suggestion for a five-minute talk about Stalin, to
be given by Iverach Macdonald, the Diplomatic Correspondent of *The
Times*, was turned down briskly by the Foreign Office: 'Stalin out for the
present; please bring up again at the end of August.'[40]

The BBC's policy in July thus remained extremely cautious. It was in the
Ministry of Information, between July and September 1941, that the central
issues of a publicity strategy were debated and a policy worked out. At first, a
central theme remained the fear that the British people might slacken their
efforts because the immediate German threat had eased. A memorandum on
home morale (21 July) discussed means of countering such a tendency, to be
based on 'one simple idea, free from any ideological implications, and safe in
that it is based neither on victory nor on defeat for the Russians': that this is
our opportunity to press on with production, training and organization,
without a pause.[41] But the head of the Ministry's Home Division, Parker,
changed the emphasis in a series of memoranda which formed the basis for
the policy which was eventually accepted.[42]

Parker's opening theme (15 July) was that the Ministry of Information had
squeezed all it could out of Churchill's speech of 22 June, and done its best
with 'interesting but innocuous' background material of a geographical and
historical kind. This line was now exhausted, and the public was demanding
stronger meat. Parker foresaw an imminent danger that the growth in the
popularity of Russia would lead to enthusiasm for Communism as a political
creed. Various factors were working in the same direction: Russia was
performing beyond expectation in the fighting, so it could not be said that
Communism was inefficient; while in Britain government control over the
economy resembled Bolshevik theory and encouraged the belief that
Communism was simply a logical extension of wartime policies. Parker
argued that if this situation was allowed to develop unchecked for six months
it would be extremely difficult to 'canalize the public mind' away from such
beliefs; but early action to do so might be successful.[43]

[39] BBC Written Archives, Talks: Russia I, Burgess to Barnes, 15 July 1941; Ryan to
Maconachie, 16 July, with attached note for Foreign Office.
[40] BBC Written Archives, Talks Policy 3, minute by ASNE, 11 Aug. 1941; Talks: Russia I,
Barnes to Sumner, 4 Aug., message from Sumner, 6 Aug., memo. by Barnes, 8 Aug.
[41] INF 1/676, Balfour to Parker, 11 July 1941; INF 1/251, memo. on home morale, 21 July.
[42] There is a valuable discussion of the debate within the Ministry of Information, covering
much of the ground which follows, in McLaine, pp. 199–202.
[43] INF 1/676, memo. by Parker, 15 July 1941.

Parker persisted with these arguments during August and early September 1941. He repeated that the public mood was one in which the government was expected to control everything: 'the general demand is not for freedom of choice but for the issue of orders'. More important, the Soviet Union, far from collapsing 'like a cranky political machine based upon illogic and phantasy', had stemmed the German onslaught. In face of this success, the public could not regard Communism as incompetent, and might well come to respect it. To counter such a tendency, Parker proposed an oblique propaganda campaign, using three lines of approach. First, there should be a 'spiritual crusade', in terms of good against evil, to provide a positive war aim for the British people. (This somewhat nebulous idea was a frequent favourite in the Ministry of Information.) Second, it should be emphasized that Britain was a country where reforms had always been brought about by constitutional means, not by revolution. Third, the Ministry should 'keep before the public mind the Draconic method of rule in the Soviet Republic, and the denial of liberty to individuals equally with the German denial, and equally repugnant to ourselves.' Parker acknowledged that this last theme would be 'more difficult to handle with subtlety'. He suggested that: 'We need not tell the public again that as Hitler has his Gestapo so Stalin has his Ogpu. But we need never let them forget it.'[44] This was indeed a fine line to draw.

Churchill intervened in this discussion at the end of August. Desmond Morton had drawn the Prime Minister's attention to evidence in the Home Intelligence reports of growing admiration for Russian fighting power, and on 30 August Churchill asked Bracken (who had recently taken over as Minister of Information) to consider what action was needed 'to counter the present tendency of the British public to forget the dangers of Communism in their enthusiasm over the resistance of Russia.' This request went to Walter Monckton in the Ministry of Information, who thought there need be no hesitation about emphasizing the difference between British political ideas and Communism, and that the Communist Party should not be allowed to take credit for the help accruing to Britain from the Russian campaign. But he thought it would be a mistake to concentrate on destructive criticism of the Soviet regime. Instead, 'It would be better to throw up in positive contrast the enduring value of our own democratic way of political life.' This proposal was endorsed by the Ministry's Policy Committee, and the Prime Minister was so informed.[45]

A.P. Ryan made a characteristically pertinent contribution to the debate, advancing, not for the first time, his view of the ordinary radio listener, who 'lives remote from Whitehall, but within easy reach of his wireless switch. He can and, all our evidence goes to show, does switch off unless he is positively interested in what is being broadcast.' What did this ordinary listener think about Russia? He admired the Russians' fighting spirit, and no-one wanted to stop him doing that. He was puzzled about what Russia was really like. Before the Nazi attack, 'only a handful of cranks and Communists' were

---

44 *Ibid.*, memoranda by Parker, 12 and 19 Aug., 9 Sept. 1941.
45 INF 1/913, Monckton to Bracken, 4 Sept. 1941, and Bracken to Churchill, 8 Sept.; INF 1/676, minute by Policy Committee, 4 Sept.

actively interested in Russia; the man in the street 'wrote them off as oppressive and incompetent'. The events of the last few weeks had not changed the charge of oppression, but incompetence was another matter. The Soviet armies had done so well that the ordinary man was 'undoubtedly asking himself how far he has been misled about the whole Russian set-up.' Ryan saw that this interest could not be prevented: 'Whether we like it or not, the public will go on taking a more kindly interest in Soviet Russia than ever before – unless she packs up.' Nor could we afford to upset the Kremlin by giving publicity to critical comments about the Soviet system. 'Can we, again without upsetting the Kremlin, remind people that Communism is as oppressive, and as alien to our ideas of right and wrong, as is Nazism? I submit that, with the battle still raging, the public are in no mood for such reminders.' And this, in Ryan's view, was crucial, because there was no point in 'putting out propaganda that listeners won't swallow.'[46]

This vigorous summing-up put the situation in rather better perspective than Parker's somewhat rarefied approach. It was believed that a keen and sympathetic public interest in Russia had been aroused by the powerful Soviet resistance to the German attack. This interest could not be switched off or conjured away, and Churchill and officials in the Ministry of Information were afraid that it might be transmuted into support for Communism. But to engage in direct propaganda about the evils of the Soviet system, or even to be lukewarm about the Russians, risked offending both the Kremlin and many of the British people. By the end of September 1941 the Ministry of Information had plotted a course between these various hazards, and a memorandum of 25 September laid down guidelines which were to govern publicity policy about the Soviet Union for a long time.

The main aims of propaganda about the USSR were to:

(a) Combat such anti-Soviet feeling in Britain as might jeopardize execution of policy defined by the Prime Minister, June 22nd. Counteract enemy attempts to split national unity over issue of Anglo–Soviet Alliance.
(b) Attempt to curb exuberant pro-Soviet propaganda from the Left which might seriously embarrass HMG. Anticipate Communist-inspired criticism and prevent initiative from falling into hands of CP.

It must be made clear to the Soviet Propaganda Ministry that the Ministry of Information had no coercive powers over the British press, but within limits the Ministry could promote publicity about the USSR, for example by distributing Soviet newsreels and encouraging cinemas to show feature films, and by securing the projection of Russia on the BBC. It should also try to get freer access to news for British correspondents in the Soviet Union. Indeed, the whole policy should be reciprocal. The Soviet government exercised censorship over material which they supplied to the British, and the British government would do the same. Equally, the British would not conduct capitalist propaganda in Russia, and would not handle or encourage Communist propaganda in Britain.[47]

---

[46] INF 1/676, Ryan to Monckton, 4 Sept. 1941.
[47] INF 1/676, Grubb to Smollett, 25 Sept. 1941.

The two objectives set out in this memorandum came to form the basis of British publicity policy on Soviet questions. They were of equal importance, though for some time the second aim ((b) above) assumed more prominence. A policy for curbing exuberant pro-Soviet propaganda and preventing the initiative falling into Communist hands was set out in a 'very secret' letter from Parker to all Regional Information Officers on 15 October 1941. The object was defined as being to conduct propaganda for Anglo–Soviet co-operation so skilfully as to 'steal the thunder' of the extreme Left. A formula was provided on which answers to questions from the press or elsewhere could be based:

> While both Russia and Britain fully maintain their very different ideals about future forms of society, and remembering clearly that they differ fundamentally over the attitude to religion, among other things, they both realize that neither can pursue their own ideals while Hitler and Germany is unbeaten. They therefore both wish to pursue the joint war effort against the enemy most energetically and to let each other's population draw as much inspiration from their Ally's efforts as possible. In order to do so the Ministry encourages and assists the distribution of factual information about Russia in Britain and about Britain in Russia.

In all activities, there should be close liaison with the Soviet Embassy, but no co-operation with the British Communist Party.[48]

Recognition of differences between the two societies; emphasis on a joint war effort; and reciprocity in providing factual information: these were the main points of the formula. The head of the Russian Department in the Ministry, Smollett, elaborated on the general directive with detailed instructions. Exhibitions about the Soviet Union were to contain equal proportions of British and Russian material, and to display large announcements that they were produced jointly by the Ministry of Information and the Soviet Embassy. Speakers about the USSR posed a problem: 'in principle we should aim at avoiding the use of both White Russians and Red Englishmen.' This did not leave much scope, and the Ministry hoped to get speakers from the Soviet Embassy, on condition that they stuck to a brief agreed between the Embassy and the British government. Regional Information Officers were firmly instructed that there was no case for general representation of the Communist Party on Information Committees. If it was thought that the strength of Communist feeling in a particular area justified such representation, the matter was to be referred to the Ministry in London.[49]

This system was put to work at once in handling many requests to the Ministry for help in organizing Anglo–Russian Weeks, Soviet Weeks, or Aid to Russia Weeks – the nomenclature varied. For example, in October 1941 the South-West Regional Information Officer reported that 'local Leftists' were proposing to arrange an Anglo–Russian Week in Bristol at the end of November. Even at that stage, the events were to include speeches by a local

---

48 INF 1/676, Parker to all RIOs, 15 Oct. 1941, 'Propaganda Policy of the Ministry in regard to Russia.' Cf. McLaine, pp. 201–2.

49 INF 1/676, Smollett to Parker, 6 Oct. 1941; Briggs to Parker, 10 Oct., including instructions to RIOs dated 24 Sept.

MP, the Lord Mayor and the Bishop of Bristol. Parker minuted that it came under the 'Stealing the thunder' clause of the Ministry's policy, and the Regional Information Office was instructed to 'capture' the Week and ensure that there was a suitable management committee. The Ministry was also to try to draw the Soviet Embassy into a joint fostering of the Week.[50] By the middle of December, the Regional Information Officer for London had received nearly fifty requests for help with similar events. He dealt with them according to the political complexion of the organizers: if they were solely Communists, they got no help; in other cases, posters, photographs, and administrative support were provided in varying degrees.[51] The initiative was not always left to others. In November a conference of Regional Information Officers proposed that the Ministry should allow them to originate Soviet Weeks as well as 'capturing' them after others had made a start; and this was quickly accepted.[52]

It may well be that the traffic in arranging and exploiting Soviet Weeks was not as one-way as the files of the Ministry of Information would indicate. The Communist Party had much practice in using individuals and organizations for its own purposes, and was doubtless able to play the Ministry at its own game. But there was no doubt about the Ministry's policy. Enthusiasm for Russia was running strongly, as was shown by the demand for Anglo–Soviet demonstrations and the zeal for knowledge about the Russian people. All this fervour was to be channelled by official guidance, and as little of it as possible was to be allowed to be diverted to the advantage of the Communist Party. In this effort, the Soviet Embassy was seen as an ally, because Ministry officials were convinced that Soviet government policy would be determined by *realpolitik* rather than ideology. In the event, the Ministry was keener to draw in the Soviet Embassy than the Embassy was to be drawn. The Ministry wanted a team of speakers, and wanted them – if they were military men – to appear in uniform; but the Embassy offered in November only three nominees, refused to allow anyone to wear uniform, and insisted that they should confine themselves to literature, art and similar non-political subjects. An Embassy official argued, with strict propriety, that he did not wish to do anything which would encourage accusations of interfering in British domestic affairs. The Ministry countered by saying that they would announce at every meeting that the speakers were invited explicitly by the British government.[53] It was an interesting tug-of-war, which at that stage the Ministry lost.

Indeed, the whole policy was clearer in conception than in execution. It proved extremely difficult to draw and maintain a line between the presentation of the Soviet Union as a powerful ally, with 'factual information' (in the

[50] *Ibid.*, Bentley to Smollett, 14 Oct. 1941, and attached papers. Other examples are given by McLaine, pp. 205–6.

[51] INF 1/676, Briggs to RIOs, 16 Dec. 1941, circulating memo. by RIO, London. Cf. McLaine, p. 206.

[52] *Ibid.*, Gates to Parker, 10 Nov. 1941; Parker to RIOs, 13 Nov.

[53] *Ibid.*, RIO, Southern Region, to Ministry, Home Division, 7 Oct. 1941; note of conservation between MOI official and Zinchenko, Soviet Embassy, 20 Oct.; memo. by Smollett, 3 Nov., with attached minute.

words of the policy formula) about the country, and the presentation of the regime which controlled that country and the political system which it embodied. Even when the material used was very closely controlled by the Ministry of Information, the task of maintaining the distinction proved impossible. For example, in autumn 1941 the Ministry sent exhibitions of photographs round the country, arranged round five themes: the Soviet Armed Forces, Soviet children, Soviet Women, Industry, and Agriculture. The first three were fairly plain sailing. The armed forces were heroic; children were appealing; women worked hard in factories and the fields, but could still be beautiful. But captions for Industry and Agriculture at once posed problems, because any reference to rapid industrialization or collectivization of farms opened controversial topics – yet how could Soviet agriculture be presented without collective farms? The attempted solution was to concentrate simply on showing the vast resources of the Soviet Union. But by the end of November 1941 the head of the Russian section wanted to end the exhibitions because of the difficulty of devising captions: 'even the most inoffensive is bound to assist Communist propaganda in this country.' But the exhibitions were too popular to allow this. The Regional offices asked for more, and they continued well into 1943.[54]

The same was true of the output of the BBC, which was entirely under official control. Thirty-five talks on Russian subjects were given on the Home Service from July to mid-October 1941. Some were readings from the classics – *Anna Karenina, War and Peace*; but others were fulsome praise of the Soviet Minister for Propaganda and a boldly titled description of 'Democracy at War'. On 4 December a meeting of officials from the BBC, Ministry of Information and the Foreign Office reviewed the treatment of Russia on the Home Service and concluded that, in spite of every care taken to avoid political bias, the presentation had been one-sided. It had proved inevitable that talks should 'dwell rather on the bright side of Soviet life and should avoid its less attractive features. A critical attitude would be resented not only by the Russians, but also by the public of this country, who, without in any way supporting communism, resent any ungenerous attitude towards our Allies.'[55]

The Home Service thus bestowed its praise somewhat reluctantly; but the European Service of the BBC had fewer inhibitions. Even in the early stages of the German onslaught, when cautious advisers were wanting to prepare audiences for Russian defeats, Newsome (the head of the European Service) would have none of it. His European News Directive for 23 July laid down that: 'We absolutely must not accept German claims to have disrupted the Soviet defence.' On 6 August he told broadcasters that: 'The Russians are extremely confident and even possessed of a feeling of superiority over Germany arising from faith in their own institutions (a faith whose possession saved us last year and the lack of which destroyed the French).'[56] The

54 INF 1/249, Home Planning Committee, 23 Oct. 1941; INF 1/676, Smollett to Parker, 28 Nov. 1941: INF 1/677, memo. by Davies, 2 Jan. 1942.
55 BBC Written Archives, Talks: Russia I, list of talks, 2 July–17 Oct. 1941; Clarke to Rÿan, 8 Dec. 1941.
56 BBC Written Archives, OS137B, European News Directives, 23 July, 6 Aug. 1941.

linking of Soviet resistance to faith in their institutions was the sort of reference which the Ministry of Information wished to avoid, but it appears to have passed unchecked. Preparing the ground for Beaverbrook's supply mission to Moscow at the end of September 1941,[57] an important General Directive declared that this conference would bring Russia 'back into the comity of civilized nations'. Broadcasts must show Russia as 'a civilized state, with a great culture of her own in the European tradition . . . It may not be a welcome fact to some, but it *is* a fact that the effect of Communist ideology on a people's culture is not, as is that of the Fascist or Nazi ideology, to disfigure and sterilize it.' Without accepting Communist economic ideas, we must convince Europe that Russia has remained civilized, and that 'an Anglo–Russian alliance holds out a fine promise of progress for European civilization towards a system combining the best features of Socialism and liberal democracy.'[58] Perhaps Newsome protested too much about civilization, but even so this launched the European News Directives on what was to be a dominant theme: that the two previously opposed ideologies of Britain and Russia would now come together in a mutually advantageous fusion. Military co-operation would lead to political and social convergence, and Britain and Russia had already shown their solidarity by their joint adherence to the Atlantic Charter.

Thus the Home Service tried to avoid the ideological issue, while the European directives acknowledged an ideological divide but rejoiced in the prospect of its being overcome, and saw the Soviet regime as part of Russia's strength. In both cases, the picture was a glowing one, and the auguries for the future were favourably interpreted.

The same was true of the presentation of the Soviet Union in the cinema newsreels. After a brief period of uncertainty, when the newsreel editors made uncomfortable references to the period of German–Soviet co-operation, the projection of the Soviet Union on the screen grew rapidly more favourable. From the beginning of September 1941 Soviet newsreels began to be received in Britain. From these, the British newsreel editors selected the footage they wanted to show, and provided their own commentaries, subject to the usual censorship procedures. This system of distribution sometimes filled the whole newsreel slot with film from the Soviet war zone. The basic material was Soviet-produced, but it was equally important that the British commentaries provided a glowing picture of the Soviet war effort and an increasingly favourable slant on the regime which directed it. There was much emphasis on the unity of the Soviet people, and the determination with which they were defending a society which they had created for themselves and in which they believed. The newsreel commentaries on the defence of Odessa did not hesitate to recall the revolutionary past which was so closely linked with that city. Soviet feature films too began to be distributed – 'Salute to the Soviet' was first shown in October, quickly followed by 'Soviet Women'. The overall image being presented by the autumn and winter of 1941 was not simply one of Russian strength and

---

[57] On the Beaverbrook mission, see below, pp. 53–56.
[58] BBC Written Archives, OS137F, Weekly General Directive, 1–8 Sept. 1941.

The friendly Bear: Good Hunting, 1941

fighting spirit, but also that of a resilient, efficient and popular regime, often held up as an example for the British people to follow.[59]

In these different modes of presenting the Soviet Union to the British public, the Ministry of Information and associated British authorities were in control of the material to be used, but the distinction which was in principle central to the Ministry's propaganda policy could not be enforced. It was impossible to distinguish between the country and the regime, even when (as in the Home Service of the BBC) the will to do so was strong. And sometimes even the will to draw the line was absent.

All this arose out of the proposal to 'curb exuberant pro-Soviet propaganda from the Left'. But the Ministry of Information's policy document of 25 September 1941 put another objective first: to combat anti-Soviet feeling which might obstruct the Prime Minister's policy of help to Russia, and to counteract enemy attempts to split national unity on the issue of Anglo–Soviet co-operation. This objective too was vigorously pursued, and

[59] On the presentation of the Soviet Union in British newsreels, see P.M.H. Bell and Ralph White, 'Images of the Soviet Union at War' (film, with accompanying booklet, Inter-University History Film Consortium, London, 1990); D.W. Spring, 'Soviet Newsreel and the Great Patriotic War', in Nicholas Pronay and D.W. Spring, eds., *Propaganda, Politics and Film, 1918–45* (London, 1982); Sergei Drobashenko and Peter Kenez, 'Film Propaganda in the Soviet Union, 1941–1945: Two Views', in K.R.M. Short, ed., *Film and Radio Propaganda in World War II* (London, 1983). On the arrival of Soviet newsreels and feature films, INF 1/622, Hogg to Radcliffe, 3 Sept. 1941, and INF 1/676, de Moulpied to Dowden, 22 Oct. 1941.

in this case the path of propaganda proved smoother than was at first expected.

Some of the most serious difficulties were expected to arise out of the question of religion. The Soviet government was publicly, and often stridently, opposed to all religion, and had long conducted an 'anti-God' campaign in its own country. In Britain, though the number of church-goers was not large, there remained a widespread respect for religion, and the churches formed a significant element in organized opinion. Most Christians, and especially Roman Catholics, were profoundly hostile to the USSR and to Communism. The problem extended overseas, where an alliance with the Soviet Union might well arouse hostility among Catholics in Canada and the USA, and among American Protestants. Up to June 1941, the Ministry of Information had itself played the religious card, promoting the idea of the war as the defence of Christian civilization against Nazism, and it had successfully enlisted the support of the churches to this end. How could the defence of Christian civilization be squared with alliance with an openly anti-Christian state, and how could the issue of religion be neutralized so as to soothe anti-Soviet feelings and avoid dangerous conflicts of opinion? It was recognized at once that the Germans would be scanning in particular the Catholic press in search of openings to exploit in their own propaganda; and the Russians themselves were quick to take offence.

The British authorities moved speedily to cope with this problem. As early as 24 June the Foreign Office set out the lines on which it was hoped that the Catholic press would comment on the German invasion of the USSR. 'It is not to be expected of course that they will – any more than the Prime Minister has done – withdraw their condemnation of Russian Communism and its anti-religious activities. But it is important that they should get the proportion right.' They should remember that Nazi Germany was the prime enemy, and not be deceived by German claims to be defending Europe against atheistic Communism. The Foreign Office hoped that Cardinal Hinsley, the Archbishop of Westminster, would give guidance along these lines. The Cardinal did so in a statement published on 28 June, recalling Papal condemnations of both Communism and Nazism, but stressing that Britain was fighting against the immediate Nazi attempt to subjugate Europe, and declaring (in almost exactly the words suggested by the Foreign Office) that no-one would be deceived by Hitler's claim to be the champion of European civilization. William Paton, Joint Secretary of the World Council of Churches, offered similar advice on behalf of Protestant churches: 'What the Prime Minister said last Sunday came not only from him but from the hearts of the mass of Christians in this country. . . . We cannot see that the kind of world the Nazi rulers would offer to the conquered nations is better than the worst the Communists could do.'[60]

[60] INF 1/790, including text of FO guidance note, Hinsley's statement (with a note by Nicolson: 'Seen by the Minister who wishes the widest publicity given to the statement'), and text of Paton's broadcast. On 26 June *The Times* published a letter from Barbara Ward, writing as Secretary to the Catholic organization, Sword of the Spirit, arguing that the Nazis would seek to exploit the anti-Communist feelings of sincere men; but the British government was lending its aid, not to Communism, but to the Russian victim of Nazi aggression. These phrases later appeared in MOI literature, and may well have been officially 'inspired'.

These early moves were quickly and adroitly followed up. Early in July the Ministry of Information prepared a memorandum offering guidance to religious opinion. 'We have not altered our opposition to Communism. We lend our aid not to Communism but to the Russian victim of Nazi aggression.' The claim to be fighting for Christian civilization remained valid: even though many people felt that this heritage was potentially menaced by Communism, it was *actually* under threat from Nazism. The Ministry was able to point out that this view had already been supported by religious leaders like Cardinal Hinsley, forbearing to point out that Hinsley's statement had been made at the Ministry's own request.[61] The Religious Division of the Ministry proved adept at securing statements from widely respected clergymen in such a way as to make them appear spontaneous. In July 1941, for example, the Moderator of the Church of Scotland publicly declared that despite differences of principle from the Soviets, it was only sensible to help Russia against the German attack. If his house was burning down, he would not ask the firemen whether they were all faithful Christians. This sturdy commonsense assertion was given a good showing in the British press, and in propaganda material for American consumption. How this particular oracle was worked was shown in the Moderator's covering letter when he sent a draft of his statement to the Ministry of Information: 'Herewith as requested. Cut it down as you think best. I hope it will serve your purpose.'[62] The same device was used in November, when William Temple, the Archbishop of York and a widely respected national figure, addressed the York Diocesan Conference along lines proposed to him by Smollett, the head of the Russian Section at the Ministry of Information. 'Their cause is ours, and our cause is theirs. Let no-one hesitate to assert our unity of purpose.' Even though the atheism of 'official Russia' remained, an honest comradeship would be possible, said Temple, following the lines suggested to him by Smollett.[63] This speech too was well reported in the press.

There was no question of these church leaders being coerced into such statements against their will. They were anxious to help what they thought to be their country's cause, and the cause of their faith. Roman Catholic, Presbyterian and Anglican alike gladly followed the lead given by the Ministry of Information. The examples given here could be supported by other cases of senior clergymen conforming to the Ministry's guidelines without the evidence of direct correspondence being extant.[64] The Bishop of Bradford was willing to go further, taking the same line as Newsome at the BBC in looking forward to better relations between the different ideologies: better understanding, more respect, a grasp that the Russians were not the

---

61 INF 1/790, Martin to Davidson, Clark and Parker, 5 July 1941, and enclosed paper.
62 *Ibid.*, Cockburn (the Moderator) to Martin, 17 July 1941; Martin to Cockburn, 21 July. The draft was in fact cut down, by omitting remarks that it was no use pretending that we would 'deliberately choose to be allies with the atheistic communists who at present rule Russia.'
63 *Ibid.*, Paton to Smollett, 22 Oct., 25 Nov. 1941.
64 The Archbishop of Canterbury (Lang), in his *Diocesan Gazette* for July countered misgivings about an alliance with the Soviet government, using the standard points that we were fighting to overthrow the tyranny of evil in Germany, and its enemies were our allies, and that Russia was fighting for its national freedom, a principle defended by Britain. He also hoped for a new toleration for religion in Russia (*The Times*, 24 July 1941).

slaves of a tyrannical regime nor the British the devotees of economic selfishness and imperialist ambition.[65] Hope and truth are both Christian virtues: on Stalin's regime the bishop's comments erred heavily on the side of hope. From the utilitarian point of view of the Ministry of Information, however, there could be no doubt that one likely source of anti-Communist and anti-Soviet feeling had been successfully nullified by skilful propaganda techniques working upon a responsive audience.

In October 1941 there was an example of what could still go wrong, despite the best efforts of the Ministry of Information. At the end of September Maisky made a speech at the American Chamber of Commerce in London, in which he rashly went out of his way to state that, despite much that was said to the contrary, religion was not persecuted in the Soviet Union. This remark drew severe comment from Catholic weekly papers, where it was described variously as hypocritical, cynical, a perversion of the truth, and akin to sneak-thieves trying to avoid punishment by lies. Maisky made a formal protest against this 'anti-Soviet campaign'; there was a flurry of exchanges between the Foreign Office and the Ministry of Information; and not for the first or last time Eden was glad to be able to explain to the Ambassador that in Britain the press was free to express its opinions. Maisky accepted this point, and later told a Ministry of Information official that he had been ill-advised to make his remarks about religion. The Russian section of the Ministry assured the Foreign Office that, with the occasional exception of the *Catholic Herald*, there was no sign that the Catholic papers were engaged in any anti-Soviet campaign. The Religions division was in regular contact with the editors concerned, who were following the line adopted by the Prime Minister on policy towards the USSR. So the incident passed off, amidst more pressing matters; but it was nonetheless a reminder of the sort of friction which could easily arise. The emollient activities of the Ministry of Information were certainly necessary.[66]

Another preoccupation of the Ministry of Information was to reassure the public that the government was serious in its intention to help Russia. Churchill's pledge to give all possible help was made on 22 June, but its fulfilment was slow to materialize. Press agitation about this began quickly. It was as early as 6 July that an article by John Gordon in the *Sunday Express* carried the headline 'Where's That Second Front?', though its demand was not for an invasion of the continent but for raids on the occupied coasts and for incendiary bombing which would set Germany on fire from end to end. Gordon claimed that action was being stifled by the 'old school tie' network, by trade union politicians, by the Foreign Office and the Treasury – in short, by a whole array of cautious and restrictive elements. The *Daily Herald* asked on 7 July: 'What is our utmost? When shall we begin to do it?' The *News Chronicle* took up the same theme, arguing on 31 July that it was now clear that Russia was not going to collapse, so the time had come to meet all Soviet requirements in arms and equipment. The *Daily Express* proclaimed

[65] *Manchester Guardian*, 27 Sept. 1941.

[66] The correspondence is in FO371/29469, N6066/3/38 and N6166/3/38. See especially Maisky's memorandum, 18 Oct. 1941, and the accompanying FO minutes; Smollett to Dew, 25 Oct. The offending articles appeared in *Catholic Herald*, 3 Oct., *Catholic Times*, 3 and 10 Oct.

on 12 August that 'We must support Russia till it hurts.' *The Times* on 6 September declared that the Russians must receive every ounce of moral and material support. On 26 September a meeting in Manchester, called by the Labour Party and addressed by a Conservative MP as well as by Liberal and Communist representatives, passed a resolution in support of maximum help for Russia.[67] On 8 September the *Daily Herald*'s leading article was headed 'Get A Move On', and demanded to know the cause of the delay in organizing aid to Russia. And so it went on.

One reason often asserted for the delay in helping Russia was that anti-Bolshevik influence (the old school tie brigade) was still strong, and that apart from the Prime Minister himself the government was only paying lip-service to a Russian alliance. This feeling was concentrated by a speech at the Trade Union Congress on 3 September, in which a delegate claimed that the Minister of Aircraft Production, Moore-Brabazon, had said that it would be best for Britain if Germany and Russia fought one another to a standstill.[68] This aroused widespread indignation in the press, especially on the Left. In the Ministry of Information, Parker thought that the episode confirmed a tendency of opinion which was already strong, and he though it urgent that the government should convince the public that it meant business about help to Russia.[69]

An attempt was made to meet the problem by speeches by government ministers, suitably reported in the press – notably Alexander, the First Lord of the Admiralty, promised every form of help to Russia, and said that the Navy was escorting convoys to Russian ports.[70] But the centrepiece of propaganda about aid to Russia was the Anglo-American supplies mission to Moscow (28 September–4 October 1941). The head of this mission on the British side was Lord Beaverbrook, the Minister of Supply and a master in the arts of publicity. Before the mission's departure, Beaverbrook launched the idea of a 'Tanks for Russia Week', to culminate while he was in Russia. His message to workers in the tank factories was dramatic, not to say theatrical:

> From Monday next . . . September 22, and for the space of seven days, the work of your hands will be sent to the Front Lines defending Leningrad, Kiev and Odessa.
> There will be no delay. The tanks you build will go forthwith into action to play their part in the battle.
> Come then, in the foundries and forges of Britain, in the engine works

---

67 *Manchester Guardian*, 8 Sept. 1941.

68 *The Times*, 4 Sept. 1941, for report of the TUC meeting. Moore–Brabazon's remark had been made at a private meeting. He wrote to Churchill asserting that he had consistently supported the Prime Minister's policy, and indeed had done so when consulted by Churchill before his speech on 22 June – Gilbert, p. 1120. What exactly Moore–Brabazon said, or what he meant, were irrelevant to the controversy which followed.

69 INF 1/676, Parker to Royde, 17 Oct. 1941.

70 Alexander, reported in *Manchester Guardian*, 15 Sept. 1941, *D. Telegraph*, 11 Oct.; Dalton, *The Times*, 18 Sept. Also other papers. In fact, only one convoy had at that time sailed, leaving Hvalfiord on 21 August 1941 and reaching Archangel on the 31st. The second (PQ. 1) sailed on 29 September. (S.W. Roskill, *The War at Sea*, vol. III, Part II (London, 1961), p. 432.

A tank called Stalin: Maisky addresses workers during 'Tanks for Russia Week'

and the assembly lines, to the task and duty of helping Russia to repel the savage invaders, who bring torment and torture to mankind.[71]

Beaverbrook's newspaper, the *Daily Express*, threw itself into the campaign:

Next week, TANKS-FOR-RUSSIA WEEK, will be the test of Britain's power to send the big stuff. . . . Next week we want you to work like men possessed. To arm Russia for attack. . . .

These tanks are going straight out to save lives and to KILL.[72]

Maisky, the Soviet Ambassador, joined in, visiting a factory to receive 'the first tank', while Mme Maisky named it, as at the launching of a ship. The newsreels made much of these activities, and a great success was claimed, with a marked increase in production over the week.[73]

Beaverbrook and his American colleague, Averell Harriman, went to Moscow and agreed on a programme of aid, Beaverbrook insisting that the line to take was not to bargain with Stalin but simply to promise him what he wanted, and thus build up Soviet confidence in Britain. There was a serious

---

[71] Kenneth Young, *Churchill and Beaverbrook. A Study in Friendship and Politics* (London, 1966), pp. 206–7. Churchill toned down an earlier draft, removing some fulsome praise of Russian fortitude, and also a passage which presented the Week as his (Churchill's) decision.

[72] *Daily Express* leading article, 20 Sept. 1941.

[73] For newsreel coverage, see Paramount, 1103, and British Movietone, 864A, both 25 Sept. 1941.

Comrades in Arms: Mrs Churchill promotes her 'Aid to Russia Fund'

side to the mission, and the agreed programme of aid was largely completed by July 1942; but the publicity lavished upon it far exceeded its actual achievements. The press was fulsome, and the newsreels presented fervent accounts of Beaverbrook's journey. Beaverbrook himself, at the key time after the nine o'clock news on 23 October, made an impassioned broadcast describing the promises of help made to the Russians and appealing for the involvement of his audience:

Men and women alike, you are all pledged to uphold the standards of Russia on the battlefront. . . . You take your part, your splendid share in the defence of Leningrad, at the outposts of Moscow, and in the citadel of Odessa. . . . We will forego food from abroad if the ships are needed for Russia. We will give up all our leisure if munitions are required to defend their cities. . . . Stalin must be sustained. The Soviet Union must be enabled to enter the spring campaign with adequate supplies of all munitions of war.

The Ministry of Information published extracts from this broadcast in a smartly produced pamphlet, *Comrades in Arms: Britain and the USSR*, with a coloured cover displaying the Union Jack and the Red Flag side by side, and pages of photographs with striking captions – pictures of Stalin and Churchill, of British tanks destined for Russia, and of the Soviet armed forces – 'WE WILL NEVER LET THEM DOWN', the text declared.[74] Later on, the Ministry also collected and publicized quotations from Soviet broadcasts, illustrating expressions of gratitude for British aid: 'Long live Great Britain for the help she is sending us'; 'The help of our friends the English increases daily'; and so on.[75] The drum was certainly banged for the Beaverbrook mission and British help for Russia. If the British public was not convinced, it was not for want of trying on the part of the Ministry of Information.

The Ministry of Information thus evolved a strategy for publicity in relation to the Soviet Union. It was not applied with absolute uniformity – the European News Directives of the BBC and some newsreel items went further in praise of the Soviet system than the Ministry envisaged. But in general it sought to keep a nice balance on a tricky tightrope. It emphasized British determination to help the Russians; it forestalled or soothed religious objections to an alliance with a Communist and atheistic state; and it sought to temper and guide admiration for the Russian war effort in such a way that it did not evolve into support for Communism in Britain. On the whole, it formed a coherent response to some very difficult problems. It is time to turn to the evolution of public opinion, and to ask how far it responded to the guidance which the Ministry provided.

The evolution of public opinion towards the Soviet Union, June–December 1941

The German assault on the Soviet Union was an event of immense magnitude which might well have produced sharp division of opinion. In the event, the response of articulate opinion in Britain was remarkably low-key and to a large degree consistent. Churchill's speech was received with universal approval. The *Daily Telegraph* praised his right judgement of the course to

---

[74] For the Beaverbrook Mission, Joan Beaumont, *Comrades in Arms: British Aid to Russia 1941–1945* (London, 1980), pp. 52–60, 112; A.J.P. Taylor, *Beaverbrook* (London, 1972), pp. 486–91. For newsreel coverage, British Movietone, 646, 20 Oct. 1941. Copies of the MOI's pamphlet were distributed to factories – report in *D. Express*, 17 Nov. 1941.

[75] Ministry of Information, Reference Division circular, 9 May 1942, with quotations from Soviet radio, Nov. 1941.

be taken; so did the *News Chronicle*. The *Daily Herald* found it 'one of the most stirring and satisfying' of all Churchill's speeches, and the *New Statesman* greeted it as a 'great and historic event.'[76] In a short debate in the House of Commons on 24 June, Eden accepted that the British and Soviet political systems were antipathetic to one another, but emphasized that this must not obscure 'the realities of the political issue which confronts us today'. Backbenchers from all three main parties went out of their way to praise Churchill's broadcast and support his stance. Lees–Smith (Labour) declared that no section in the country would see Hitler as a crusader against Communism. As if on cue, Bower (Conservative) made a brief but remarkable statement, claiming to speak on behalf of 'His Majesty's many millions of very loyal Roman Catholic subjects'. He began with a *caveat*: 'We hate Communism and Nazism equally, for one reason and one reason only, that both are pagan and both atheistic.' But he went on: 'As regards the political and military measures which may be necessary, as long as the Prime Minister and Foreign Secretary stand by the assurances which they have given today that they do not wish in any way to withdraw their condemnation of Communism as a creed, we also will be behind them and will have our eyes on the target, which is the utter destruction of Hitler and of Nazi Germany.'[77] It was an impressive display of unity from a House of Commons which was still essentially that which had been elected in 1935, and in which sympathy with the Soviet Union had not been strong. Outside Parliament, the National Council of Labour, representing both the political and trade union wings of the Labour Party, issued a statement on 25 June condemning Nazi aggression and sending greetings and assurances of support to the Russian people; though it commented in passing that the Russians were sharing the experience of all who trusted Hitler's word, which was a reminder of the Nazi–Soviet Pact.[78] Among the press, the *Daily Mail* had been among the most ardently anti-Communist and anti-Soviet. The *Mail*'s leading article on 23 June recalled Stalin's recent record: he was now paying the price for a policy of 'brutal cynicism'. It rehearsed the catalogue of the Nazi–Soviet Pact, the attack on Poland along with the Germans, the war against Finland, and the seizure of the Baltic states. But after all this it concluded, albeit grudgingly: 'In the struggle between Russia and Germany, Russia's interests are ours. It is a pity Stalin failed to see this two years ago.' The *Mail* agreed that Britain would give help to Russia, but without weakening herself. On the 24th the *Mail*'s leader, perhaps to alleviate the grudging tone of the previous day, claimed that if Hitler hoped to split the British and American democracies over the issue of Bolshevism he was mistaken. This was a theme widely taken up in the press, across political boundaries: Hitler's claim to be the defender of civilization against Bolshevism was generally and publicly rejected.

A broadcast by Stalin on 3 July, in which he welcomed Churchill's 'historic speech' and declared that the struggle of the Russian people was linked to that of the peoples of Europe and America, was extensively reported and

76 Newspapers all 23 June; *New Statesman*, 28 June.
77 *HC Deb.*, 5th series, vol. 372, cols. 971–1006.
78 Text in *The Times*, 26 June 1941.

welcomed in the British press. The *Daily Telegraph* praised Stalin's 'iron determination', and the *Manchester Guardian* found his speech remarkable for its 'frankness, clarity and spirit'.[79] The Anglo–Soviet declaration of mutual assistance (12 July), pledging no negotiations for a separate peace, was greeted by *The Times* as 'tantamount to an alliance', implying the necessity of agreement on terms of peace. The *Manchester Guardian* again praised Churchill's statesmanship, and reflected how fortunate it was that he was Prime Minister and leader of the Conservative Party in this crisis. The very fact of his previous opposition to Communism enabled him to carry everyone with him in the understanding that Hitler was not making war upon Communism but upon the state of Russia and its people. When the war was over, it might well be that the British and Russian peoples 'can serve the world in peace by their sympathy', as they would in war by their courage.[80] The *Spectator* argued that the agreement would forestall a German peace offensive. *The Economist* thought it contained nothing to upset even the most apprehensive opponent of Communism, but recognized that if Russian resistance was successful there might be almost insoluble problems at the peace: Britain must resolutely refuse to sacrifice the small peoples of eastern Europe to considerations of strategy or self-interest. The *New Statesman* was more hopeful in its long-term views. 'The Alliance may gradually lead to modifications of outlook both in Britain and in Russia.' Russia might become more democratic in its political system, while Britain moved towards a socialist economy – 'it is not Utopian to seek a narrowing of economic and ideological conflict.'[81] But these questions appeared distant and hypothetical in the immediate crisis. The House of Commons accepted the Anglo–Soviet declaration on 'no separate peace' with almost no comment.[82]

All this showed a quite unexpected degree of agreement. The opposition to a Soviet alliance which was anticipated from anti-Communist MPs, newspapers and the churches did not materialize. This was presumably the result of Churchill's speech of 22 June, superbly timed, phrased and delivered; of the adroit work of the Ministry of Information, especially with religious leaders; and above all of the circumstances, in which British self-interest was so clearly bound up with Russian resistance. However, this near-unanimity could not last, and during the second half of 1941 two serious conflicts of opinion arose, one on an immediate issue of strategy, the other on a distant question of peace-making and principle.

The strategic question was that of a 'second front'. John Gordon opened the public controversy in the *Sunday Express* on 6 July 1941, calling for immediate raids on the European coastline to distract German forces from Russia. The *Daily Herald* quickly commented (8 July) that more was needed than 'a chain of petty Gallipolis'; though it offered nothing more positive than exhortation – 'Our strategists must think hard, big and quickly'. On 19 July the *New Statesman* pointed out that what Stalin wanted above all was 'a

---

[79] Both 4 July 1941. Other papers used similar language.
[80] *The Times*, 14 July 1941; *Manchester Guardian*, 17 July.
[81] *Spectator*, 18 July 1941; *Economist*, *New Statesman*, 19 July.
[82] *HC Deb.*, vol. 373, cols. 463–4.

second active front' against Germany, but this raised questions which only the general staffs could answer. 'No layman ought to offer advice on so technical and dangerous an adventure.' If this sage advice had been universally followed, there would have been no controversy; but of course it was not, and these early exchanges set a pattern for what was to follow.

On the one hand was the 'Do something' school. Britain must create a diversion in western Europe, by means which might vary from small-scale commando raids to an invasion in force. The main support for such ventures was to be found in articles in the *Daily Express* and *News Chronicle*, with echoes in other papers. There were public meetings, held usually by Left-wing groups: one at the Garrick Theatre in London on 20 October was addressed by Michael Foot, Frank Owen and Harry Pollitt; there was another in Trafalgar Square on the 26th. The Communist Party was also active, and on 12 October issued a statement that 'The honour of the British people is at stake. If we let Russia down history will demand a most terrible retribution. It is time to open a second front in the west.'[83] The campaign built up during September and reached a peak in October 1941, when there was general agreement in the press, even among opponents of the agitation, that opinion in the country was deeply disturbed. On the other hand was the school which advocated caution and held that strategic decisions should be left to the experts. The *Spectator* (17 October), while acknowledging the intensity of the anxiety to help Russia, observed that an invasion of western Europe demanded men, ships and ports – to attempt invasion with less than 40 divisions would invite disaster. The *Sunday Times* (28 September, 12 October) argued that the only way to help Russia in the long run was to win the war – there was no point in a generous gesture which would lose it. Such arguments were by no means confined to the Right wing in politics. The President of the TUC, Frank Wolstencroft, speaking at Liverpool on 14 September, said that Britain should not throw thousands of lives away on the continent merely to provide a 'stage show'. The *Manchester Guardian* (22 September) soberly pointed out that there was one vital condition for a second front: that the force should be so large and well supplied that the Germans would not defeat it. Only the irresponsible would tell the government what it must do in such a matter. When Parliament debated aid to Russia on 23 October, the whole trend of the debate was that the question of a second front must be left to the government and the Chiefs of Staff. Even Gallacher, the Communist member, said there might be a front in Italy or the Near East, not only in the west.[84] Commenting on the debate, the *Manchester Guardian* thought the government's case was unassailable; though it should not ignore the real desire to help Russia (25 October). By the end of the year, with the certainty that nothing could be done in winter, and

[83] For example, *Daily Express*, 12 Aug. 1941; *Sunday Express*, 14 Sept. (article by John Gordon); *Daily Herald*, 18, 23 Sept.; *News Chronicle*, 10, 11, 14, 21 October (including letters from soldiers). The CPGB statement, *Manchester Guardian* and other papers, 13 Oct. It is worth noting that Churchill's first reaction to the invasion of Russia had been, on 23 June, to propose to the Chiefs of Staff a raid by 25–30,000 men on the coast of France – Gilbert, vol. VI, p. 1122.

[84] *HC Deb.*, vol. 374, cols. 1943–2010.

with the immense problems raised by the Japanese war in the Pacific, the agitation and the dispute largely died away. It was to resume the next year, under stronger leadership and with greater force.

The other controversy was a mere sketch of things to come, but none the less significant as an augury. Leading articles in *The Times*, written by E.H. Carr, the Deputy Editor, began very early to stress the theme that after a victorious end to the war Russian influence must prevail in eastern Europe. He began on 5 July, with an article on the error of keeping Russia out of the peace agreements of 1919: a settlement without regard for Russia's interests was unlikely to endure. 'That error at any rate will not be repeated.' This argument was presented with great emphasis in a long leading article on 1 August, headed 'Peace and Power'. Starting with the uncompromising premiss that 'No peace settlement can last which is not rooted in the realities of power', the article went on to argue the necessity for an objective assessment, free from ideological prejudice, of Russia's role in eastern Europe. This assessment was stark: 'Leadership in Eastern Europe is essential. . . . This leadership can fall only to Germany or to Russia.' Neither Britain nor the United States had the will or the capacity to exercise a predominant role in the area; and since German influence was unacceptable, this left only Russia to fill the bill. This article set alarm bells ringing among the governments of eastern European states, most obviously the Poles, but also the Turks and Greeks. Correspondents to *The Times* letter columns (6 August) questioned the diagnosis that eastern Europe could only accept German or Soviet leadership, and raised the possibility of a bloc of Slav states, from the Baltic to the Adriatic. *The Times* diplomatic correspondent, Iverach McDonald, tried to explain that 'leadership' did not mean predominance, but this cut no ice. The hostile reaction was well summed up in a leading article in *The Economist* (16 August), 'The Eastern Fringe'.[85] The problems of eastern Europe seemed far away; yet it was that area which had brought Britain into the war, and Britain already had specific war aims in eastern Europe, notably the restoration of Poland and the curbing of German strength. Those who accepted the inevitability of great power domination saw the solution for the area in Russian leadership, but this meant 'absorption into an ideological framework quite incompatible with Europe's traditional conception of freedom'. The assumption of unlimited Russian leadership in the area was contrary to British pledges, and also inexpedient, because it would lead many to accept German control as preferable to Russian. Europe, the article concluded, was struggling to be free, not to exchange tyrannies. *The Economist* reflected the point on 13 September, accusing *The Times* of merely offering eastern Europe 'the choice of Germany or Russia as *Fuehrer*'.

Carr was unrepentant, writing to Barrington–Ward, the editor of *The Times*, 'I'm depressed by the obtuseness of people in this country who don't understand that, if Russia helps to win the war for us, we neither can nor should dictate an Eastern settlement except on her terms.'[86] But in

---

[85] Articles on eastern Europe in *The Economist* at that time were often written by Isaac Deutscher.

[86] *The Times* archive, E.H. Carr Box, Carr to Barrington–Ward, 9 Aug. 1941.

any case the question seemed remote, not only in terms of distance but of time and probability. The prospects of a victorious end to the war in eastern Europe or anywhere else were not bright in August or September 1941, and the issue could be left to simmer. However, the lines of confrontation had already been drawn between an approach based on naked *realpolitik*, disregarding ideological considerations, and a stance which rejected the assimilation of eastern Europe into an alien and unwelcome ideological system – or in plain language an exchange of tyrannies.[87]

The reaction of general opinion in Britain to the German attack on the Soviet Union, as reflected in the Home Intelligence reports, was at first restrained and low-key. The reception of the news over the first three or four days was summed up as 'jubilant, with a strong undercurrent of caution'. The jubilation arose mainly from relief that the Germans were so heavily occupied in the east that they would have little to spare to attack Britain. The caution sprang from what seem to have been deep-seated feelings – an ingrained reluctance to believe good news, which was doubtless the result of disappointments in the past, and a feeling (again the result of recent experience) that Hitler always knew what he was doing. There was little confidence in Russian military capacity, which tended to be judged on the Soviet performance against Finland in the Winter War. There was a widespread belief that the best that could be hoped for was that Russia would hold out long enough for Britain to gain some advantage. Churchill's speech on 22 June was much admired, and his pledge of help to Russia was accepted as practical and logical. It appears that the British people reacted soberly to the drama in the east; though there was one rather pleasing touch of fantasy which recalled the previous great war – a rumour that Russian soldiers had landed at Dover. There was no mention of snow on their boots.[88]

This comparative restraint on the part of the public evaporated as the struggle in the east unfolded and began to grip men's minds and engage their emotions. The German offensive opened with brilliant and sweeping successes, catching the Soviet air force on the ground and cutting great swathes through the Russian armies. Despite contradictions between the German and Soviet communiqués, place-names told their own tale of the German advance. Then the German forces paused from mid-July to mid-August before launching their far-reaching autumn offensive. These first few weeks of the campaign, to the middle of August, propelled British opinion on a switchback ride of doubt and hope. Were the Russians strong enough to survive? People remembered that before the Nazi–Soviet Pact Russia had been presented as a colossus – many, of course, remembered the 'Russian steam-roller' which was a common phrase in 1914. Then there had been the war with Finland, in which the Red Army had done very badly. Now Soviet strength was being played up again by press and radio, and the public did not

[87] The question of whether Carr was influenced solely by questions of power politics or whether he had a latent sympathy for Communism and the Soviet regime is an open one. See the valuable discussion on *The Times* by Alan Foster, '*The Times* and Appeasement: The Second Phase', in Walter Laqueur, ed., *The Second World War: Essays in Military and Political History* (London, 1982).

[88] INF 1/292, HI Report 38 deals with 18–25 June 1941.

know what to make of it, fearing another let-down. People were deeply sceptical about official versions of events, and produced for themselves a series of arbitrary periods as likely limits for Russian resistance. When three weeks had passed and the Russians were still fighting, the limit was shifted to six weeks; when they were still going at six weeks, they might hold on until the autumn or winter. At the beginning of August, it was commonly held that if they lasted until September all would be well. The choice of these intervals of time seems to have been spontaneous, and to have been similar in different parts of the country. The slowly growing confidence in Russian resistance which accompanied the passage of the weeks produced one of the reactions of which the government was afraid: a feeling that, as the Russians fought on, there was scope for the British to relax and let someone else carry the burden of the war.

As to general attitudes towards the Soviet Union and its regime, about which the Ministry of Information was growing anxious during July, these were summed up by Home Intelligence in mid-August as 'great admiration tempered by some doubt'. The admiration was largely for courage and fighting power, but there were also reports of 'a latent working-class sympathy for the "workers' republic" ', and of comments that the Soviet army, whose officers had been purged and which had done so badly against the Finns, was now doing better than the British had ever done. This was one of a number of signs of a reaction against earlier criticism of the Soviet Union. But there were also doubts about Russia. Distrust of Communism was reported as persisting in many quarters; and there was also anxiety about Soviet demands at the final peace settlement, which emerged despite much favourable comment on the Anglo–Soviet agreement of 12 July. That there should be questions about peace terms when there was no sign that the war could even be won, and before the press took up the issue of eastern Europe at the beginning of August, is an intriguing phenomenon, and a sign that general opinion did not simply follow leads given by propaganda or the media. Similarly, the idea of a 'second front' (though not the phrase) also appeared in public reaction before it was canvassed in the press. In the first three or four days after the German invasion, Home Intelligence reported an eagerness that Britain should somehow strike at once, while the Germans were tied up in the east. In the first week of July there was a considerable demand for diversionary attacks in the west, and a feeling that Russia should not be allowed to collapse without Britain doing something to help. These were the first signs of the 'second front' movement in the country, and of course they soon merged with agitation in the press.'[89]

If admiration tempered by doubt summed up public attitudes towards Russia in mid-August 1941, over the next four-and-a-half months to the end of the year the admiration increased enormously and the doubts appear to have dwindled away. The German offensive which resumed in late August came as a shock to many people, who had been reassured by the lull in late July and early August. Then the ensuing battle for Moscow began to

[89]   This survey of opinion in July and the first fortnight of August is drawn from INF 1/292, HI Reports 39–45.

dominate public attention. It assumed an epic quality, and concentrated public attention upon Russia to the exclusion of almost anything else in the war news. This was repeatedly reported in October, and the Home Intelligence report for 17–24 November noted that the British victories in Libya had done nothing to diminish concern about the Russian front. The vast scale of the fighting and the tenacity of the Russian resistance made a deep impression and inspired a remarkable confidence. Even when the fate of Moscow seemed in the balance there were no reports of any expectation that the Russians would surrender. 'Russia is not France' was how feeling was summed up in the week of 13–20 October. The recapture of Rostov at the end of November was seen as the first major setback for the Germans – the turn of the tide. Even then, at the height of the drama, there were signs that the public's critical faculties were still awake: people wondered whether the press and radio were not exaggerating the Russian successes, noting that places said to be of no importance when they were captured by the Germans assumed great significance when they were recaptured.

During this period, admiration for Russian endurance and fighting power was being extended to the Soviet regime. In mid-September there were occasional reports of resentment by people who felt they had been deceived by earlier stories of Soviet backwardness. In October there were general indications of the 'realization of the moral strength of a country which was formerly somewhat disparaged officially'. And at the end of December Home Intelligence registered 'increased demands to know more of the regime which appears capable of producing such supermen'. So far, these reports were not overwhelming, and were often matched by others which showed that concern with Russia arose from a substantial basis of self-interest. There were widespread comments that 'the Battle of Britain is being fought on the Eastern front' (first week in October); that 'every Russian killed is one Englishman less to die' (late November); and that while Russia held on there would be no heavy air-raids (end of November). These sentiments were accompanied by a sense of gratitude to the Russians – people were described as being 'deeply grateful', and the word 'gratitude' appeared with increasing frequency in the Home Intelligence reports. (In retrospect, this may seem overdone: after all, the Russians were fighting in self-defence, not to help the British. But at the time it was a very natural reaction, particularly among those who remembered the slaughter of 1914–18, and were relieved – and yet perhaps felt guilty – to see the casualties being borne by someone else.)

These feelings of admiration, relief and gratitude were accompanied by a desire to do something to help the Russians. At the end of August and in early September there were widespread reports of discontent at British inactivity, concern that not enough help was being sent to Russia, and a growing feeling that Britain should make Germany fight on two fronts. In the second week in September, dissatisfaction at the absence of land operations in the west was the strongest current of feeling noted by Home Intelligence, and this sentiment persisted for the rest of the month. There was a sense of irritation – if the British couldn't do anything then, with 90 per cent of the German army in Russia, when could they manage anything? At the end of

September and the beginning of October these reports died away, because public attention was caught by the 'Tanks for Russia Week' and the Beaverbrook mission to Moscow. These two acts of showmanship on the part of Beaverbrook achieved a striking success in persuading people that something was being done, in spite of a good deal of cynicism about 'Tanks for Russia' – there was much comment to the effect that it was no use pretending that every tank produced that week either could or should be sent to Russia. The speed and apparent success of the Moscow conference were warmly welcomed, and generally linked to Beaverbrook's capacity for hustle.

The battle for Moscow brought a revival of demands for landings in the west between 6 and 20 October, but this was followed by a striking change. The Home Intelligence report for 20–27 October noted that demands for a second front were dying down, not because of any decline in concern about Russia, which continued unabated, but through a growing realization of the difficulties involved. There were reports of resentment against the 'second front' campaign on the part of those with sons or husbands in the army: the journalists who were so enthusiastic about an invasion would not have to take part in it. Home Intelligence picked out three principal reasons for change: the publication of Lord Gort's despatch covering the Dunkirk evacuation in 1940, which stirred memories of a disastrous continental campaign; a reaction against the press and Communist agitation for a second front, which appeared to be counter-productive; and a belief that Britain's best role was to provide supplies for Russia. The following week (27 October–3 November) saw these tendencies strengthening, with sharp criticism of 'the London papers' for agitating about a second front, and impatience with Communist attempts to use the movement for their own political ends. During the next fortnight the demand for a second front diminished still further, and was reported to be dying away by mid-November – when it was also fading away in the press. There remained some lingering frustration at British inactivity, even when it was recognized as inevitable, and this found an outlet in attacks on anything smacking of lack of zeal in helping Russia, or 'anti-Soviet feeling in high places'. Suspicions of inertia, incompetence or deception in the government (from which Churchill was usually exempted) were reported as intensifying in mid-November, when demands for a second front were diminishing. Not until Eden visited Moscow in December 1941 and made an impressive broadcast on his return, which was also featured on the newsreels, were these suspicions recorded as diminishing.[90]

The Home Intelligence reports showed some evidence that admiration for Russian fighting power was developing into approval of the regime which produced it, but this process was as yet very limited. Another anxiety of the Ministry of Information was that credit might accrue to the British Communist Party, but of this there was little sign. Occasional mentions of the Communists reflected annoyance caused by the 'second front' agitation,

[90]   This survey of developments in public opinion between mid-August and December 1941 is based on INF 1/292, HI Reports 48–66 inclusive. For Eden's broadcast, see HI Report 67.

and by a feeling that 'the Communists will work to save Russia, but not Britain'. Home Intelligence formed the impression in late October that the majority of people did not associate the British Communists with Russia, and thought that Stalin would do well to disown them. In November one report specifically noted that there was praise for Stalin and admiration for Russian resistance, but no apparent growth in sympathy for the British Communists.[91] This may have indicated some success for the Ministry of Information's efforts in this direction, but was more probably a sign that the Ministry was pushing at an open door.

The Home Intelligence reports can be supplemented by a number of questions put by the Gallup Poll between August and November 1941.

> *August 1941.* Are you satisfied or dissatisfied with the amount of military help Britain is giving Russia?
> Satisfied 37   Dissatisfied 30   No Opinion 33
> If not satisfied, what more should we do? (To this question, 70 per cent of the 'Dissatisfied', i.e. 21 per cent of all respondents, replied that they favoured an attack in the west.)[92]

The wording of the main question was unfortunate, since presumably none of those being interviewed knew how much help was being given, so that the only sensible answer was 'Don't Know', which was in fact given by one-third of the respondents. However, for what they are worth, the replies showed only minority dissatisfaction with what were believed to be British efforts to help Russia, and even smaller support for a second front.

In October and November Gallup put another, rather general question twice over:

> *Oct./Nov. 1941.* Do you feel that Britain has taken or has not taken full advantage of the opportunities offered by the German attack on Russia?
>
> | | Has taken full advantage | Has not | Don't know |
> |------|------|------|------|
> | Oct. | 29 | 49 | 22 |
> | Nov. | 35 | 32 | 33[93] |

The question did not mention the second front issue directly, so the answers can only be presumed to bear upon it. In so far as there is some relation, the fall in the proportion replying that Britain had not taken full advantage of the opportunities coincided with the findings of Home Intelligence that public support for a landing in the west diminished in November. But in general, the Gallup evidence for autumn 1941 is scanty and unsatisfactory.

Mass-Observation asked its volunteer observers to keep diaries, which are now in the organization's archives. The following quotations appear in two of these diaries for 22 June 1941.

91 *Ibid.*, HI Reports 56, 57, 59.
92 Gallup Archive, BIPO Survey 79; *News Chronicle*, 12 Sept. 1941.
93 Gallup Archive, BIPO Surveys 80, 81.

Naomi Mitchison (at Carradale, Scotland):

I feel so excited today, I can hardly think what happened. [Listening to the one-o'clock news]. As it went on I began to sob and shake with hysterics. I began to realize how I had been expecting another appeasement or worse. Now at last we are on the same side; this ache I have had all the war because of the Soviet Union is now healed.

Miss Oakley (Glasgow):

The news – Germany's attack on Russia, of course . . . . comments – Charlie, 'Quite the most interesting news we have had for a long time.'[94]

On the whole, the immediate British reactions to the German invasion of the Soviet Union were much nearer to that of the stolid Charlie than to the hysterics of the Left-wing intellectual Miss Mitchison. Expectations of sharp and dangerous divisions of opinion which might imperil national unity and impede the war effort were not fulfilled. The response to Armageddon was to carry on much as usual, with a considerable sense of relief that it was taking place elsewhere. In part this steadiness was due to the prompt and well-judged intervention by Churchill in his speech on 22 June. It owed something too to sensible action by the Ministry of Information, particularly in relation to religious leaders. But not least, and not for the first or last time, it proved that 'the British public shows a very high degree of common sense'.[95]

A more intense reaction followed later, as the British people began to watch the struggle on the eastern front with a degree of concern and involvement which were quite unusual for events in a foreign country and over a thousand miles away. Admiration for Russian fighting power, gratitude for taking the weight off Britain, and anxiety to do something to help built up to a remarkable extent in the latter part of 1941. As the new year of 1942 began, the question was raised as to whether these developments in public opinion would affect British policy.

[94] Mass–Observation Archive, War Diaries, June 1941: Women.
[95] The phrase was Stephen Taylor's in a memorandum on wartime morale, INF 1/292, HI Report 52, Appendix; cf. McLaine, p. 240, where the author uses the phrase as a chapter heading.

3

Sword of Honour? British Public Opinion and the Soviet Union, 1942–45

To the steel-hearted citizens of Stalingrad, the gift of King George VI, in token of the homage of the British people.
(Inscription on the Stalingrad Sword, presented by Churchill to Stalin at Teheran, 29 November 1943)

During the latter half of 1941 the British government evolved a balanced propaganda policy in relation to the Soviet Union. It sought to control and take advantage of admiration for Russia without promoting support for Communism, and at the same time to check any anti-Soviet elements which might divide opinion in the country. From 1942 onwards this policy was subjected to severe ordeals, first by excesses of enthusiasm for the Soviet Union and later by problems posed by the rapid growth of Soviet power in eastern Europe. The force of events became too great for any measured propaganda policy; and yet public opinion assumed greater importance than before. In the 'second front' campaign of 1942 a deliberate attempt was made to use public opinion to decide a crucial question of strategy; the Russomania at the time of the battle of Stalingrad seemed an uncontrollable tide; and for much of the time any attempt to distinguish between Russian fighting power and the Soviet/Communist regime seemed a forlorn hope – if indeed it was still being seriously pursued.

During this long period of just over three years, from the beginning of 1942 to early 1945, the fortunes of war changed drastically. The first nine months of 1942 marked for Britain the nadir of the war, including the fall of Singapore to the Japanese in February and of Tobruk to the Germans in June. At the end of the year came a sudden reversal of fortune, with the battle of Alamein in October, the Anglo-American landings in North Africa in November, and the Soviet victory at Stalingrad (November 1942–February 1943). Then, in a remarkable transformation, the calamities of defeat were speedily followed by the problems of victory and the anxieties of how to reach agreement on a post-war settlement. In examining this complex period from the point of view of British public opinion and the Soviet Union, we shall discuss four separate aspects: the development of government propaganda policy; the agitation for a second front in 1942; the height of enthusiasm for the Soviet Union which was reached during the battle of Stalingrad and the celebration of Red Army Day in February 1943; and the growth of public doubts about Soviet policy which developed from 1943 onwards.

The development of government propaganda policy

On 3 November 1941 the Press Attaché at the Soviet Embassy called at the Ministry of Information to enquire what public recognition was to be accorded to the twenty-fourth anniversary of the Russian Revolution, which would occur on the 7th of that month. There was a fluttering in the offices and some anxious telephoning. In fact, the Ministry had cautiously suggested the publication of messages by the Prime Minister and Service Ministers, and had asked the BBC to treat the event simply as a news item. The Soviets were persistent in their questions, and Maisky took the matter up with the Foreign Office, where a compromise was produced: the anniversary should be treated as more than merely a news item, but it should be made clear that what was being marked was the Soviet National Day, not the birthday of the Revolution.[1]

It was an intriguing game of thrust and parry, and on this occasion the British were able to find a formula which enabled them to maintain the distinction between the Soviet state, which was to be supported as an ally, and the ideology for which it stood, which was not to be encouraged. Suitable publicity was given to a telegram from Eden to Molotov offering cordial greetings on the twenty-fourth anniversary celebration of the Soviet National Day, and Maisky left it at that. But by the time the anniversary again approached, it was clear that such somewhat distant politeness would no longer suffice. The Ministry of Information was still trying to manage public opinion in relation to the Soviet Union, but by autumn 1942 the intensity of feeling about the eastern front and the admiration for the fight put up by the Red Army were so strong that the government's hand was forced.[2] Bracken, the Minister of Information, alerted the War Cabinet a month before the anniversary came round, and it was agreed that there must be official celebrations, because otherwise other organizations would take over, and 'so many difficulties arise from large-scale ceremonies of unexceptionable purpose but ambiguous parentage'. After consultations with Eden, Bracken proposed another compromise, which again offered a chance of sidestepping the issue of the Revolution: that the government should put on a great official show for Red Army Day, 23 February 1943. This, in principle, would concentrate attention on the military achievements of the Soviet

---

[1] INF 1/676, minutes by Smollett, 3, 4, 5 Nov. 1941; note of telephone call from FO, 5 Nov.

[2] For the development of public opinion during 1942, see below, pp. 88–96.

Union, which was right and proper; and the War Cabinet agreed on 25 January 1943 that 'the tribute of the British people' should be paid at a series of official functions, to which all allied governments and organizations concerned with Anglo-Soviet relations should be invited. The government would thus take the lead, and as Bracken wrote: 'it is hoped that by this means the effective celebrations of the day will be left to official organizations'.[3]

In the event, the celebrations were more spectacular than the War Cabinet had envisaged. The armed forces paraded through city centres, all kinds of organizations turned out in strength, and attendances were large. The main event at the Albert Hall on 21 February included a speech by Eden, music by the bands of the Brigade of Guards and the Royal Air Force, a specially commissioned fanfare by Arnold Bax (Master of the King's Music), and readings by Laurence Olivier and Ralph Richardson – the full ceremonial resources of the British establishment, except for the Royal Family. It was splendidly official, but the effects almost inevitably outstripped the government's intentions. It was after all *Red* Army Day. The Red Flag flew over public buildings; the *Internationale* was played repeatedly, with the inhibitions of 1941 thrown to the winds; Stalin, the central figure of world Communism, was presented as a hero. Fine distinctions between Russia and Communism could not survive this kind of treatment, and the result was a hymn of praise both for the Red Army and for the regime which had created it. Unofficial accompaniments to the celebrations had the same significance, even when there was not the slightest sign of fellow-travelling. The recording company Decca, impeccably capitalist, put out a special set of gramophone records: Soviet Fatherland Song, Soviet Airmen Song, Song of the Heroic Airmen, Through the Moonlit Meadow, Under the Soviet Flag, Anti-Nazi March, Red Army Cadet March, At the Call of Lenin March.[4] Apart from the moonlit meadow, the theme was certainly Red.

The episode was significant. The government had succeeded in applying the means of its propaganda policy – official control of the ceremonies was strong – but it was quite unable to control the effects, which reflected glory upon the Soviet regime. In some publicity material produced by the Ministry of Information, all serious restraint on praise for the regime seems to have been abandoned. The Ministry's 'Speakers' Notes' distributed in February 1943 provided a highly favourable and selective account of Soviet history since 1917, with a long passage on the 'strikingly liberal constitution' of 1936. It conceded that it would be wrong to imagine that there existed in the USSR 'intellectual and political liberty comparable to our own in peacetime', but claimed that communism in the Soviet Union today was 'not a malignant Marxist bogey, but much more a Russian answer to a Russian problem'. Stalin's reforms showed that 'while Russia is certainly not a democratic state as we understand it, it is a state moving towards the

---

[3] CAB 65/32, WM(42) 131st. Conclusions, 5 Oct. 1942; CAB 65/33, WM(43) 16th Conclusions, 25 Jan. 1943; CAB 66/33, WP(43)37, memo. by Bracken, 22 Jan. 1943; INF 1/73, Executive Board, 21, 26 Jan. 1943. For practical reasons, the celebrations were actually held on Sunday, 21 February.

[4] Advertisement in *Spectator*, 26 Feb. 1943.

democracies'.[5] A briefing document for press and radio, again in February 1943, was supposedly devoted to describing the mineral and industrial resources of the Soviet Union, but became also a tribute to Soviet economic planning. 'Thanks to the far-sightedness of Soviet economic policy before the war the organization of the area between the Urals and the Altai had reached an advanced stage'; and more to the same effect.[6] Another paper in the same series expatiated upon the status and role of women in the Soviet Union, and the equal rights accorded to them under the Soviet constitution – they were thus better prepared than women in any other belligerent country for full and immediate participation in the war effort.[7] Although in these and other examples, a genuflection in the direction of restraint or balance can sometimes be seen, the general effect was highly favourable to the Soviet system.

At the BBC, the European News Directives, now under the general control of the Political Warfare Executive, continued to be strongly, indeed wholeheartedly, pro-Soviet. For the week 1–8 March 1942 the General Directive laid down that 'If we are to reflect, as we *must*, the feeling of the great mass of this nation, we must make the following facts clear': that we regard Russia as 'a great fighting nation and a mighty ally in war', and also see the Russians as 'a people who have set us an example of how to pursue an ideal with wholehearted sacrifice'[8] Broadcasters were strongly urged to use a *Times* leader in honour of Lenin describing how Russia had been reborn through his leadership, which had laid the foundations of an edifice which had withstood the utmost fury of Hitlerism.[9] The abolition of the post of political commissar in the Red Army in October 1942 was warmly welcomed. The line was to be that from the first the 'Soviet experiment' was designed to educate the people and the army to the point where they would behave in the right way without pressure from above: that had now been reached. The change was to be represented as 'a complete vindication of the Soviet system', and proof that the Bolshevik regime 'always aimed at introducing genuine self-government among the Russian peoples'.[10] A special directive on the occasion of the dissolution of Comintern in May 1943 described this Soviet action as 'by far the most important political event of the war'. It signified that the Soviet government intended to win the war and secure the peace, not by class war, but by co-operation between nations with different political, economic and social systems. 'This brings Moscow absolutely into line with London and Washington and all the Allied Governments.'[11] When in September 1943 the Soviet government re-established the Holy Synod of the Russian Orthodox

[5] Ministry of Information, 'Speakers' Notes', SN92, *The USSR*, copy in BBC Written Archives, Talks: Russia I. Cf. INF 1/677, memo. by Collins, 18 Feb. 1942, where it is noted that 425 copies of this paper were distributed.

[6] Ministry of Information, Reference Division, *The Soviet Economy in the Urals, Western Siberia and Central Asia. The Basis of Russian Resistance and Offensive.* (27 Feb. 1943).

[7] *Ibid.*, *Soviet Women at War* (31 August 1943).

[8] BBC Written Archives, OS137F, Weekly General Directives.

[9] *Ibid.*, OS137B, European News Directive, 23 April 1942. It is true that the article said that much of Lenin's teaching was hostile to fundamental British traditions, but it ends 'there need be no incompatibility'.

[10] *Ibid.*, OS137B, news directive, 10 Oct. 1942.

[11] *Ibid.*, OS137E, Special Directives, 22 May 1943.

Church, Newsome wrote that this showed that Stalin was 'practising toleration in accordance with the spirit of the Four Freedoms. . . . We now have a chance to take the offensive in projecting a liberalized Russia. We ought to be able to kill the Bolshevik bogey stone dead.'[12] The directives combined praise for the Soviet regime with claims that it was being drastically liberalized. Their most consistent theme, as Newsome himself insisted, was that western democracy, modified by greater state control, and Sovietism, modified by greater recognition of the liberty of the individual, could work together and were set on converging courses.[13]

In the Home Service the tone was much more muted, but the underlying message remained favourable to the Soviet regime. The BBC's regular contribution on the USSR, "Russian Commentary" was written by Alexander Werth and read by Joseph Macleod (a highly respected news reader) at the peak listening time just after the nine-o'clock news. Werth was a Left-wing journalist, strongly sympathetic to Communism and the Soviet system and determined to present it in the best possible light.[14] His talks emphasized patriotism, the industrial war effort and military operations, and repeatedly drew attention to cultural life – operas and plays being performed to packed houses, and the great works of art which, he claimed, Russia alone was capable of producing during the war. The first six months of 'Russian Commentary', beginning in July 1942, told listeners quite a lot about the Soviet system, and the general impression, if not completely Red, was at least rose-coloured. One talk, 'Member of the Komsomol', went further than most. Werth told his listeners about Olga, 'one of the most active members of the local Komsomol (Union of Communist Youth) in one of Moscow's largest textile factories'. He had accompanied Olga to a dance held to celebrate receiving the second prize for a month's production among all the textile factories in the Soviet Union. There was a brass band and vigorous dancing; and, Werth wrote, 'in the background stood Stalin, laughing and clapping.' Later, he went with Olga to the ballet, and as they stood at the tram-stop they looked up at the moonlight on the Kremlin. 'Olga said pensively, "Our beloved leader working there"'. Fifty years later this reads like caricature; but Werth presented it straightforwardly as an insight into 'the life and mood of the Russian working-class youth.'[15] In other talks, listeners met a Stakhanovite turner who produced four times the standard daily output, and learned that the 'real driving force in "socialist competition" is the Party and the Komsomol'; and they heard about an anti-aircraft battery whose range-finders were manned entirely by girls, all volunteers and all members of the Komsomol, who in their off-duty hours read scientific books and the Russian classics.[16] After mid-1943 the content of Werth's talks became more concerned with the Russian victories, conveying a picture of

12   *Ibid.*, OS137B, news directive, 5 Sept. 1943.
13   *Ibid.*, OS137B, news directive, 9 March 1943.
14   See Leopold Labedz, 'Alexander Werth' in *Survey*, vol. 30, Nos.1–2, March 1988, pp. 126–34. Incidentally, Joseph Macleod had been a study group convenor in the Left Book Club: see John Lewis, *The Left Book Club* (London, 1970), p. 14.
15   Alexander Werth, 'Member of the Komsomol', *Listener*, 27 Aug. 1942, pp. 263–4.
16   *Listener*, 5 Nov. 1942, pp. 589–90, and 13 May 1943, p. 559.

confidence, pride and not least a spirit of vengeance against the Germans, which was in Werth's eyes a subject of admiration. The general picture remained one of a society which had suffered terribly but had come through with devoted heroism, inspired by a benign leader and an omnicompetent Party.

As well as Werth's regular 'Commentaries', the BBC provided a number of special programmes. On 21 December 1942 Stalin's birthday was marked by the first performance in Britain of Khachaturyan's 'Ode to Stalin', with the BBC Symphony Orchestra and BBC Chorus conducted by Sir Adrian Boult.[17] On 8 November 1943, the anniversary of the Revolution (though the BBC was careful to call it Russia's National Day), both domestic programmes (Home and Forces) devoted the whole evening to features 'In Honour of Russia'. The Home Service spent an hour invoking 'The Spirit of Russia', followed by talks on 'Russia at War', while the Forces Programme put on 'Factory Floor Show' and 'Russia Sings and Dances'. After the eight o'clock news the two programmes combined for 'The Red Army' and 'War Songs of the Soviet Peoples'. It was a mark of public interest that the listening figures were high – 35 per cent for the earlier part of the evening, falling away after the news. As often, it was hard to confine the admiration to the country and its army without involving the regime which lay behind both.[18]

Occasional stirrings of anxiety and scepticism in the BBC hierarchy only confirmed that presentation of the Soviet Union on the radio was over-whelmingly favourable, and that nothing could be done about it. Sir Richard Maconachie, the BBC Controller (Home), was a constant but unavailing critic. He wrote to Harold Nicolson, then a Governor of the BBC, in June 1942:

> . . . you recently said you were touched and disconcerted by the public attitude towards Russia. I have been worrying about this for some time, and the particularly disquieting symptom, as I see it, is not the demand for information about the Russian way of life, but the demand for nothing but praise for it. While I feel the BBC ought to do something about this, as it seems a popular misconception with great potentialities for harm in the future, neither Barnes [Director of Talks] nor I can as yet see what or how.

Nicolson agreed, replying that the public were 'putting all their eggs in the Russian basket. . . . All that they think about is the glory of Russia and they have a completely distorted and legendary idea of what Russia really is.' He took the matter up with Bracken at the Ministry of Information, and received a humorously dusty answer, duly passed on to Maconachie:

> Bracken is not at all in favour of our starting a series on the truth about Russia. He says that if we once started on that Maisky would send a band of dynamiters to blow up Broadcasting House. The more I think of it the more I feel that he is right in this opinion and that we shall have to keep silent and let the false legend prevail. I hate this as much as you do but I

---

[17] *Manchester Guardian*, 21 Dec. 1942.
[18] BBC Written Archives, Audience Research, Special Reports, LR/2204, 30 Nov. 1943.

think we would find that once we got down to it we would find ourselves edged by tact and discretion into something almost as untruthful as the legend itself.[19]

Maconachie returned to the charge on later occasions. He took exception to a proposed programme on the Soviet Five-Year Plans (November 1942), which he thought laudatory in tone and question-begging in substance. He would have no objection, he said, if it could be stated frankly that the Plan had been 'put through by autocratic methods at an enormous cost in life and happiness of the Russian people, but had been proved to be well worth while in its effect on the military strength of Russia'; but he recognized that this was 'of course impossible'.[20] In February 1943 Maconachie complained that talks and schools broadcasts about Russia painted a rosy picture – pretty much what the audience was asking for, but hardly worth while. He again recognized, however, that the Foreign Office would object to anything which would provoke protests from the Soviet Embassy. The Directors of Talks and Schools Broadcasting defended their respective services. The Director of Talks agreed that 'we cannot admit at the microphone the importance in the life of the individual of the secret police'. He wondered if they were not 'a little too sensitive to Foreign Office direction', but his general conclusion was that nothing could be done.[21] Maconachie kept nagging, with some strongly argued notes at the end of 1944, but to no avail.[22] There was no question of the BBC drawing attention to the darker side of Soviet life. All that Maconachie's objections did was to bring out that the BBC was *knowingly* broadcasting rose-coloured impressions of the Soviet regime. For overwhelming political reasons, balance was out of the question.

In a similar way, but with the power of the visual image added to the spoken word, the newsreels presented a highly favourable picture of the Soviet Union. The period from late 1941 to early 1943 saw a powerful concentration on Russia by the newsreels. Much of the coverage was battle-front material, and so dealt primarily with the Soviet military effort; but the message was frequently implicit and sometimes explicit that here was not just a great army but a strong society, drawing inspiration from its ideals. An occasional newsreel issue went much further, with footage devoted entirely to the virtues of the Soviet regime and the society which it had created.[23] All of this output was passed by the censorship machinery of the Ministry of Information.

Another example of the same tendency can be found in the treatment of religion in the Soviet Union. In 1941 the Ministry of Information had

19 BBC Written Archives, Talks: Russia I, Maconachie to Nicolson, 2 June 1942; Nicolson to Maconachie, 5, 17 June.

20 *Ibid.*, Maconachie to Barnes, 14 Nov. 1942.

21 *Ibid.*, Maconachie to Barnes and Somerville, 1 Feb. 1943; replies by Barnes (2 Feb.) and Somerville (8 Feb.).

22 BBC Written Archives, Talks: Europe and Ourselves, Maconachie to Barnes, 25 Nov. and 13 Dec. 1944 – 'Random Thoughts of an Idle Fellow', as Maconachie called them.

23 Bell and White, 'Images of the Soviet Union at War'. British Movietones's issue No. 739A, presented by Charles Ridley, was devoted to Soviet culture and its links with the war effort.

trodden very delicately round this subject, but with the passage of time it permitted a distinctly favourable presentation of the Soviet position. Within the Ministry, the Religions Division maintained a balanced outlook, noting in 1943 the relaxation of Soviet policy towards the Orthodox church but insisting also that there had been severe persecution in the past, and that religious liberty in the western sense was still not allowed in the Soviet Union. However, an approach from the Metropolitan of Kiev for an exchange of visits between the Orthodox church and the Church of England had to be given some sort of welcome. The Ministry of Information recognized that the purpose of the move was political, but accepted that it must be pursued; the Archbishop of Canterbury, Temple, apparently hoped that the object might be primarily religious. The result was a visit to Russia by the Archbishop of York, Garbett, in September and October 1942, dates which coincided with the Soviet government's granting of permission for the Russian Orthodox church to hold a Synod and appoint a Patriarch, an office which had been unfilled since 1925. On his return, Garbett held a press conference, introduced by Brendan Bracken, who thus emphasized the Ministry of Information's association with the journey and its conclusions. The Archbishop certainly had his private reservations, and he tried to sustain a note of caution: but the general trend of his remarks was favourable to the Soviet regime in the present, and optimistic for the future. He was sure that he had seen signs of a genuine revival of religion in Russia. He recognized that Stalin might have had political motives for making an appointment to the office of Patriarch, but thought that his main reason was his acceptance (because he was 'a wise statesman') that religion had deep roots in the lives of his people. His conclusion was as follows:

> However much we may condemn some of the methods used during and after the Revolution, and I think we should all condemn some of them, we should now watch with sympathy the working out of a great social and economic experiment, even though we may feel much of it may be inapplicable to our own country. [24]

This sentence tried almost painfully to hold the balance and to discourage sympathy with Communism in Britain; but the central emphasis was surely on 'a great social and economic experiment', which was the conventional language of support for the Soviet regime. Bracken, by his very presence, gave government endorsement to the Archbishop's attitude.

There is no sign that the principles laid down by the Ministry of Information, enjoining a guarded and balanced approach to publicity about the Soviet Union, had been formally abandoned. But in practice during 1942 and 1943 the attempt to distinguish between Russia as a powerful ally and the Soviet regime largely broke down. All the aspects of the Ministry's work

[24] Garbett's statement quoted in McLaine, p. 216; *The Times*, 11 Oct. 1943; Ministry of Information, *Orthodox Church Bulletin*, No. 20, Nov. 1943, included a favourable account of the visit. See Charles Smyth, *Cyril Forster Garbett, Archbishop of York* (London, 1959), pp. 299–307, where the author emphasized Garbett's cautious approach both to the visit and to the press conference. Some of the points, unfortunately, were too subtle to come across effectively in press reports.

Molotov in London, May 1942: a walk in the garden of 10 Downing Street

surveyed above show not merely acceptance of but admiration for the Soviet system; though the British Communist Party was still treated with reserve and distaste.

This change in attitude and emphasis must be seen in its context, which was a transformation of Anglo-Soviet relations at the highest level and in the most public manner. Eden visited Moscow in December 1941, returning in the New Year to give a glowing account of his journey. In the years that followed, Churchill went twice to see Stalin in Moscow (August 1942 and October 1944), and twice took part in three-power summit meetings with Stalin and Roosevelt (Teheran, November–December 1943 and Yalta, February 1945). All these meetings were presented in press, radio and news-reel coverage in eulogistic terms, and indeed were described by the Prime Minister himself in the most favourable and hopeful language. In May 1942 Molotov, the Soviet Foreign Minister, came to Britain, and when the need for security had passed his reception was awarded vivid treatment by the newsreels, using footage shot by the RAF Film Unit for publicity purposes. At a lower level, delegations of Soviet trade unionists, servicemen, and school-children toured Britain. British airmen and sailors received the Order of Lenin and other awards for gallantry. From May 1942, a formal Anglo-Soviet alliance was in being. In the short run, it was clearly a military necessity. In the long term, a stable peace settlement depended on its preservation after the war was over. Churchill wrote to Stalin on 21 November 1941 that he expected Soviet Russia, Great Britain and the United States to meet at 'the council table of the victors', and make a good plan for their mutual safety.[25] On 30 December 1943, after the Teheran Conference, Churchill telegraphed to Stalin: 'I only wish we could meet once a week. Please give my regards to Molotov. If you will send me the music of the New Soviet Russian Anthem, I could arrange to have it played by the BBC on all occasions important Russian victories were announced.' The music indeed arrived, and Churchill ensured that it was played before the nine-o'clock news on Sunday, 16 January 1944, by the BBC Symphony Orchestra.[26] It is true that this was the new Soviet anthem, not the 'Internationale', to which Churchill had objected so vehemently and persistently in 1941. The Soviet government had made a gesture by abandoning the 'Internationale' in favour of something patriotic, and Churchill seized the opportunity to display solidarity with Soviet Russia. A symbol of distrust was replaced by a symbol of unity. Differences certainly persisted, but they were thrust firmly into the background.

In these circumstances, 'stealing the thunder of the Left' was no longer a metaphor with much meaning. Lines and distinctions grew blurred, and it was generally accepted that praise for Russian strength would merge into what was at least acceptance of, and often admiration for, the regime which produced such strength. The culmination of this process may be seen in the gift of the Stalingrad Sword. This symbolic weapon drew the King, formally the author of the presentation, into the current of pro-Soviet feeling. The sword was displayed in public buildings up and down the country for the admiration of vast crowds, which trooped quietly past to gaze on this ceremonial, almost cultic object. The inscription on the blade ran:

> To the steel-hearted citizens of Stalingrad, the gift of King George VI, in token of the homage of the British people.

Homage to the courage and tenacity of the defenders of Stalingrad, certainly; but the city itself bore the name of Stalin, who was not only the ruler of Russia but the embodiment of Communism. Admiration for the city could not be separated from admiration for the man, and the man personified the regime as well as his country and its peoples. All these aspects were so merged together that few could be expected to distinguish between them when Churchill presented the sword to Stalin at the Teheran Conference, with the newsreel cameras in attendance to record the event for the world to see.[27]

'Second Front Now', 1942

In the autumn of 1941 some newspapers, along with the Communist Party, had raised a cry for an immediate 'second front' in western Europe, in the form of either substantial raids or a large-scale invasion.[28] By the end of the

---

[25] Churchill to Stalin, 21 Nov, 1941, in Churchill, *Second World War*, vol. II, p. 472. Cf. FO 371/29472, N6799/3/38.

[26] Gilbert, *Churchill*, vol. VII, pp. 630, 650.

[27] *Ibid.*, pp. 577–8; FO 372/3531 contains fascinating correspondence on the design of the sword and the wording of the inscription. At the presentation ceremony, Stalin handed the sword to Voroshilov, who very nearly dropped it.

[28] See above, pp. 58–60.

year this had died away, and on 27 January 1942, facing defeats in North Africa and the Far East, Churchill asked rhetorically where we would have been if the government had yielded to the clamour and attempted an invasion of France. At the time, there was no answer, and soon afterwards, when Singapore fell, Beaverbrook found himself under attack in the press for sending to Russia equipment which might, it was said, have saved the island from the Japanese.

However, from February 1942 onwards this situation changed, and there developed a public campaign of a remarkable intensity and range, designed to force the government into an invasion of western Europe at an early date – or in the simple slogan of the time, 'Second Front Now!' This campaign was to some degree led and stimulated by the Communist Party, but extended far beyond that tight-knit body. *Tribune* ran a series of articles by Frank Owen (disguised under the pseudonym of 'Thomas Rainboro'). In March the *News Chronicle* again took up the call for large-scale raids, and perhaps the temporary establishment of bridgeheads, to divert German forces from the east. The *Daily Herald*, though generally cautious, pointed out that the Polish leader, General Sikorski, had argued that a second front should be opened before the Germans launched their spring offensive in Russia. If Britain was genuinely unable to mount an invasion, why did her allies keep calling for one?[29] On 25 March Maisky, the Soviet Ambassador, made a speech covered prominently by the newsreels in which he emphasized that 1942 was the vital year for the Allied cause – the inference about the second front was left implicit, but was not hard to discern.[30] Sir Stafford Cripps, who had returned to England at the end of January 1942 at the close of his spell as Ambassador in Moscow, threw himself into an effort to heighten public awareness of the desperate nature of the struggle in Russia and to urge closer co-operation with the Soviet government. He made an impressive broadcast after the nine-o'clock news on 8 February. 'I want you to realize', he said, 'the differences between the fortunes of war as you have experienced them and as they have been suffered by millions of our Russian allies. These sufferings are going on at this very moment, while we sit in comparative safety and comfort. . . .' He criticized a lack of urgency in the British war effort at home, and called for help to be sent to Russia in arms, raw materials and food. In this and other speeches he stopped short of advocating an immediate second front, but his general commitment to the Soviet cause gave an extra impulse to that campaign.[31]

The most important influence in the revived second front agitation, however, was that of Beaverbrook. According to an unpublished account written at Beaverbrook's own request, the entry of the United States into the war changed his mind as to the feasibility of an invasion of France. He became convinced that the British and Americans together could achieve what Britain alone had previously been unable to attempt. At the end of February

29 *News Chronicle*, 23 March 1942 (article by Philip Gribble); *D. Herald*, 28 March.
30 Maisky, *Memoirs*, pp. 269–70. Newsreels released, 30 March.
31 Colin Cooke, *The Life of Richard Stafford Cripps* (London, 1957), pp. 277–8; Eric Estorick, *Stafford Cripps* (London, 1949), pp. 292–4.

"WHAT NEWS FROM THE SECOND FRONT?"

'Second Front Now', July 1942

1942 he resigned from his office as Minister of Production and was free to launch into public controversy. His most dramatic intervention was made from across the Atlantic, during a semi-official visit to the United States. At a big public dinner in New York on 23 April he spoke with intense vehemence:

> Strike out to help Russia. Strike out violently. Strike even recklessly. How admirably Britain is equipped in weapons of war for directing an attack on Germany I well know. Britain should imitate Russia's spirit of attack by establishing somewhere along the two thousand miles of occupied coast-line a Second Front.[32]

The speech created a sensation on both sides of the Atlantic. It received widespread support in the American press, and in Britain it was strongly endorsed by the *Daily Express*, *News Chronicle* and *Daily Mirror*.

There was a strong tendency to assume that, since Beaverbrook had only recently left the War Cabinet, he knew something that others did not. In fact, he did know something of the mission to London by Harry Hopkins, Roosevelt's personal representative, and General Marshall, the American Chief of Staff, in April. During these conferences, the British had agreed to an invasion of France in 1943, and to an emergency operation if necessary in

---

[32] Beaverbrook Papers, *The Second Front*, typescript by David Farrar, ff. 23–44; for the speech, f. 38; Young, *Churchill and Beaverbrook*, p. 243.

1942 (Operation SLEDGEHAMMER). Hopkins had approved the passage on the second front in Beaverbrook's speech, which was a deliberate attempt to use public opinion to make a retreat from these commitments impossible. This attempt continued after Beaverbrook returned from the United States. According to the account commissioned by Beaverbrook:

> it became Beaverbrook's endeavour, after he returned to England and sensed that Churchill and his military advisers were hanging back, to secure that public opinion would mould strategy. That was the purpose of his every public action that summer of 1942.[33]

There followed the climax of the Second Front movement. In May Beaverbrook created a body called 'The Centre of Public Opinion', which held its first meeting at the London Hippodrome and was in effect devoted to the Second Front agitation. In June, during Molotov's visit to Britain, an Anglo-Soviet treaty of alliance was signed and a communiqué was issued stating that 'in the course of conversations full understanding was reached with regard to the urgent tasks of creating a second front in Europe in 1942 – phrasing which was in fact carefully obscure, but was widely taken to mean that a definite decision had been reached. On 21 June a number of rallies were held in great cities to mark the anniversary of the German attack on the Soviet Union. Beaverbrook spoke in Birmingham to a vast crowd (one estimate, in an account favourable to Beaverbrook, was 50,000). He described the sufferings of the Russian people, proclaimed his faith in the Russian leaders, and declared that the opening of a second front would win the war in a year. In fact, Beaverbrook had learned just before making his speech that Tobruk had fallen to the Germans and that his cause was lost – nothing would now turn Churchill's attention and British resources away from North Africa. But this was far from ending the campaign. The *Express* newspapers continued their advocacy. At the end of July there was a great meeting in Trafalgar Square. On 30 July Maisky addressed a well-attended meeting of MPs in a committee room in the Palace of Westminster, and urged on them the necessity for a second front in 1942. He gave the same message to a meeting of newspaper editors on 31 July.[34] But then events intervened.

On 19 August there took place the disastrous raid on Dieppe. The landing forces, mostly Canadian, sustained heavy casualties. This shook the advocates of a second front and gave ammunition to their opponents. Indeed, Beaverbrook appears to have at least half-believed that the Chiefs of Staff had agreed to the operation in order to demonstrate that a cross-Channel attack was impossible. In September a resolution at the Trades Union Congress calling for an immediate second front was heavily defeated. Churchill's visit to Moscow in August was widely interpreted as indicating that a decision on a second front had been reached between the two leaders, so that further agitation was out of place. (In fact, Churchill had gone to tell Stalin that there would be no cross-Channel attack that year; but this

---

[33] Beaverbrook Papers, Farrar typescript, f. 45.
[34] *Ibid.*, ff. 50–2; Maisky, *Memoirs*, pp. 294, 301–2; King, *War Diaries*, pp. 185–6.

remained a secret). In October there was a flurry of activity by the second front movement, stimulated by Stalin indicating publicly that he disagreed with the British government's strategic assessment on the practicability of an invasion. *Tribune* responded to Stalin's intervention in a leading article on 23 October, claiming that influential anti-Soviet elements in Britain were still obstructing co-operation with the Soviet Union. The masses supported Russia, but lacked leadership, which it was clearly implied should come from Stalin himself over the heads of the British government. *Tribune* was right in at least one respect: the second front movement had lost its direction and leadership. Beaverbrook had for a time withdrawn from the fight. He fell silent after June for a long period, and a *Daily Express* leading article on 28 October on the theme of helping Russia dealt only with sending more supplies, making great efforts, forming fresh plans: all was left vague, and there was no call for a second front. In November there came the Anglo-American landings in North Africa, which met the need for action of some kind in the west. By the end of the year, the 'Second Front Now' movement had lost its impetus.

There was thus a prolonged and vociferous campaign to persuade or even compel the government to launch an invasion of France in 1942. It was a deliberate attempt, by a strange and heterogeneous coalition, to use public opinion to force the hand of the government. To this end, all the means and arts of publicity were deployed: influence behind the scenes, or in supposedly private meetings like that between Maisky and MPs; articles in the press, especially Beaverbrook's own papers and the highly sympathetic *News Chronicle*, *New Statesman* and *Tribune*; public meetings in great cities; and powerful coverage in the newsreels, which took the message of public meetings to the vast cinema audiences of the day. How much response did this agitation receive in terms of popular support? As usual, a fairly full answer can be deduced from the Home Intelligence reports and Gallup Poll results.

Home Intelligence began to pick up comments about a second front, after a period of quiescence, at the end of February 1942, when a slight revival of the previous year's demands was noted. At the end of March Maisky's speech calling on the Allies to stake everything in 1942 (which was given much coverage in the newsreels) was said to be supported by a general desire to take the offensive.[35] In April and May something of a contrary reaction was being reflected in the reports. In April a growing minority in Scotland was complaining that Maisky and others had been unhelpful in stimulating a demand for a second front which could not be fulfilled. Another report recorded a continuing demand for an invasion in some quarters, but also increasing anxiety about the practicability of a landing and some fear that the government might be persuaded to take excessive risks. On 10 May Churchill made a broadcast which was reported to have reduced the demands for a second front, but only because people thought it was now on its way.[36] At the end of May and beginning of June, public opinion as

---

[35] INF 1/292, HI Report 74, 23 Feb.–2 March 1942.
[36] INF 1/292, HI Reports 81 (13–20 April 1942), 83 (27 April–4 May), 85 (11–18 May).

reflected by Home Intelligence seemed to have reached a point of balance: there was a general desire for a second front, but not before everything was prepared. There was considerable irritation against the 'open-at-any-price brigade', and it was specifically noted that 'Where the Communist demands are vociferous, general opinion tends to harden against it' (i.e. against a second front). 'No more Dunkirks' was one summary of the desire to be absolutely ready before opening an attack. By the week of 2–9 June a decrease in the public demand for a second front was reported from many regions.[37]

In the same period, February–May 1942, Gallup put four questions bearing on the second front issue.

February 1942. Do you think the Allies will be able to open a front in Western Europe this year?
Yes 22   No 38   Don't Know 40
April 1942. (Open questions)
(i) What do you think is the most important problem the Government has to solve during the next few months?
    Second Front   20
    Shipping Losses   13
    Production   10
(ii) How do you think Great Britain can best help to defeat Germany this year?
    Open another front, develop an offensive somewhere   36
    Help Soviet Union in every way we can   15
    Increase bombing offensive against Germany   13
May 1942. Some people say that even if invading the Continent this summer might cost more than invading next summer, the results would make the cost worth while. Do you agree or disagree that the cost would be worth while?
Agree 49   Disagree 17   Don't Know 34[38]

The first set of answers, in February, showed a marked lack of belief that the Allies could mount a successful invasion that year. The open questions of April produced answers which are difficult to interpret ('develop an offensive somewhere' is a vague concept); but in so far as they were direct they showed only minority support for an invasion. The question posed in May was convoluted and hard to follow; but it appeared to show 49 per cent acceptance of the cost of a landing in 1942 rather than waiting until the next year. This at least indicated a growth in the support for a second front. Broadly speaking, these Gallup results were in line with the Home Intelligence reports.

June and July saw a clear change in public mood. In June the published communiqué on the talks with Molotov, referring to 'full understanding . . . with regard to the urgent tasks of creating a second front in Europe in 1942', was understood by most people as a promise of immediate action. Only a few noted the ambiguous phraseology of the statement. Even with this stimulus, which was generally welcomed, there remained sharp divisions of opinion. At the end of June and the first half of July there was much feeling in favour

37 *Ibid.*, HI Reports 86, 87, 88 (18 May–9 June 1942).
38 Gallup Archives, BIPO Surveys 84 (Feb.), 86 (April), 87 (May).

Second Front: still waiting

of an invasion and a sense that it was long overdue. But at the same time the defeats in North Africa and the fall of Tobruk reinforced the fear of failure. What was the use of starting a second front when 'we can't hold what we've got', or 'we can't manage the fronts we've got'?[39] But then the success of the German summer offensive in Russia brought renewed and sometimes grave anxiety about the situation on the eastern front, and with it an increased desire to do something to take the weight off the Russians. Confidence in the Russians' ability to hold out began to falter, and there was some talk of the consequences for Britain if Russia collapsed. In these circumstances, it was reported that calls for a second front, even at great risk, were being made with renewed vigour. 'Why the hell don't we do something about it?' was a simple way of putting the matter. Belief that the British inactivity was due to obstruction by 'people in high places' was reported from six regions at the end of July. Even at this stage, however, there were strong elements of caution – the same report referred to an even more widespread belief that Britain was not in fact in a position to open a second front. The Home Intelli-

[39] INF 1/292, HI Reports 89 (9–16 June 1942), 91, 92, 93 (23 June–14 July).

gence report for the end of July and beginning of August concluded that the agitation for a second front had not spread to more people, but those who were involved in it had grown more desperate.[40]

This conclusion was not borne out by the Gallup results, which in July and August showed a clear majority in favour of an invasion in 1942, which held firm for three successive polls.

July 1942. Do you think the Allies should or should not try to invade Europe this year?
Should 62   Should not 12   Don't Know 26
Undated, but near to the above. Do you think that the Allies should try to invade Europe this year?
Should try 58   Should not 19   Don't Know 23
August 1942. Do you think that the Allies should try to invade the Continent this year?
Should 60   Should not 17   Don't Know 23[41]

This was the first time that the question had been put in an unequivocal manner, so that direct comparisons with earlier results are impossible, but it seems clear that these three consistent answers showed increased, rather than simply intensified, support for an early invasion of Europe.

This marked the height of public support for the second front campaign. In August the situation was changed by two events. The first was Churchill's journey to Moscow to meet Stalin. The Prime Minister arrived in Moscow on 12 August, but already during the week of 4–11 August there were widespread rumours that he was in Russia, and that he had gone to make plans for a second front. When the news of Churchill's visit was made public, this reaction was confirmed, and many believed that the conference foreshadowed an invasion. Even at this stage, the Home Intelligence reports still showed a division in the public mind between a desire to strike hard at the Germans by an invasion of Europe and anxiety that the Allies were not actually ready to do so.[42] The second event then intervened: the Dieppe raid of 19–20 August. At first, in spite of government statements to the contrary, there was a widespread belief that the invasion had begun. Then, in the week of 25 August–1 September, there were rumours of very heavy casualties, which continued for some weeks – at the beginning of October there were reports from the Isle of Wight of commandos who had come back from Dieppe with their nerves shattered by the massacre they had witnessed. A statement in Parliament by Churchill on 8 September referred guardedly to 'a reconnaissance in force', and indicated that most of the landing force had returned. On 30 September he said that the losses had been 'very heavy' – almost one-half of those involved. Home Intelligence reported almost as soon as the raid was over (in the week 25 August–1 September) that the desire for a second front was now mingled with a 'considerable

40 *Ibid.*, HI Reports 94, 95, 96 (14 July–4 Aug. 1942).
41 Gallup Archive, BIPO Surveys 89, 89A (undated), 90.
42 INF 1/292, HI Reports 97, 98 (4–17 Aug. 1942).

dread' of its cost.[43] During the week of 8–15 September it was reported that the demand for an immediate second front had almost died away except among Communist elements. This did not prove permanent, and revived talk of an invasion was reported towards the end of the month; but in October the reports, while indicating a continued division of opinion, maintained consistently that the majority was prepared to leave the matter to the judgement of the responsible experts. A Home Intelligence summary prepared for the War Cabinet on 9 October claimed that as a political issue the second front 'has ceased to count'. There was a much greater awareness of the gravity of such an undertaking. 'No single factor has contributed more powerfully to bring this about than the news of the Dieppe raid.' The public had seen what were thought to be the opening phases of an invasion go wrong, and 'they appear to have drawn a grim moral from what they saw'. By the end of October the victory at Alamein had done something to meet the need for action, and demand for a second front continued to diminish.[44]

Gallup put no question about a second front in September 1942, and a question posed in October took the indirect form of an enquiry into opinion about the public discussion of an invasion.

> *October 1942.* Do you approve or disapprove of public discussion of whether or not there should be a Second Front?
> Approve 37 Disapprove 46 Don't Know 17[45]

This showed a substantial degree of disapproval of public discussion of the subject, and thus indicated a reaction against the second front agitation; and it seems reasonable to infer a decrease in support for the operation itself.

On 8 November the Anglo-American landings in French North Africa began, giving further evidence of Allied success. On 11 November Churchill spoke in the House of Commons, saying that the communiqué of June about the second front had been a ruse to deceive the enemy. He went on to claim that in July measures had already been in hand to take decisive offensive action, though nothing could be said.

> See then how silly it is for people to imagine that Governments can act on impulse or in immediate response to pressure in these large-scale offensives. There must be planning, design and forethought, and after that a long period of silence, which looks – I can quite understand it – to the ordinary spectator as if it were simply apathy or inertia, but which is in fact steady indispensable preparation for the blow.

He added, in words which must have drawn a weary sigh of assent from his military advisers: 'I am certainly not one of those who need to be prodded. In fact, if anything, I am a prod.'[46] It was a reproof to the second front agitators

---

[43] *Ibid.*, HI Reports 99, 100 (17 Aug.–1 Sept. 1942), 104, 105 (22 Sept.–6 Oct.). It should be noted that large-scale newsreel coverage of the Dieppe raid was released on 27 August. Churchill's statements in *HC Deb.*, vol. 383, cols. 84–5, 768–9.

[44] INF 1/292, HI Reports 102 (8–15 Sept. 1942), 104 (22–29 Sept.), 106, 107, 108 (6–27 Oct.); CAB 66/29, WP(42) 454, 9 Oct. 1942, Report on Home Opinion, 9 Oct.

[45] Gallup Archive, BIPO Survey 92.

[46] Quoted in Gilbert, *Churchill*, vol. VII, p. 255; see *HC Deb.*, vol. 385, cols. 20–39.

and an appeal to the wisdom of the strategic experts, now supported by the evidence of successful action.

Actions spoke louder than words, but the words still counted for something. The *Daily Herald* (12 November) held that Churchill's speech proved the wisdom of the TUC resolution passed in September, refusing to demand a second front within a stated time but pledging full support for an operation when the competent authorities should decide. Equally, however, there was no need for those who supported the agitation to reproach themselves, because Beaverbrook had given a lead in saying that a second front was a feasible proposition. The *Daily Telegraph* (same date) declared outright that no amount of clamour should force the government into unwise courses, and hoped that public opinion would now ensure that the second front commotion came to an end. It did indeed become only a minor element in the Home Intelligence reports. The great battle of Stalingrad held public attention in the winter of 1942–43, but it had only a limited effect in reviving demands for an invasion of Europe. Some desire to give further help to Russia appeared in the reports at the beginning of December. Early in January 1943 the question 'Are we doing enough to help?' was reported from six regions, but without specific reference to a second front. When Beaverbrook, after a long silence, renewed his demand for a second front, he did so not at a great public meeting but in the sober surroundings of the House of Lords. Reaction in the country was divided between approval, specifically noted as coming from 'Left-wing people' and resentment against Beaverbrook's belittling remarks about Britain's own efforts. Of the two feelings, resentment was said to predominate.[47] In March, widespread comments about a second front were again being reported, but the tone was said to be 'expectancy rather than clamour'. The general belief was that Britain had undertaken to carry out an invasion, and preparations were nearly complete. There was a strong hope that it would not be long delayed, but this was not translated into a wish to push the government into action. Only a small minority of what were described as 'noisy second-fronters' continued their agitation, and these aroused some resentment. Greater impatience and livelier demands for a second front were reported in mid-March, but in April both the regional reports and the postal censorship recorded a decline in comments about Russia and a general expectation that an offensive in Europe would follow final victory in North Africa.[48]

The Gallup Poll asked no questions about the second front between October 1942 and the end of February 1943, a period in which the fortunes of war were transformed. When questions were resumed, they were not in the direct form of enquiring about support for a landing.

End February/1 March 1943. Do you think that the Western Democracies (USA and Britain) are or are not doing everything possible to help the Red Army?

[47] INF 1/292, HI Reports 114 (1–8 Dec. 1942), 119–22 (5 Jan.–9 Feb. 1943), 126 (23 Feb.–2 March).
[48] *Ibid.*, HI Reports 127–33 inclusive (2 March–20 April 1943).

Yes 61   No 26   Don't Know 13[49]
March 1943. Do you expect an Allied invasion of the Continent this year?
Yes 67   No 14   Don't Know 19
April 1943. What do you think this is the most important war problem the Government must solve during the next few months?
Second Front 29   Shipping losses 21   Food rations 7[50]

The first two sets of answers showed a widespread belief that everything possible was already being done to help the Red Army (the phrasing is significant, the poll being taken just after the celebrations for Red Army Day), combined with an expectation that an invasion would come during the year. In these circumstances, it is natural to infer that public pressure to open a second front at once was diminishing, though the result for April showed a continuing recognition of the importance of the issue in itself. The Gallup evidence thus confirms, somewhat indirectly, that of Home Intelligence. The second front issue had died away by early 1943, with a fairly general view that enough was already being done to help the Russians.[51]

To sum up on the 'Second Front Now' campaign, it is clear that its high point came in July and August 1942, when Gallup showed a clear majority (between 58 and 62 per cent) in favour, and Home Intelligence reported the greatest intensity of feeling on the issue. Three reasons for this are apparent. The meetings and propaganda reached a peak at the end of June and during July; the German summer offensive in Russia revived the public desire to help the Russians in their time of need; and the Allied communiqué in June, despite its ambiguous language, appeared to be a government promise of a second front in 1942. All these three influences worked together, in proportions which are quite impossible to assess, to produce a large volume and marked intensity of public feeling. Even at its height, however, and more obviously at other times, this sentiment was opposed by a current of opinion made up of fear of casualties, the desire to avoid another débâcle like Dunkirk, and resentment against those who chalked on walls or wrote articles in the press but would not be doing the fighting. At the end of August the failure at Dieppe gave a powerful impulse to this movement, which in terms of fear of casualties represented something very deep-seated in British consciousness. This marked, in all probability, a decisive setback for popular support for the second front campaign. Then in October and November the victories at Alamein and in French North Africa showed that the British were in fact taking the offensive and doing something to take the weight off the Russians. The tide of war was visibly turning. Confidence in the government and its conduct of affairs revived, and with it the belief (never far beneath the surface) that the decision about an invasion of the continent was best left to

---

[49] INF 1/292, HI Report 129, reporting BIPO survey completed 1 March. This survey does not appear in the Gallup Archive.

[50] Gallup Archive, BIPO Surveys 97, 98.

[51] A retrospective Mass-Observation note on public opinion in 1943, by J. Ferraby, concluded that the feeling of guilt that the British were not doing more to help Russia came to an end with the final conquest of North Africa and the invasion of Sicily (May–June 1943). By June 1943 approval for the idea of an invasion was almost unanimous, but people were generally willing to leave the timing to the experts. (Mass-Observation Archive, FR2022, Notes on Public Opinion in 1943, 25 Feb. 1944.)

the experts. In autumn 1942 the campaign for a second front in the press and public agitation ceased to find a response among the majority of the population, and Beaverbrook's attempt to revive it in February 1943 was both half-hearted and unsuccessful.

The purpose of the second front campaign was to force the government's hand on a major strategic issue. In this, not surprisingly, it failed, though it caused some exasperation in government circles. On 1 July 1942 General Brooke, the Chief of the Imperial General Staff, wrote in his diary:

> Russia, USA, and the Press, all clamouring for a 'Western Front', without thinking what it means, or what its implications are! One might think we were going across the Channel to play Bacara at Le Touquet, or to bathe at Paris Plage! Nobody stops to think what you can possibly do with some 6 divisions against a possible 20 to 30.'[52]

Brooke's comment reveals one of the ways in which the agitation might have achieved some serious effect: by acting in conjunction with pressure behind the scenes from the American and Soviet governments. Soviet pressure for a second front was continuous from Stalin's very first message to Churchill in 1941; and in the spring and summer of 1942 the Americans were strong advocates of Operation SLEDGEHAMMER, a quickly-mounted invasion, probably of the Cotentin peninsula, in 1942. In theory, it was just possible that public agitation in Britain, added to the influence of the two great allied powers, might tip the balance in favour of such an operation. But in practice the British would have to provide most of the troops and nearly all the landing-craft, and they therefore had the final word on what could or could not be done. As long as the professional advice given to the British government by the Chiefs of Staff remained firm – and it did – there was no chance of it being overruled. The only other chance of success for the second front campaign lay in the possibility that Parliamentary support for the government might crumble. The first half of 1942 saw an almost unbroken catalogue of disasters for the British forces, in the Far East, in Libya and Egypt, and even in home waters, where in February the *Scharnhorst* and *Gneisenau* sailed up the Channel to German ports in broad daylight. On 1 and 2 July a motion expressing 'no confidence in the central direction of the war' was debated in the House of Commons. In the event, the supporters of this motion showed themselves to be divided, and the government won the vote of confidence by 475 votes to 25.[53] There was a good deal of uneasiness in the House, but the coalition between the major parties stood firm. Here too the second front campaign beat against the stone wall of a government which proved to be invulnerable in the House of Commons.

In retrospect it appears surprising that those who led the campaign even thought it might succeed. There is, of course, a strong tendency for newspapermen to overestimate the power of the press, and this surely played a part in the miscalculation. It is also true that the motives of those involved were very divergent. Some doubtless simply wanted an immediate invasion of western Europe as the most likely way to win the war; and in this they

---

[52] Alanbrook Diaries (MS), 5/6A/1.
[53] *HC Deb*, vol. 381, cols. 609–14.

were not necessarily pro-Soviet, but merely advocates of a particular strategy. The Communists, on the other hand, were trying to exploit popular sympathy with Russia to build up political support for themselves, and the second front issue seemed a good card to play. Others on the left – Bevan in *Tribune*, Kingsley Martin in the *New Statesman* – genuinely believed in the dangerous influence of ultra-conservatives in the government, still more hostile to the Soviet Union than to Nazi Germany, and they seized on the second front as a means of breaking the power of these die-hards and 'guilty men'. Beaverbrook, who never lost his affection or admiration for Churchill even in the midst of their differences, believed for at least some of the time that he was helping the Prime Minister against the excessive caution of the Chiefs of Staff and the armed services.[54] In view of these differences in motives, it may well be that some of those involved in the campaign did not actually expect to see an invading army set sail for France in 1942, but hoped rather for some other advantages to accrue from their efforts.

For the most part, however, the advocates of a second front doubtless meant what they said, and were misled (particularly by Beaverbrook, who after all was a senior minister until February 1942) into thinking that the government was open to pressure. In this they were mistaken, but their motive was straightforward and honourable: to help Russia by drawing German forces off to the west, and thus to secure Britain herself from the disastrous consequences of a Russian collapse. This motive drew much of its strength from the immense concern with and admiration for Russia which flourished in 1942 and the early part of 1943. It is to this sentiment, which thrived at much the same time as the second front movement but was much more spontaneous, that we must now turn.

The Height of Russomania, 1942–early 1943

Throughout 1942 and to the end of the battle of Stalingrad in February 1943, the Home Intelligence reports recorded widespread and often deeply felt admiration for the Soviet Union among the British people. This was primarily a matter of respect, amounting sometimes to wonder, at the vigour and tenacity of Russian resistance against the previously all-conquering German armies. Such admiration was already strong in 1941, and it increasd in 1942. A report by the postal censorship authorities in March 1942 stated that 'The majority of writers seem to pin their faith almost entirely on the Russians – "the chaps who don't talk but keep on killing Huns".'[55] In February 1942 a special report on 'Home Morale and Public Opinion' at the turn of the years 1941–42 noted that 'The gratitude and admiration for the

---

[54] Beaverbrook told General Pile on one occasion that he meant to 'go on beating the drum for 1942, otherwise no one will do anything to get things ready'. Young, *Churchill and Beaverbrook*, p. 241.

[55] INF 1/292, HI Report 76 (9–16 March 1942). The postal censorship dealt with mail going abroad, which primarily meant correspondence with the Irish Free State and the USA. Many of the writers were doubtless either Catholic or well-disposed to America (or both), and they did not form the most natural constituency for pro-Soviet sentiment.

Symbol of Soviet sacrifice: a military cemetary outside Stalingrad

great fight of the Russians far exceeds the feeling for any other foreign country.'[56] At the beginning of July, when Sebastopol fell to the Germans after a siege of nine months, this prolonged resistance was widely contrasted with the rapid German capture of Tobruk from the British in June.[57] This bleak disparity between Soviet staying-power and British surrenders was noted in a number of reports in the first half of the year.

At the end of August the monthly report on home opinion submitted to the War Cabinet indicated that anxiety was gaining ground: 'Although sympathy and admiration for the Russian people remain great, the possibilities of a Russian collapse are now very much in peoples' minds'.[58] Admiration and anxiety alike came to be focused upon the battle of Stalingrad. At the end of September there were rising hopes that the city might hold out. Admiration for Russia was said to be 'as widespread and intense as at the time of the defence of Moscow', and events on the eastern front, and especially Stalingrad 'overshadow all others in the public mind'. In early October the battle of Stalingrad had 'almost become an obsession', dominating public interest virtually to the exclusion of any other war news. The postal censorship in Edinburgh found praise for the Russians in every letter.[59] The battle of Alamein and the Anglo-American landings in North Africa, which occurred in October and November, ended this total concentration on Stalingrad, but as the siege and dogged defence turned to

---

56 *Ibid.*, HI Report 71 (2–9 Feb. 1942), Appendix.
57 *Ibid.*, HI Report 92 (30 June–7 July 1942).
58 CAB 66/28 WP(42) 385, 28 Aug. 1942, memo. by Bracken.
59 INF 1/292, HI Reports 104, 105 (22 Sept.–6 Oct. 1942).

victory the British admiration for the Russian armies became virtually unqualified. Between November 1942 and February 1943 the German forces in and around Stalingrad were first surrounded and then forced to surrender – the first capitulation of a German army in the course of the war. 'Supermen' was a word which Home Intelligence picked on as embodying British praise for the extraordinary Russian powers of recovery, and throughout January and February 1943 enthusiasm and admiration for the Russians were reported to be intense.[60] The public celebration of Red Army Day (23 February, 1943), which came immediately after the German surrender at Stalingrad, provided an appropriate climax and release for these feelings. As we have seen, the government made a great effort in terms of parades and public functions, and while Home Intelligence reported that some people thought that it was all done with tongue in cheek, the predominant view was that the celebrations were 'a fitting sign of our feelings for the Red Army'.[61]

Much of this admiration was extended to the regime which had produced so strong an army and so formidable a fighting spirit. In January 1942 Home Intelligence registered 'considerable enthusiasm for the regime in Russia', and the postal censorship mentioned numerous letters to the same effect.[62] At the end of that month a delegation of Soviet trades unionists was received with great enthusiasm at factories in Nottingham, Derby and Lincoln; though some of their outspoken criticisms of British production methods were less welcome.[63] In March reports from all over the country agreed that a trend towards socialism had been given a distinct impetus by the Russian military successes. The 'ruthless speed of Russia's dictatorship' was admired in north-east England, and from Scotland there was reported an awakening of interest in the Communist Party, which had gained 1,200 members in the first six weeks of the year.[64] In May a special report on public feeling in south-west England emphasized a unanimous admiration for the Russian people, accompanied by 'an almost equally unanimous belief that the success of the Russian armies is due to the political system in that country'. The same report remarked on a constant reiteration that after the war things could not go on as they had been in Britain.[65] The next month, Home Intelligence again noted a decided 'slant to the left', despite widespread suspicion and resentment of the Communists, and attributed this movement of opinion to a belief that the Russian political system was responsible for their victories in battle.[66] The battle of Stalingrad elicited more comment along the same lines. In December it was reported that sympathy for Russia was deep-seated among the working class – Russia was 'the true country of the ordinary people'. In January 1943 industrial workers were said to be keenly interested

---

[60] *Ibid.*, HI Reports 113–16 (24 Nov.–22 Dec. 1942, 121–3 (19 Jan.–9 Feb. 1943). All the reports during these months contain some mention of admiration for the Russian successes.

[61] *Ibid.*, HI Report 125 (16–23 Feb. 1943). See above, pp. 68–69.

[62] *Ibid.*, HI Report 67 (5–12 Jan. 1942).

[63] *Ibid.*, HI Reports 68, 69 and 70 (Appendix I), 12 Jan.–2 Feb. 1942.

[64] *Ibid.*, HI Report 77 (16–23 March 1942), Appendix on 'Home-made Socialism'.

[65] *Ibid.*, HI Report 85 (11–18 May 1942).

[66] *Ibid.*, HI Report 88 (2–9 June 1942).

in the Russian social and political system, for which people were prepared to fight so hard. In February there was some speculation as to whether a victorious Russia would spread communism outside its borders: some were alarmed at the prospect, but others thought it would be good if post-war conditions in Britain were modelled on Russian lines.[67] A Mass-Observation report at the end of November 1942 presented very much the same picture. There was almost unanimous admiration of the way Russia had fought, but different opinions as to the reasons. There was a minority view that 'the Russians were simply fighting for themselves, not us'. But the majority thought they fought so hard because they believed in 'the Russia they've created themselves'. There must be something in the Soviet system and its ideals to produce so great an effort.[68]

At the head of this regime, and the cynosure of all eyes, stood Stalin. He was seen as the director of Russia's military efforts (he was after all Marshal Stalin), but he was also the wise, benevolent, even jovial figure of 'Uncle Joe'. In the newsreels he was smiling, unobtrusive yet obviously reliable. We have met him in Werth's 'Russian Commentary', smiling and applauding at a workers' dance. Perhaps above all he was an image for the cartoonists, with his pipe (a symbol of calm and dependability) and a general air of being an unassuming practical man – a wood-cutter, for example. Sometimes he appeared as a bear, strong yet almost cuddly; and in a famous cartoon in *Punch* by Bernard Partridge the Russian bear had borrowed the British lion's top hat and frock coat as together the two animals went into the forest to tackle Nazism. When a sterner side appeared to his character, it was still held up for admiration – there was much support for ruthlessness in dealing with the Germans. It is not surprising that Home Intelligence picked up reports of Stalin's great popularity in the country during 1942, or that he was described as the most applauded figure on the cinema screens when he appeared on the newsreels. In May 1942 Gallup put the question 'Who is the world's greatest living man?' and produced the following results:

Churchill 42   Stalin 24   Roosevelt 20   Hitler 4   Cripps 3

It is remarkable to see Stalin thus placed ahead of Roosevelt, who had for so long been a commanding figure in all forms of British publicity.[69]

Other Gallup polls gave clear evidence of public admiration for Russian vigour and fighting power.

February 1942. From all the things Russia has done to fight Germany, what do you think is the most useful lesson for us in Britain?
Go all out, deal drastically with slackers and racketeers   23
Achieve unity of people, Army and Government   15

---

[67] *Ibid.*, HI Reports 114 (1–8 Dec. 1942), 119, 120 (5–19 Jan. 1943), 124 (9–16 Feb.)
[68] Mass-Observation Archive, FR1492, 20 Nov. 1942. The report gives no indication of the evidence on which it was based. It was not a Gallup-type poll.
[69] See INF 1/292, HI Reports 67, (5–12 Jan. 1942); 74, 75 (23 Feb.–9 March); Gallup Archive, BIPO Survey 87.

Stalin the great and benevolent: a portrait of Stalin as Marshal of the Soviet Union

Thoroughness and determination of military
command – guerrilla warfare   14[70]
March 1943. Consider what each of these countries could do, which one do
you think is trying hardest to win the war: Russia, China, USA or Britain?
Russia 60   China 5   USA 3   Britain 33[71]
April 1943. Which country of the United Nations do you think has so far made
the greatest single contribution towards winning the war?

[70] Gallup Archive, BIPO Survey 84.
[71] Home Intelligence, 'British Public Feeling about America', q. 25. This survey was
conducted by BIPO, using its usual methods.

Russia 50   China 5   USA 3   Britain 42
(In answer to a supplementary question, 'Why do you think this?', 39 per cent
of those naming Russia gave answers summarized as 'Her great losses and
suffering; she is bearing the biggest burden; acts not merely talks; fighting the
hardest; war on her own soil'.[72]

The general impression is one of respect for Russian energy, determination
and efficiency. The last two sets of answers effectively placed Russia top
among the allies for both effort (March) and achievement (April), ahead of
Britain, and with the United States an also-ran. The questions were put, of
course, in the immediate aftermath of the victory at Stalingrad – the best
possible time for an interim report on the Russian war effort.

An interesting point of comparison with the Home Intelligence and Gallup
Poll evidence is provided by a survey conducted by the Listener Research
Department of the BBC in July 1942. Eight hundred and fifty of the BBC's
local correspondents were asked to comment on a list of possible subjects for
broadcast talks about the Soviet Union, and on another list of issues which
might cause misunderstanding and distrust of the USSR. These local correspondents were volunteers, and by definition people who were keenly
interested in broadcasting; they were in no sense a representative sample of
public opinion, though they were asked to give their views on general listener
reaction. The main conclusion drawn from the survey by the Listener
Research Department was that current feelings about Russia were 'a
combination of profound gratitude and admiration, coupled with a
considerable sense of frustration that more overt help cannot be given to her'.
These feelings had been produced by recent events; but behind the
experience of the past year lay a period of some twenty-five years in which
'public opinion about the Soviet regime oscillated with bewildering rapidity
between sympathy and repugnance'. The result was a sense of bewilderment,
for which the public blamed the organs of opinion, including both press and
radio, which had said too many contradictory things in a fairly short space of
time. The result was a great demand for information about the Soviet Union,
and above all that such information should 'carry an unmistakeable stamp of
authenticity'. (The report did not enlarge on how this authenticity could be
provided, though it emphasized that the public would not accept 'mere
propaganda'.)

From the list of subjects on which people might welcome information, the
correspondents placed as an easy first 'the ordinary lives of ordinary people',
with second 'the political and social system of the USSR'. From the subjects
which were suggested as possible 'barriers to full understanding of the Soviet
Union', the clear first was the Soviet attitude to religion, and second the post-
war policy of the USSR. On religion, the report was emphatic: 'More than
any other problem, it has been a cause of misunderstanding and deep
mistrust, and there is a genuine need for clarification, particularly on the
question of persecution.' The main questions were whether there was freedom of worship, and whether the government was hostile or merely indiffer-

---

[72] Gallup Archive, BIPO Survey 98; also INF 1/292, HI Report 139, which gives the
answers to the supplementary question as well as the main results.

ent to religion. (This overriding concern with religion is one of the points where the particular nature of the BBC's panel of correspondents stood out. There is little reference to religion in the Home Intelligence reports). On post-war policy, there was said to be much speculation on whether Russia would identify her interests with those of Britain and the allies, whether she would 'attempt to convert the world to her way of thinking', and whether her influence would be 'subversive rather than pacific'. These two problems were followed, in the correspondents' order of importance, by questions relating to the Soviet attacks on Poland and Finland in 1939, and about the secret police – 'Why is such a system necessary if Russia is really a democracy? . . . What has it in common with the Gestapo?'[73]

The BBC's local correspondents were an articulate and sophisticated group, and the picture they painted was varied and revealing. Admiration, bewilderment, a search for authentic enlightenment, and a considerable measure of doubt about the present and anxiety about the future: these were the main features.

The elements of doubt and anxiety were also present among a wider public, even at the height of the enthusiasm for Russia which ran so strongly in 1942 and early 1943. Home Intelligence picked up some signs of uneasiness in June 1942, at the time of the signature of the Anglo-Soviet treaty. Amid the general welcome for this agreement, 'a questioning minority' foresaw difficulties in the post-war settlement, notably over the territories which Russia had taken from Poland in 1939. There were even suggestions (in five Regions) that at some future date Britain might find herself in conflict with Russia.[74] In October 'a clearly defined minority', perceptible in five Regions and stronger among older people, was saying that the Russian pact with Germany had brought the war about in 1939, and so Britain too should consult her own interests in relation to Russia. This was particularly linked to the second front question – 'It's a pity Russia didn't think about a second front in 1939.'[75] In December there were reports of growing scepticism about Soviet claims for their military successes, especially their figures for German casualties – if these were true, why was the German army still so strong? A minority was also expressing fear about Russian power after the war.[76] In January and February, with the developing Soviet victory at Stalingrad, there were signs of anxiety about what would happen at the peace if Russia was allowed to win the war alone and then dominate the settlement. 'We shall have to fight Russia yet' was one remark recorded. 'Will Joe stop at the Channel?' was another, with an authentic ring of gloomy humour. In Scotland, the anti-Russian sentiments of the Polish troops stationed there were reported to be irritating to many but impressive to some others, who were inclined to say that the Poles had been neighbours of the Russians for so long that they knew more about them than the BBC.[77]

[73] BBC Written Archives, Audience Research: Special Reports, LR/1175, 11 Sept. 1942.
[74] INF 1/292, HI Report 89 (9–16 June 1942).
[75] *Ibid.*, HI Report 107 (13–20 Oct. 1942).
[76] *Ibid.*, HI Reports 114 (1–8 Dec. 1942), 116 (15–22 Dec.).
[77] *Ibid.*, HI Reports 119, 120 (5–19 Jan. 1942), 123 (2–9 Feb.)

Similar doubts and reservations among the general admiration were revealed by Gallup Poll questions.

January 1942. Would you like to see Great Britain and Russia continuing to work together after the war?
Yes 86   No 6   Don't Know 8
Do you think they will?
Yes 53   No 18   Don't Know 29[78]

Presumably only the most strong-minded (or curmudgeonly) anti-Soviet respondents replied 'No' to the first part of the question – almost anyone would surely *like* to see the two countries working together. But the question on expectations produced a very different response, with much higher level of uncertainty.

In December 1942 Gallup put a sharply worded question, though about a hypothetical situation in the future:

December 1942. If after this war you HAD to choose between an alliance with Russia or with America, which would you choose?
Russia 32   America 46   Don't Know 22[79]

Other questions about the post-war situation were put in March 1943.

March 1943.
Will USA try to boss Britain after war?
Yes 31   No 44   Don't Know 25
Will Russia try to boss Britain after war?
Yes 18   No 58   Don't Know 24
After the war, which country do you think will be more anxious to get on with Britain: the USA or Russia?
USA 34   Russia 25   Same 24   Don't Know 17
Which country do you think it will be easier for us to get on with after the war: USA or Russia?
USA 46   Russia 22   Same 17   Don't Know 15[80]

Taken together, these answers reveal a rather complicated state of opinion. On the one hand, it was thought more likely that the USA would try to 'boss' Britain when the war was over than that Russia would; though should we necessarily attach an unfavourable meaning to the word 'boss'? On the other hand, there was a strong impression that the USA would be easier to get on with than Russia. When a hypothetical choice of an ally was pressed, the USA emerged as the favourite by some distance, with the Don't Knows also running strongly. These questions were all put at a time when the battle of Stalingrad was being fought or had just been won, and when admiration for the military effort of the Soviet Union was at its height; and

[78] Gallup Archive, BIPO Survey 83.
[79] *Ibid.*, BIPO Survey 89. It is good to see the resolute persistence of the 'Don't Knows', even though the wording of the question tried to exclude that option!
[80] Home Intelligence, *British Public Feeling about America*, questions 53, 54, 57, 58.

yet the answers demonstrate significant reservations in British opinion about the likely post-war policy of the USSR.

The cumulative evidence about popular opinion leaves no doubt as to the extent and intensity of admiration for the Soviet Union, concentrated primarily upon its military performance, and rubbing off on the regime and the personal reputation of Stalin. But even at this stage, ending about March–April 1943, there were doubts and anxieties about the past record and the future intentions of the Soviet Union. Even at the height of Russomania, a picture of total and undifferentiated popularity for the Soviet Union would be inaccurate. As time went on, the doubts were to increase.

The growth of doubt, March 1943–March 1945

By the spring of 1943 the tide of war had visibly turned. The surrender of the German Sixth Army at Stalingrad was a tremendous blow. In North Africa, the Axis forces held on in Tunisia until May, but then they too capitulated. It was true that the Axis still dominated most of Europe, but there was an air of optimism abroad in Britain. In April 1943 Gallup put a question, as it did from time to time, on how long people expected the war to last.

April 1943. How long do you think the war will last from now?

Up to 6 months	7	Up to 2 years	26
Up to 1 year	27	Up to 3 years	9
Up to 18 months	22	Longer	6
	Don't Know 3[81]		

So as many as 34 per cent of respondents thought the war would be over inside a year; 56 per cent within 18 months; and 82 per cent in two years at the latest. In these circumstances, it was natural that opinion in the country should look forward to the end of the war, and that in relation to Russia attention should move towards the political aspects of the Anglo-Soviet alliance and the likely shape of the post-war world. Of course, the war went on, and the struggle on the eastern front gripped people's attention from time to time, but not with the same intensity as in late 1941 and 1942. In October 1943, the Conference of Foreign Ministers (British, American and Soviet) at Moscow, and then the meeting of the Big Three at Teheran at the end of November confirmed this shift of attention from the military to the political.

During 1943, four main themes may be discerned in popular opinion about the Soviet Union: continuing admiration for the Russian war effort and fighting power; diminishing interest in the second front issue; anxiety about the working of the 'grand alliance'; and fear of Soviet intentions at the peace and in the post-war world.

The degree and intensity of admiration for the Soviet Union fluctuated considerably during 1943. At the end of March Home Intelligence reported that comment on Russia had diminished markedly, and only the warmest admirers showed no decline in their interest. In April this slackening of

---

[81] Gallup Archive, BIPO Survey 98.

interest was again noted by both the regional and the postal censorship reports, and two regions mentioned signs that 'the emotional regard for her (Russia) may be burning itself out'.[82] Soviet victories during the summer led to a revival of interest during August, with delight at the good news coming when in previous summers the Germans had made all the running. This was accompanied by a return of the feeling that the Russians were making all the big sacrifices and the British were not doing enough to help; but this tended to be matched by a countervailing irritation at Russian unwillingness to acknowledge the extent of British help, and especially the strain and losses involved in the Arctic convoys.[83] In October there was something like a revival of the old enthusiasm with the displaying of the Stalingrad Sword in cities up and down the country. The response to this event – in itself distinctly dull, because all one could do was glance briefly at the sword before shuffling on – was remarkable. The Sword (always dignified by the capital letter) was sent on two tours of the provinces, and ardent requests from towns which were excluded from its route had to be turned down by the Ministry of Information. Even Torquay wanted to see the Sword, and made a claim for its affinity with the heroic city of Stalingrad. In all, according to the official figures, a total of 491,457 people filed past this symbolic weapon during the 33 days during which it was on display.[84] At the beginning of November one Home Intelligence Report spoke of enthusiasm for Russia being 'higher than ever'.[85] But this was exceptional, and the general picture for the year was of a marked slackening of interest and enthusiasm.

The public pressure for a second front had already lost its impetus before the end of 1942, and the following year saw no more than an occasional stirring of the old ardour. In mid-March Home Intelligence reported a considerable increase in impatience at British inactivity, but noted also that there was no desire to risk defeat through lack of preparation, and no sympathy with 'second front agitators'.[86] This mixture of feeling persisted during March; and in April it was widely expected that an invasion of Europe would follow the mopping up of the enemy forces in Tunisia.[87] In May, the welcome for the German surrender in Tunisia was at once followed by speculation as to where the attack on Europe would come – agitation for a second front was reported to have virtually ceased, except for some continuing 'communist clamour'. Italy was generally predicted as the probable area for an invasion, with Sicily or Sardinia tipped as the first points of attack – Sicily it was, though not until 10 July.[88] The successful invasion of Sicily then aroused a general expectation that further landings were imminent, either in the Mediterranean or across the Channel. The only signs of anything like a second front agitation were reported as coming from the

82 INF 1/292, HI Reports 130 (23–30 March 1943), 132, 133 (6–20 April).

83 *Ibid.*, HI Reports 150–2, (10–31 Aug. 1943).

84 *Ibid.*, HI Reports 160 (19–26 Oct. 1943); FO 372/3532, and especially TI5138/2396/372, Ministry of Information memo., 4 Dec. 1943.

85 INF 1/292, HI Report 162 (2–9 Nov. 1943).

86 *Ibid.*, HI Report 128 (9–16 March 1943).

87 *Ibid.*, HI Reports 130–132 (23 March–13 April 1943).

88 *Ibid.*, HI Reports 136 (4–11 May 1943), 139 (25 May–1 June).

extreme left.[89] In September there were reports of a feeling that the British were still not doing enough to help Russia, but there was also increasing resentment at the continued Russian demands for a second front – it seemed that they only wanted a second front as they themselves defined it, and took no notice of the landings in Italy.[90] Finally in the middle of November Home Intelligence reported that demands for a second front had disappeared.[91] At no time in the year had they amounted to anything serious, for obvious reasons: the victories in North Africa, Sicily and Italy were enough for most people, and in any case the Russians were doing very well.

The third strand of public feeling emerged in anxiety about problems within the wartime alliance, and particularly in an apprehension lest Russia was being excluded from Anglo-American consultations. There was some uneasiness in February 1943 that Stalin had been absent from the meeting between Churchill and Roosevelt at Casablanca the previous month, and some comment on lack of understanding between the three allies during March and April. But the main expression of concern and disapproval came when Stalin was again missing from the Anglo-American conference at Quebec in August. Public attention focused upon this personal issue, but there was also the wider point that there was no Russian representation at the conference at all. Why, people asked, was 'our favourite ally' not taking part? This sort of comment persisted for about three weeks, and at one point was reported to be 'the most discussed aspect of the Conference'. At the end of August the simultaneous recall to Moscow of the Soviet Ambassadors in London and Washington made a far greater impact on public consciousness than would be expected of any diplomatic gesture, because it was seen as confirming the fears that there was a serious rift within the alliance. Talk of Russia making a separate peace was reported from six regions. Home Intelligence recorded a difference of opinion between those who felt that the Russians were right to feel aggrieved, and thought there was little real sympathy for Russia in British governing circles (except for Churchill, who was usually excluded from these criticisms), and on the other hand those who believed that the Russians were being unreasonable – they had no understanding of the problems of naval warfare, and Stalin was only interested in Russian ambitions. But whoever was held to be at fault, the lack of co-operation within the alliance was held to be plain, and was much lamented.[92]

Churchill was well aware of difficulties with the Russians, and was trying to draw Stalin into a three-power meeting. In a speech on 31 August, broadcast in Canada and reported verbatim in Britain, he went out of his way to pay tribute to recent Russian victories, explained that a Soviet presence at Quebec would not have been suitable because much of the discussion was taken up with the war against Japan (in which Russia was not engaged), and expressed his and Roosevelt's desire for a three-power meeting. This had a marked effect in Britain, where anxiety over the state of the alliance

---

[89] *Ibid.*, HI Report 151 (17–24 Aug. 1943).
[90] *Ibid.*, HI Report 154 (7–14 Sept. 1943).
[91] *Ibid.*, HI Report 163 (9–16 Nov. 1943).
[92] *Ibid.*, HI Reports 151, 152, (17–31 Aug. 1943).

diminished over the next fortnight.[93] Eventually, the news of the three-power conference of Foreign Ministers in Moscow, released at the end of October, was greeted with 'delight and relief'; and then the meeting of Churchill, Roosevelt and Stalin at Teheran, which became known early in December, caused general satisfaction. The three great men had met at last, and the anxiety about the exclusion of Russia from the Allied counsels was assuaged.[94]

The fourth strand of opinion, however, reflected an uneasiness which had been present even at the height of Russia's popularity in 1942: that the Soviet Union would prove a difficult, perhaps a dangerous, partner in the post-war settlement. In March 1943 there was a good deal of talk about Russia winning the war, but then posing new problems. Had they really given up interfering in the internal affairs of other states? Did they have plans for 'bolshevizing the world'? From three regions remarks were reported about there being 'too much boosting of Russia'. These reports continued until the end of March, with uneasy speculation about Russia's post-war role, and anxiety about Russian silence on their objectives.[95] In April remarks were picked up suggesting that 'Russia is not necessarily fighting the same war as we are'. In the same month the story of the German discovery of the mass graves of Polish officers at Katyn was given wide publicity. The story was rapidly followed by the Soviets' breaking off diplomatic relations with the Polish government in London. These matters will be discussed in detail in the following chapter, but in sum they caused a sharp division of opinion (the majority siding with the Russians, a minority supporting the Poles), and reinforced anxieties about the post-war situation. 'If a thing like this can start in the middle of a war, what on earth will happen afterwards?' was one way of putting it; and similarly, if the Russians and Poles broke off relations while they were still both fighting the Germans, how would they get on after the war?[96] After this, a current of uneasiness about Soviet-Polish relations continued, even when relations between the three great allies were improving. A widespread minority was reported as noting that the communiqué after the Moscow Conference of Foreign Ministers failed to mention the Polish problem. Some people were anxious as to whether Poland would be fairly treated, and even the small Baltic states (Estonia, Latvia and Lithuania) surfaced in public discussion.[97]

1944 was a dramatic year for the British people. The Normandy landings on 6 June and the sweeping victories which followed during August, when Paris was liberated and the Allied armies advanced into Belgium, brought a wave of optimism in the country. Home Intelligence reported at the end of August that people were laying bets that war would be over in October, and were hunting out flags and bunting to put out when the day came.[98] But it was also a year in which Britain once again came under attack from the air,

93 *Ibid.*, HI Reports 153, 154 (31 Aug.–14 Sept. 1943).
94 *Ibid.*, HI Reports 161, 162 (26 Oct.–9 Nov. 1943), 166, 167 (30 Nov.–14 Dec.).
95 *Ibid.*, HI Reports 128, 130 (9–16, 23–30 March 1943).
96 *Ibid.*, HI Reports 133–136 (13 April–11 May 1943).
97 *Ibid.*, HI Reports 162, 163 (2–16 Nov. 1943).
98 *Ibid.*, HI Report 204 (22–29 Aug. 1944).

this time from the alarming new devices of the V-1 flying bombs and the V-2 rockets. For these reasons, popular attention was diverted away from Russia and the eastern front, especially during the latter part of the year (from June onwards). The Home Intelligence reports recorded much less comment about Russia than in earlier years, and the former admiration for Russia showed itself only in fitful bursts. In January 1944 the headlong Russian winter offensive, crossing the old Soviet-Polish border, aroused 'widespread admiration and delight', along with hope that the advance would continue into Germany.[99] In April there were again indications of general pleasure at the rapid progress of the Russian armies, and a spate of jokes that at the present rate the Russians would get to Calais before the British did.[100] In August and early September there was again widespread admiration for the Russian advances, especially into Rumania, but this was clearly at a lower pitch, and the eastern front commanded less attention than the campaign in the west which filled the newspapers, and the flying bombs which occupied many minds. In October there occurred the last references to 'deep admiration' for Russia before the end of the year brought with it the winding up of the Home Intelligence reports.[101]

This slackening current of admiration for Soviet victories had as its counter-point an increasing degree of concern about Russian ambitions and their effects on the post-war settlement. The centre of this anxiety was Poland, which had already attracted public attention during 1943. In January 1944 there was much discussion of Soviet-Polish relations in the light of statements about the Teheran conference and under the stimulus of the Red Army's advance across the pre-1939 Polish frontier. The crossing of this border was reported on the BBC and in the press early in January, arousing widespread interest and a marked division of opinion. It was generally understood that the Poles were likely to insist on their pre-war boundaries, while the Russians would not give up the territory they had occupied. In this dispute, those who took the Russian side tended to say that because the Russians were doing all the fighting they must decide the question. Without the Russian efforts, Poland would now simply be part of Germany. 'We must face facts' was a frequent attitude. There were also assertions that the Curzon Line was a reasonable frontier, and a political current of opinion to the effect that the Polish government in exile was reactionary and unrepresentative. (One marvels at the geographical and political sophistication of such comment, but of course the issues were widely discussed in the press.) Those who supported the Poles took the position that Britain had gone to war for Poland in 1939, and that the war was being fought for the rights of small nations. There was also some comment to the effect that the Russians were determined to have their own way, and had no real intention of discussing the frontier question. For most of January, majority opinion was reported to be on the Russian side, but by the end of the month feelings appeared to be more evenly divided, and 'a considerable minority' was said to take the Polish side.[102]

99   *Ibid.*, HI Report 171 (4–11 Jan. 1944).
100   *Ibid.*, HI Report 185 (12–18 April 1944).
101   *Ibid.*, HI Reports 204, 205, (22 Aug.–5 Sept. 1944); 212 (17–24 Oct.).
102   *Ibid.*, HI Reports 171–175 (4 Jan.–8 Feb. 1944).

An event which made a marked impact in late January was the publication by *Pravda* of a story about secret Anglo-German peace negotiations, which was itself widely reported in the British press. This caused general bewilderment, anxiety and resentment. The story was almost universally rejected, the common sentiment being that any government trying for a separate peace would be thrown out of office, but there was much questioning as to why the Russians should appear to believe the rumour, and why they chose to publish it. The episode became another focus of anxiety about Russian behaviour and intentions.

On 22 February Churchill declared in the House of Commons that it was reasonable and just for Russia to have the Curzon Line as its frontier with Poland, with the Poles being compensated with other territory from Germany. This strong lead from the Prime Minister met with widespread, though not universal, acceptance in the country. For five weeks running in March and early April the Home Intelligence reports indicated 'minority anxiety' about Russia's ultimate aims and the danger of Soviet domination of Europe after the war.[103] This trend of thought was brought to a head by the events of the Warsaw Rising in August – September 1944, when the Polish underground army in the capital held out against the Germans for two months. The Soviet forces, though only a few miles away, gave almost no help to the desperate Poles, and for a long time also refused to grant landing facilities to British or American aircraft flying supplies to Warsaw. This episode is examined in detail in Chapter 5, but in brief, British public suspicions of the motives behind Soviet inactivity increased as the weeks passed. By the end of August there was widespread concern about the situation in Warsaw, and bewilderment that British aircraft were having to fly there from Italy when the Russians were so close. Admiration for the heroism of the Poles was general. By mid-September it was reported that a majority was suspicious about the Russian attitude, and early in October Home Intelligence recorded that 'Feeling appears to have crystallized against the Russians, who are now chiefly blamed for the city's fall'.[104]

This sentiment does not appear to have led to widespread disillusion with the Soviet Union, but rather towards a mixture of perplexity and resignation. Churchill and Eden visited Moscow in October, which revived a rather vague hope that some settlement of the Soviet-Polish issue might be reached, but this came to nothing. The rights and wrongs of the problem left people baffled, but Home Intelligence recorded that 'everyone agrees that it is in a hell of a mess'. For two weeks in mid-October opinion remained mixed and confused, with sympathy for the Poles and distrust of the Russians on the one hand mingling with continuing praise for the Red Army and criticism of the Polish government on the other. Not surprisingly, there was some tendency to give the whole affair up, and some people were said to be 'fed up with all Poles'.[105] On 14 December Churchill confessed to the House of Commons his disappointment that no settlement of the Soviet-Polish dispute had been

---

103 *Ibid.*, HI Reports 178–183 (22 Feb.–4 March 1944).
104 See below, Chapter 5, and specifically INF 1/292, HI Reports 204 (22–29 Aug. 1944), 207 (12–19 Sept.) and 210 (3–10 Oct.).
105 *Ibid.*, HI Reports 211, 212 (10–24 Oct. 1944).

reached. Comment in the country was muted. Those with strong views remained divided between supporters of the Poles, who spoke of betrayal and the government knuckling under to the Russians, who were being allowed to do as they liked, and others who sustained Russia's claim to the Curzon Line. By the end of the year majority opinion was reported to support the government's position, which itself favoured the Soviet claim; while a few voices were recorded as saying gloomily that 'Russia will have her own way anyway.'[106]

Something of the uneasiness about Soviet intentions was reflected in the Gallup Polls, though questions about the Soviet Union became very infrequent during the last two-and-a-half years of the war. Between March 1943 and March 1945 four questions were asked on the issue of post-war co-operation between the great powers.

> *March 1943*. Do you think that Britain, the USA, Russia and China will work together when the war is over?
> Yes 55   No 22   Don't Know 23
> Those who answered 'No' were asked why not, to which the following categories of answers were given:
> Conflicting interests   1 1
> Tories won't   6
> Russia won't   4
> USA won't   2[107]

The next question was prompted by the Moscow Conference of Foreign Ministers in October 1943:

> *November 1943*. At the Moscow conference the Allies have agreed to continue during peace the co-operation they have established during the war. Do you expect that they will, or will not, be able to work together after the war?
> Will 55   Will not 21   Don't Know 24[108]

A question put in April 1944 was of a completely different kind, though raising the general issue of post-war co-operation:

> *April 1944*. After the war, should Britain and the USA concern themselves with Western Europe while Russia concerns herself with eastern Europe, or should Britain, Russia and the USA co-operate together concerning all Europe?
> Britain and USA West Europe, Russia East Europe   9
> Co-operate   76
> Don't Know   15[109]

The Yalta Conference in February 1945 led to a Gallup question the following month:

106 *Ibid.*, HI Reports 220, 221 (12–27 Dec. 1944).
107 Gallup Archive, BIPO Survey 97. The percentages under the 'If No' heading add up to 23, not 22: this was presumably due to rounding up of fractions.
108 *Ibid.*, BIPO Survey 103.
109 *Ibid.*, BIPO Survey 108.

March 1945. At the Crimea Conference the Allies said that they would continue to co-operate during peace, as they have during the war. Do you think that they will or will not be able to work together after the war?
Will 58   Will not 21   Don't Know 21[110]

The general pattern of these answers is consistent over a period of two years, and corresponds broadly with a poll in January 1942, which showed 86 per cent of respondents wishing to see Britain and Russia working together after the war, but only 53 per cent thinking that they would actually do so.[111] The poll of April 1944 similarly showed 76 per cent in favour of general co-operation between the main allies (as distinct from a 'spheres of influence' approach to post-war problems). But only between 55 and 58 per cent, as registered in the polls of March and November 1943 and March 1945, actually *expected* the allies to work together, with 21 or 22 per cent thinking that they would not. In view of the margin of error inherent in the polling methods, these proportions show effectively no change over the two-year period. Only the poll of March 1943 attempted to probe into the reasons for these doubts, and that showed a remarkably low proportion of distrust of the Soviets. The later polls shed no light on this question, revealing only a steady one-fifth of respondents professing a cautious uncertainty. What is clear is that there was distinctly more hope than expectation abroad on the matter of post-war co-operation between the great allies. In a broad sense, this corresponds with the Home Intelligence findings.

Popular opinion, having passed through widespread and intense admiration for Russia in 1942 and early 1943, showed increasing doubts about Soviet post-war intentions during 1943 and 1944. These anxieties increasingly gathered round the question of Soviet-Polish relations, on which by the end of 1944 opinions were confused and disillusioned. The Yalta Conference of February 1945 and the full-dress debate on it in Parliament which followed, focused public opinion on these difficult questions. But we must leave the Yalta debate to a later chapter.

Reflections

British public opinion concerning the Soviet Union – considered at present mainly in the sense of general opinion – provides a particularly instructive case for the study of the links between public opinion and foreign policy. Its significance is evident in three principal aspects.

First, the British government was concerned from a very early stage – as soon as July 1941, immediately after the German attack on the Soviet Union – that popular opinion was likely to become closely engaged with the role of Russia in the war. Admiration for Soviet success in battle might well be translated into respect for the Soviet system, and so into enthusiasm for 'Communism as an idea and, by further extension, emerge as support for the Communist Party in Britain. This view was held by Churchill, who

---

110 *Ibid.*, BIPO Survey 117.
111 See above, p. 95.

intervened strongly in August to encourage action to prevent such developments. Officials in the Ministry of Information were already thinking on the same lines, and between July and October 1941 the Ministry evolved a sophisticated and carefully balanced strategy on the question of publicity about the Soviet Union. This was to encourage support for Russia as an ally, and inhibit anti-Communist elements which might obstruct the working of the alliance, while at the same time so guiding and channelling enthusiasm for Russia that British Communists should not be able to exploit it for their own ends. This was called 'stealing the thunder of the Left': admiration for Russian courage and fighting power was to be welcomed and endorsed, but its extension to the Soviet regime and social system was not. In 1942 and 1943 this policy was applied in an increasingly diluted form, and with diminishing hope of success. The celebration of Red Army Day in February 1943 was an outstanding example of the government putting substantial official resources into a propaganda event in the hope of keeping control of it away from the Communists and other unofficial pro-Soviet groups. Ostensibly, everything was directed towards recognition of Russian military achievements and martial valour; and yet even in government hands the ceremonies veered towards praise for the regime – after all, why was it the *Red* Army?

But whether successful or not, the very existence of this publicity strategy reflected an acute anxiety about the state of public opinion in relation to a foreign power. The development of public opinion towards the Soviet Union was seen by the British government as a serious and urgent problem, and great efforts were made to guide and control that opinion.

Secondly, a number of other elements sought to influence and exploit public opinion about the Soviet Union. The Soviet Ambassador, Maisky, used his considerable skills as a communicator in public and an operator behind the scenes to mobilize MPs, the press, and the public at large in support of the campaign for a second front. In this process he received, and took advantage of, a greater licence than was normally allowed to the ambassador of a foreign power – a fact which was itself an indication of the public standing which had been achieved by the Soviet Union. The historian G.M. Young drew a pessimistic analogy with the past: 'never since Gondomar have we allowed a foreign ambassador to interfere so much in our domestic affairs.[112] Maisky was actively, though not always adroitly, assisted by the Press Attaché and Tass representative, Rothstein; and the Embassy produced various English-language publications, notably *Soviet War News*, to influence British opinion. The British Communist Party also threw itself into the second front agitation, and seized the opportunity provided by the newly kindled enthusiasm for the Red Army and Russian fighting power to recruit new members – in which it had some success. From a very different political standpoint, Lord Beaverbrook also took up the issue of the second front, and deliberately tried to use public opinion to influence government policy on a crucial strategic issue.

[112] G.M. Young to Barrington-Ward, 4 May 1943: *The Times* archive, Barrington–Ward box. Gondomar was the Spanish Ambassador to the court of James I; his influence at court has been generally judged to have been both excessive and malign.

Thus Maisky, the Communist Party, and Beaverbrook all believed that public concern and admiration for the Soviet Union could be turned to their own purposes and advantage. Their point of view was very different from that of the British government, but all were agreed that public opinion on this subject was significant, and tried to exploit or control it according to their different outlooks and expectations.

Thirdly, the views of all these different parties were justified, in so far as popular opinion did indeed become widely and sometimes intensely involved in events on the eastern front and with the Soviet Union, in a way which is distinctly unusual. The British public does not easily or often become interested in foreign countries. The first crucial development was the successful Soviet resistance in 1941. After reeling at the shock of the German attack, the Russians became the first people to hold out against the all-conquering Nazi forces, and the British watched their stand with an admiration which was powerfully reinforced by the recognition that the eastern front relieved their own country from both aerial bombardment and the threat of invasion. These sentiments became heavily concentrated, first upon the defence of Moscow in the winter of 1941–42, and then upon the siege (and subsequently the victory) at Stalingrad in 1942–43, which captured public attention to a remarkable degree. In this way, there was indeed a profound current of opinion and feeling, which might, as the British government feared and others intended, be influenced or exploited.

Yet in the event this popular opinion proved more independent than some feared and others hoped. The careful strategy of the Ministry of Information did not prevent admiration for Russian fighting power spreading out into respect for the Soviet regime and praise for Stalin. On the other hand, the second front agitation, though skilfully and emotionally mounted, was only briefly successful in its appeal to general opinion, and popular support faltered rapidly when the disaster at Dieppe struck home – a notable example of the public grasping the nature of a defeat in spite of a muted presentation by the government. Moreover, public opinion about the Soviet Union was never wholly united or solid. Even at the height of admiration for the deeds of the Red Army there were doubts and anxieties about Soviet post-war intentions, and these grew in 1943 and 1944, especially with regard to the position of Poland. Pro-Soviet zeal was never boundless, and it never produced quite the effects that the British governments feared and the Soviet Embassy hoped.

INTRODUCTION TO THE CASE STUDIES

The two previous chapters have taken a wide and sweeping view of developments in public opinion and policy towards the Soviet Union, in an attempt to establish the broad pattern of developments. In the early stages, two elements stand out: the government's attempts to influence and exploit public opinion; and the emergence of a great surge of public admiration for the Soviet war effort. With the passage of time, the picture changes, with the evolution of a balance between continuing enthusiasm, especially for the speed and scale of Soviet victories, and the growth of doubt about the aims and methods of Soviet policy. Both aspects of this balance command our attention. In one sense, the growth of doubt is the more interesting, because it runs counter to a widespread impression of a virtually undiluted Russomania. Yet the large degree of continued support for the Soviet Union, and belief that Britain and the USSR could and should continue to work together after the war, in the face of some serious and disturbing contra-indications, is surely equally significant. We need to look more closely at this balance between doubt and admiration, in the context of particular circumstances.

Similarly, the broad, panoramic view of events reveals some of the general and continuous contacts between public opinion and foreign policy, and between censorship, propaganda and opinion. But there are other and more detailed questions to be asked about these interrelated issues. The links between public opinion, in its different forms, and foreign policy can be brought into sharper focus by looking at the day-to-day conduct of affairs. The evolution and the effectiveness of policies on censorship and propaganda take on a different aspect when we see how their practitioners tried to cope with specific problems. How in detail did government try to influence opinion? What specific use was made of censorship 'stops' and guidance memoranda, and how far were they effective? How was general propaganda policy adapted to particular circumstances? What was the role of the press, and how far could it influence events? At what points did parliamentary opinion become important?

Any attempt to subject the whole of Anglo-Soviet relations to this kind of microscopic examination would make almost impossible demands upon a researcher's time, not to mention a reader's patience. The only practical method is to select particular examples, and two such case studies follow, on the affair of the Katyn graves (April–May 1943) and the Warsaw Rising (August–September 1944). The reasons for choosing these two episodes are reasonably plain. They arise out of the triangle of Anglo-Soviet-Polish relations which lay at the heart of the problems in the Anglo-Soviet alliance. Their nature is stark and dramatic, engaging public attention at the time and since, right up to the present day. The time-span encompassed by each is fairly short, making a day-to-day treatment of events feasible. Moreover, each episode was in an important sense public in nature. This is not to say that some aspects were not secret or obscure, as indeed they were and still are; but to emphasize that the affairs of the Katyn graves and the Warsaw Rising were played out very much before the public eye. Other interesting and fruitful case studies can be envisaged (the long and painful story of the Arctic convoys, the occasional reports in the press of separate peace negotiations, and the public treatment of particular wartime conferences come to mind), but none seem to offer the same advantages as the two here chosen.

In writing the following chapters, much use has been made of the detailed and illuminating Foreign Office correspondence, which shows what a close eye officials kept upon the press, and how they followed the Home Intelligence reports. The press has been widely, though not exhaustively, scanned, taking a generous sample of national dailies (from *The Times* to the *Daily Mirror*, both of which have much to tell us), some non-London papers (notably from Scotland, where Polish affairs were followed closely), the Catholic weeklies (which also took a keen interest in Poland, and were always a likely focus for anti-Soviet opinion), and the excellent weekly reviews which contributed so much to British political thinking at the time – the *Economist*, the *New Statesman*, the *Spectator* and *Tribune*. The BBC written archives are, as always, invaluable, and have been exploited in detail – for example, by examining the news bulletins from day to day.

The development of these detailed case studies involves some repetition of points made in earlier chapters, which is necessary if the studies are to be coherent in themselves.

Earlier in this book, in Chapter 2, it was explained that British propaganda policy towards the Soviet Union had two main aims: to curb anti-Soviet and anti-Communist sentiment, so that it did not obstruct the working of the Anglo-Soviet alliance; and to prevent pro-Soviet feeling from getting out of hand and spilling over into support for the Soviet system and the Communist Party. In 1941 and 1942, the second of these tended to take precedence, and much effort was put into 'stealing the thunder of the Left'. These two case studies, located in 1943 and 1944, mark a change of emphasis, and illustrate the problems posed to propaganda policy by Soviet actions which were likely to alienate public opinion from the USSR. It was not quite a question of how to keep pro-Soviet opinion going, because in April–May 1943 it was still powerful, and in August–September 1944 by no means exhausted. But it was certainly a matter of controlling a resentment against Soviet actions which if unchecked might lead to dangerous consequences for the future of the alliance. In 1941 and 1942, the notion of public opinion getting out of hand meant that it might swing alarmingly towards Communism. By 1943, and even more 1944, it meant that the public might condemn Soviet actions in such a way as to imperil the alliance and the post-war settlement. It is this change in strategic emphasis, as well as the day-to-day tactics of publicity policy, which the case studies illustrate.

4

Case Study 1: The Katyn Graves Revealed, 1943

It is our job to help to ensure that history will record the Katyn Forest incident as a futile attempt by Gemany to postpone defeat by political methods.

(Political Warfare Executive Directive, 28 April 1943)

The sombre story of the mass graves at Katyn, filled with the corpses of murdered Polish officers, has left a lasting scar on the history of the twentieth century. The echoes of that story, and of the question of the responsibility for the massacre, have reverberated down the years and are not yet stilled. The subject of this chapter is not the graves themselves nor the issue of who killed the officers; though it must be said at once that the evidence of Soviet guilt leaves no room for doubt.[1] Our purpose here is to go back to April and May 1943, and to consider the problems posed for British censorship, propaganda and public opinion by the revelations about the graves at Katyn. The diplomatic crisis produced by the German publication of the story was one in which publicity was freely used as an instrument of policy – indeed sometimes policy and publicity were indistinguishable. Those who controlled British censorship and propaganda, and attempted to guide public opinion, were faced with acute and wide-ranging problems. If it were indeed true that thousands of officers in the army of one ally (Poland) had been massacred by the secret police of another ally (the Soviet Union), then serious questions arose. In most circumstances, important sections of the British press and public opinion would be expected to take up such an accusation, to raise cries for enquiries to be made and justice to be done. If British public

---

[1] See J.K. Zawodny, *Death in the Forest: The Story of the Katyn Forest Massacre* (London, 1971), and compare the discussion of the evidence in two despatches by the British Ambassador to the Polish government, O'Malley to Eden, 24 May 1943 and 11 Feb. 1944, both in PREM 3/353. The evidence indicates overwhelmingly that the officers were killed by the Soviets.

opinion was thus engaged, then danger would threaten in at least two ways: to the Anglo–Soviet alliance, which would be sorely strained; and to national unity in Britain, because pro-Soviet opinion would not easily accept the thesis of Soviet guilt for the massacres.

This was a potential crisis in the relationship between public opinion and foreign policy, and for Anglo-Soviet relations. This chapter examines how the British government dealt with the problem, and traces the reactions of the press and public opinion as they developed in April and May 1943. In doing so, we must first briefly review the course of events as the Germans made their revelations; then analyse the nature of the problem posed to the British government, and the range of opinions involved; and finally examine the government's policy and the degree of its success in guiding public opinion in its various forms. At the time, this was a test for the government's capacity to control and guide public opinion; for us, looking back, it forms a case study in the interaction between foreign policy and public opinion.[2]

The graves revealed

On 12 April 1943 the German news agency Transocean announced that German troops had discovered mass graves in the Katyn forest, some twelve miles west of Smolensk, containing the bodies of about 10,000 murdered Polish officers. Berlin radio broadcast the story on 13 April, and during the next few days the press and radio across Europe – Axis, occupied and neutral – took up the tale. The various reports contained a number of elaborations and inconsistencies, notably concerning the number and condition of the corpses (the number eventually proved to be between 4,100 and 4,500); but all agreed that the men had been shot in the back of the neck, and that the killings had been carried out by the Russians in the spring of 1940. The accounts were accompanied by lists of names of the dead, compiled from papers found on the corpses.[3]

The Soviet government issued a denial of the German stories on 15 April, claiming that some Polish prisoners of war had been captured by the Germans near Smolensk in 1941. The Germans had evidently shot these men, and were now trying to cover up their crime.[4]

On 16 April the Polish government in London issued a statement setting out in some detail a story of which it had long been aware. Since 1941, when

---

[2]   This chapter is a revised version of a paper read to the Royal Historical Society on 22 April 1988, and published in the Society's *Transactions*, 1989, pp. 63–83. I am grateful to the Council, first for its invitation to read a paper, and next for its kind permission to reproduce much of the text here.

[3]   PWE prepared (29 April 1943) an analysis of Axis reports, with a note on discrepancies between them: FO 371/34565, C4891/258/55. Collections of newspaper reports from several countries may be found in the Chatham House press cuttings collection, British Library Newspaper Library, and at the Polish Institute in London.

[4]   The denial was published in English in *Soviet War News*, 17 April 1943, and published or summarized in the British press on the same date. It may also be found in General Sikorski Historical Institute, *Documents on Polish-Soviet Relations, 1939–1945 (DPSR)*, vol. I, (London, 1961), No. 306.

The dark side of the Soviet alliance: grave-pits and fir trees at Katyn

a Polish army began to be formed in Russia from released prisoners of war, it had become apparent that about 15,000 troops, including over 8,000 officers, from the army of 1939 were missing. The Poles had made great efforts to trace these men, without success; and the Soviet authorities had given conflicting accounts of their whereabouts: for example, that all officers had in fact been released, or on the other hand that 15,000 prisoners had escaped to Manchuria in 1941. The statement concluded by saying that the Poles were accustomed to the lies of German propaganda and understood the purpose of these revelations, but in view of the details which they contained it was necessary for the graves to be investigated and the facts verified. The Polish government had therefore approached the International Red Cross at Geneva to send a delegation to the site to verify the facts. On 17 April a further statement repeated that the Polish government had asked the IRC to conduct an enquiry, but changed the emphasis by listing German crimes against the Polish people and denying the Germans any claim to use crimes attributed to others as arguments in their own defence.[5]

Any Red Cross investigation would have been limited to identifying the bodies; but the Poles hoped for some advantage even from this. In the event, however, the Polish appeal played into the hands of their enemies. The German government seized the opportunity to announce (on 17 April) that they too had asked the Red Cross to intervene. On 19 and 20 April a leading article in *Pravda* and a communiqué by Tass asserted that the simultaneous approaches to the Red Cross by the Polish and German governments showed that the two were working in collusion. Following this accusation, the Soviet

[5] Texts of the two statements, in English, *DPSR*, I, Nos. 307, 308. They appeared in the British press, 17 and 19 April.

government broke off diplomatic relations with the Polish government, by a note delivered on 25 April and published on the 26th.[6]

Publicity was thus the essence of the Katyn affair. Each of the three governments principally involved created or sought public attention. The Germans produced a propaganda *coup* designed to sow dissension among their enemies, making a strong appeal to anti-communist sentiment. Bolshevism was a regime of murderers, and in the event of a communist victory in Europe the same thing would happen, for example in France, as had happened to the Poles at Katyn; yet it was to this regime that the British and Americans were giving their full support.[7]

The Polish government for its part faced the grim evidence of the list of names, which tallied with names on their own rolls of those missing in Russia. Already, through diplomatic channels, by direct appeal to Stalin, and by the tireless investigations of Captain Czapski, the Poles had done all they could by private enquiry to trace their missing officers. They now had to face the reaction of General Anders's Polish army in Iraq, which had only recently left the Soviet Union and in which these officers were known as comrades-in-arms and fellow prisoners. There were already ominous reports from the British authorities in the Middle East that Anders's troops were losing confidence in the Polish government; and the Foreign Office believed that, with the news of Katyn, there was danger of serious trouble among these troops. These warnings were known to the Polish government.[8] Recent reports reaching London from Poland indicated that any concessions by the Polish government to the Soviet Union would mean that it no longer represented the nation: these referred to territorial questions, but were likely to apply equally strongly to the Katyn graves.[9] In Britain, General Sikorski, the Prime Minister, was already under attack from those who claimed that he was unduly compliant towards the Russians. In these circumstances the Polish government had to be *seen* to be taking action to investigate the stories about Katyn. Inquiries behind the scenes would not do. So the Poles acted publicly, rapidly and independently.

The Soviet government had to issue a denial of the German stories, because silence would be taken as assent. Its action in breaking off relations with the Polish government, however, might have been kept quiet for a time. Churchill appealed to Stalin to refrain from making the decision public, 'at any rate till every other plan has been tried'. The British Ambassador in Moscow, Sir Archibald Clark Kerr, tried hard to persuade Molotov to defer publication. Both failed. Stalin wrote to Churchill on 25 April that the note had been delivered and publication could not be avoided, giving reasons

6 Soviet note, in English, *DPSR*, I, No. 313; published in the British press, 27 April.

7 For the German propaganda effort, see Balfour, *Propaganda in War*, pp. 332–4; for references to France, see e.g. *Le petit Parisien*, 17–18 April 1943.

8 FO 371/34593, C3375/335/55, Hopkinson to Strang, 17 March 1943, and attached papers; C3583/335/55, Minister of State, Cairo, to FO, 31 March 1943; C3623/335/55, same to same, 1 April; C3742/335/55, FO to Washington, 20 April. Count Edward Raczynski, *In Allied London* (London, 1962), p. 133.

9 FO 371/34383, C3345/50/62, BBC Survey of European Audiences: S-E Europe, 10 March 1943. The Germans used loudspeakers in the streets of Warsaw to broadcast the news of Katyn.

which were themselves in the public domain – attacks on the Soviet Union by Polish papers in Britain, and the reaction of public opinion in Russia, indignant at the ingratitude and treachery of the Polish government.[10] Whatever the real reason, the Soviet government moved swiftly to publish a decision which could have been kept quiet for a time, to give British diplomacy a chance to find a way out of this phase of the Soviet-Polish problem.

The three governments all used publicity as a weapon, and the British were caught in the crossfire of statements and accusations. The problem was very public, and its handling had to be a matter of publicity.

The problem for British policy

To appreciate the nature of the British government's difficulty, we must examine its main elements: the question of Polish-Soviet relations, including recent public skirmishes, the machinery of censorship and propaganda available to the British authorities; and the range of public opinions which were involved in the Katyn affair.

Polish-Soviet relations early in 1943 were very difficult, partly through the legacy of several centuries of history, and partly as a consequence of the events of the previous four years. In September 1939 Germany and the Soviet Union partitioned Poland between them. The Red Army occupied about half the country, taking 230,000 prisoners of war in the process; and at the end of October the USSR annexed these territories. In the next eighteen months, somewhere between a million and a million-and-a-half people were deported from eastern Poland to the Soviet Union. After the German attack on the Soviet Union in June 1941, British mediation helped in the negotiation of an agreement (30 July 1941) which restored diplomatic relations between the Polish and Soviet governments; but this agreement made no specific reference to the frontier between the two states. The Soviet government continued to insist on the boundaries of June 1941, while the Poles held to those of August 1939. These events thus left two major sources of friction between the two governments: the frontier question, and the fate of the Poles (prisoners of war and deportees) in the Soviet Union.[11]

The British government stood uneasily between the Poles and the Soviets. In 1939 Britain had committed itself to maintain the independence (though not the territorial integrity) of Poland; and in 1940, after the fall of France, General Sikorski's government had been welcomed to London. Polish airmen fought with courage and dash in the Battle of Britain, and substantial land and naval forces served alongside the British. On the other hand, since June 1941 the Soviet Union had borne the brunt of the war, and was clearly going to play a crucial role in the peace settlement. Both Poland and the

---

10 Churchill to Stalin, 24 April 1943, and Stalin to Churchill, 25 April, Warren F. Kimball, ed., *Churchill and Roosevelt: The Complete Correspondence* (Princeton, 1984), II, pp. 193–6; Kerr to Eden, 26 April, FO 371/34569, C4646/258/55.

11 On the background of Soviet-Polish relations, see Anthony Polonsky, *The Great Powers and the Polish Question, 1941–45* (London, 1976), especially pp. 13–23.

Soviet Union were now allies of Great Britain. Poland was the older ally, but the Soviet Union was by far the stronger. Moreover, the British government was dubious about both the ethnic basis and the practicality of Polish claims to territories in the east of inter-war Poland. By early 1943 opinion in the Foreign Office was moving towards the idea of Poland accepting losses in the east (probably to the so-called Curzon Line proposed in 1920) in return for compensation in the west; though Eden warned of the danger that Sikorski's government might be repudiated by the underground movement in Poland if it accepted such a loss of territory.[12]

In January and February 1943 the Polish-Soviet frontier conflict was again emerging into the open, with an exchange of public statements between the two governments about the status of the disputed territories and their inhabitants. The British government tried to limit the damage done by this verbal duel by preventing discussion in the British press and foreign newspapers published in Britain. A Ministry of Information guidance memorandum of 2 March 1943, issued at the behest of the Foreign Office, requested the press to use no material on the frontier problem other than that provided by British government sources. The Ministry of Information thought this would not work, and it was indeed only partially successful.[13] Polish-language papers independent of the Polish government published articles on the frontier question, and British Catholic journals vigorously supported the Polish case. On the other side, the London *Evening Standard* (4 March) published a cartoon by Low attacking 'Polish Irresponsibles', and on 10 March *The Times* first leader (by E.H. Carr) took the striking line that 'If Britain's frontier is on the Rhine, it might just as pertinently be said . . . that Russia's frontier is on the Oder, and in the same sense.' The Communist *Daily Worker* reprinted articles from *Soviet War News*, published by the Soviet Embassy in London, bitterly critical of the Polish government. The Polish and Soviet Ambassadors both complained to the Foreign Office; but the Controller of Censorship at the Ministry of Information only lamented that he could do no more than write to offending newspapers to remind them that they had disregarded the guidance memorandum, whose effect had been to curb comment by those who observed it, leaving the field free for those who did not.[14] It was a salutary illustration of the limitations of the British system of censorship and guidance, which was about to be further tested by the gruesome story of the Katyn graves.

The main aspects of this system, in the shape of Defence Regulations, Defence Notices and Guidance Memoranda have already been described in an earlier chapter.[15] It may help to recall here that there was no compulsory censorship of the press before publication, and that D Notices, with their

---

[12] Polonsky, pp. 24, 121–2; CAB 66/34, WP(43)69, note by Eden for War Cabinet, 17 Feb. 1943.

[13] Guidance memo., FO 371/34566, C2905/258/55; MOI Executive Board minutes, 2 March 1943, INF 1/73.

[14] The Catholic journals were *Catholic Times*, 4 March, *Catholic Herald*, 5 March, and *The Tablet*, 6 March. Chief Censor's remarks in FO 371/34565, C2509/258/55, minute by Nash, 10 March 1943.

[15] See above, pp. 12–15.

warning against public discussion of 'matters prejudicial to the good relations between ourselves and any neutral or allied country', were for guidance only. These arrangements were far from watertight. A.P. Ryan had written in June 1941, with his usual vivacity: 'The Ministry of Information is a sop to Cerberus, and the history of animal management contains no more dismal record of failure. No dog has been stopped barking by the Ministry of Information.'[16] Like many *bons mots*, this was an exaggeration, but its substance was correct. Most of the dogs could be restrained for most of the time, but when they chose to bark, as some did about the Polish frontier question, they could not be stopped.

The graves at Katyn posed questions which were both sharper and more profound than those raised by the frontier problem. There had recently been much public discussion of Nazi war crimes, drawing heavily on evidence from Poland, and accusations of similar crimes against the Soviets might well result in clamour and recrimination on a dangerous scale. This was an acute problem in the management of news and opinion, which the British government faced with instruments which were doubtless formidable in appearance but often defective in operation.

The problem was compounded by the number and variety of forms of public opinion which were involved. For British opinion, the Katyn story came only a very few weeks after admiration for the Soviet Union reached its height with the victory at Stalingrad and the celebration of Red Army Day.[17] The degree of popularity enjoyed by the Soviet Union at that time was such that the British government would have found it hard to take a public stance against the USSR on the question of Katyn, even if it had wished to do so. Yet, as we have seen, there were also doubts and anxieties about the Soviet Union. The BBC's audience research enquiry of September 1942 revealed concern about the Soviet secret police, and there was a constant undercurrent of worry arising from the Soviet attack on Poland in 1939 and the territorial dispute between the two countries. The presence of Polish troops in Scotland had a distinct, though minority, effect on opinion there.[18] There was a group of MPs (mainly but not solely Conservative who supported Polish interests; and Catholic opinion, led by Cardinal Hinsley and the Catholic press, was strongly sympathetic to the Polish cause. There was scope here for anti-Soviet opinion, which had been feared by the government since June 1941, to develop. A public debate in Britain about Katyn and the NKVD was an unwelcome prospect for the government.

As well as British opinion, there were the various centres of Polish opinion in Poland itself, in Britain and the Middle East, and among Polish-Americans in the United States. The Poles were naturally profoundly moved by the news of Katyn, and the reactions might well be severe enough to damage further the morale of General Anders's army and endanger the stability of General Sikorski's government. The British authorities were also conscious of an ill-defined but significant public opinion in occupied Europe. In eastern

16 Ryan to Monckton, 4 June 1941, BBC Written Archives, 830/37; cf. Asa Briggs, *History of Broadcasting in the United Kingdom*, III, p. 32.
17 See above, pp. 68–69.
18 See above, pp. 93–95.

Europe, where the prospect of Soviet occupation was beginning to loom, the Katyn graves cast a chilling shadow: while in the west, where relations between the communists and other resistance groups remained uneasy, old fears and doubts were likely to be revived. The British, who had undertaken a prominent propaganda role through the European broadcasts of the BBC, had to say something to their listening public across the continent. Indeed, the British government had to cope with the news about Katyn for all its different constituencies, and what it said to one could not differ markedly from what it said to another. It was a hard nut to crack.

Censorship, propaganda and public opinion

Before looking at how the British dealt with this problem, we must ask what the policy-makers believed about Katyn at the time. With varying degrees of certainty, Churchill, Cadogan and Roberts in the Foreign Office, and Clark Kerr in Moscow all concluded that that Soviet Union was responsible for the massacre. Eden appears to have left no written opinion, but there is no sign that he disagreed.[19] On 24 May the British Ambassador to the Polish government, O'Malley, analysed the evidence in what was rightly described as 'a brilliant, unorthodox and disquieting despatch', which makes painful reading even many years later. His conclusion was that Soviet guilt was a near, though not an absolute, certainty. The minutes on this despatch within the Foreign Office, while criticizing some points in its style and approach, did not dissent from its conclusions. It was given very restricted circulation, to members of the War Cabinet and the King; and Churchill sent a copy to Roosevelt. All this implied acceptance.[20] This in turn meant that British senior ministers and the Foreign Office, in their handling of this matter in terms of news and propaganda, were consciously engaged in deception, or in later jargon, a 'cover-up'.

British ministers who were acquainted with the evidence believed that the Soviets had carried out the massacre, but they could not allow this to affect their policy. British policy in the immediate crisis was simply to prevent Katyn from damaging Anglo-Soviet relations and to keep the way open for a Polish-Soviet reconciliation. Churchill assured Stalin on 24 April that Britain would oppose any investigation by the Red Cross, which in territory under German control would be a fraud. Moreover, he wrote, 'we should never approve of any parley with the Germans or contact with them of any kind whatever'. Eden persuaded Sikorski to regard the appeal to the IRC as

---

[19] For Churchill, see FO 371/34568, C4230/258/55; Raczynski, *In Allied London*, p. 141; cf. Elisabeth Barker, *Churchill and Eden at War* (London, 1978), p. 249. For Cadogan, see David Dilks, ed. *The Diaries of Sir Alexander Cadogan, 1938–1945* (London, 1971), p. 523. For Roberts, see FO 371/34569, C4464/258/55. For Kerr, see Clark Kerr to FO, 21 April 1943, FO 371/34569, C4464/258/55.

[20] O'Malley to Eden, 24 May 1943, and accompanying minutes, FO 371/34577, C6160/258/55. Cf. Louis Fitzgibbon, *Katyn Massacre* (London, 1977), pp. 193–213, where the despatch and minutes are printed.

having lapsed, though neither he nor Cadogan could induce the Poles to withdraw it.[21]

Little more could be done behind the scenes. Publicity continued to dominate the Katyn affair, and it was clear that one of the main things the British government had to do was to devise a policy for the public domain, using its instruments of censorship, propaganda and guidance. What could it do?

Censorship, in the sense of preventing the story of the Katyn graves being given any circulation in Britain or British-controlled areas, proved impossible. On 13 April, the day after the first German reports, the semi-official Polish daily, *Dziennik Polski*, proposed to publish the story and approached the British press censor, who said that there was no legal power to stop it. The Foreign Office News Department then persuaded the editor to hold the story up for twenty-four hours, but they could do no more. The Polish Embassy rightly pointed out that the news was already widely known among Poles in Britain – its telephone had been ringing constantly. If *Dziennik Polski* did not print it, other papers certainly would, and official silence would do more harm than good. In effect, though a Foreign Office official grumbled about the censorship selling the pass, there was no pass to sell. The censors had no power to stop the story of the graves, and if they had it would have served little purpose, with the news all over the European radio stations. There was a suggestion in the Foreign Office for at least a voluntary truce on public *comment*, with the Polish press and *Soviet War News* agreeing to keep quiet, and the British restraining the papers which might act as champions for the two sides. But, as Roberts observed, 'Since the Germans are speaking to the world, we cannot expect the Russians and Poles to keep quiet.' If the Poles did not take a firm line in public, he doubted if there would soon be a Polish government at all; and since the *Soviet War News* had not accepted British guidance on the frontier question, it could not be expected to do so on Katyn.[22] The idea of a truce was rapidly given up.

The Middle East, a particularly sensitive area because of the presence of General Anders's army, seemed to offer rather more scope for censorship. Certainly the British military and civil authorities had greater freedom of action than the government at home, and sometimes they could act effectively. On 18 April Anders issued an Order of the Day instructing all units to celebrate a requiem mass for the souls of their comrades who had been prisoners of war in the camps at Kozielsk, Starobielsk and Ostashkov (from which officers had been transferred to Katyn); for all those who had died in Soviet prisons and labour camps, or who had been deported and died of hunger, cold and disease; and for all who had died in the struggle against the Germans. Maisky, the Soviet Ambassador in London, speedily protested to Eden, and the British Commander-in-Chief in the Middle East, General

21 Churchill to Stalin, 24 April 1943, Kimball, II, pp. 193–4; Sikorski's record of conversation with Eden, 24 April, *DPSR*, II, pp. 696–702; FO 371/34573, C4919/258/55, minute by Cadogan, 30 April.

22 FO 371/34569, C4478/258/55, minutes by Lancaster and Roberts, 13, 14 and 15 April 1943; FO 371/34570, C4664/258/55, minutes by Ridsdale and Roberts, 21 April.

Wilson, went to see Anders and ordered him to restrain all 'hot-headed talk', and to ensure that nothing critical of the Soviet Union appeared in writing. Anders accepted what Wilson insisted was a direct order, and his next formal Order of the Day, referring to the Soviet breach of diplomatic relations with Poland, was moderate in tone, emphasizing the need to keep up the struggle against Germany. The British also imposed censorship on the Polish troops' internal army newspaper – though they could not stop the soldiers talking among themselves and with others.[23] In Persia, the British Minister in Teheran, Sir Reader Bullard, instructed the British censors (20 April) not to release any message about the Katyn graves, but two days later he reported that Tass statements on the subject were circulating freely, infuriating the Poles, who were prevented from replying by the censorship stop. If anything effective was to be done, he concluded, it must be at a higher level.[24] But when, on 21 April, the Minister of State in Cairo, Richard Casey, proposed to issue a censorship stop for the whole Middle East area, forbidding any mention in the press or on the radio of either the Katyn graves or the frontier question, the Foreign Office told him that the story had gone too far to be hushed up, and that to bottle up all news would only encourage rumour.[25] This was true. Wilson could assert his military authority over Anders, but it was impossible to insulate the whole area from the Katyn story. Even in apparently favourable circumstances, censorship was of little avail.

Turning to propaganda, the problems were almost as severe. A propaganda line of some kind had to be produced for the Political Warfare Executive (PWE) Directives for Europe, and the closely linked BBC European News Directives. On Polish-Soviet relations just before the Katyn story began, the stance to be adopted was already a matter of great delicacy. One directive laid down that broadcasters should say nothing to offend the Russians, nothing to cause despair in Poland, nothing to arouse discontent among Polish troops – indeed, if at all possible, to say nothing. However, behind the tact the main position was clear: Britain had decided unequivocally to collaborate with Russia during and after the war. 'The Red bogey is a red herring', played up only by Germans and traitors – this was the PWE line, and a joint PWE and Ministry of Information committee agreed in March that the German propaganda campaign to exploit the Bolshevik danger was reaching a crescendo.[26]

When the Katyn story emerged, the line was thus largely prejudged. The expected crescendo had arrived. The PWE Central Directive of 21 April laid down that the story of the graves was part of a German political counter-offensive to offset Allied military successes. PWE must not get involved in

23 Minbranch Bagdad to Minister of State, Cairo, 29 April and 2 May 1943, FO 371/34571, C4828/258/55 and 34572, C4897/258/55; Minister of State, Cairo to FO, 29 April, FO 371/34570, C4743/258/55. M. Josef Czapski, who edited the newspaper for Anders's army, said in an interview in May 1987 that the British excluded comments on Katyn from that paper, though the main effect of this was merely to anger the troops.

24 Bullard to FO, 20 and 22 April 1943, FO 371/34569, C4383 and 4458/258/55.

25 Casey to FO, 21 April 1943, and attached papers, FO 371/34569, C4458/258/55.

26 PWE Central Directives, 3 and 24 Feb. 1943, FO 371/34381, C907/50/62 and C1884/50/62; PWE Weekly Directive for BBC Polish Services, 26 Feb., FO 371/34555, C195/129/55. Special Issues Committee, 15 March, FO 371/34383, C3686/50/62.

controversy, but treat the affair as an attempt to revive the Bolshevik bogey and split the alliance. The BBC Polish services were instructed to adhere rigidly to the Central Directive – 'Silence is the Golden Rule'. News of the Polish appeal to the Red Cross was to be broadcast only in Polish government air time, and on no other service.[27] With the breach in Soviet-Polish relations, this policy of near-silence began to appear unrealistic and unprofitable, and at the BBC Newsome tried to produce a more subtle approach in his European News Directives. He argued that listeners could be divided into three categories: (1) those whose sole concern was to get rid of the Germans, and who feared that the Soviet-Polish rift would lead to a more dangerous split between the western allies and Russia; (2) those who saw the affair as a test case for British attitudes as between smaller states and the USSR; and (3) those who hoped the rift might save Germany from defeat. The main task of broadcasters was to reassure the first category – there would be no split between the allies; this would also disappoint the third, pro-German group. The middle category would have to go unreassured. This was if anything rather too subtle; but its main tenor was clearly pro-Soviet. PWE continued to elaborate its existing line about German propaganda, comparing the Katyn story to that of the Reichstag fire, i.e. a case of the Germans blaming others for what they had done themselves. 'It is our job', stated the Directive of 28 April, 'to help to ensure that history will record the Katyn Forest incident as a futile attempt by Germany to postpone defeat by political methods.' On 4 May a special European News Directive declared that the supreme political crisis of the war had been passed, and the main task now was to ram home the failure of the German attempt to split the alliance.[28] This was one of many occasions when a forced optimism was the duty of the propagandist.

In dealing with home opinion, there was less urgency to produce a directly propagandist line, but the double issue of the Katyn graves and the Soviet-Polish breach was sensitive and dangerous, and it was also an area in which both the Soviets and the Poles were keenly alive to any slights which appeared in the press. The British authorities had to devise guidance for the press. The main lines were the same as those used in Europe. On Katyn, Foreign Office advice was that the story should be treated as a German attempt to undermine allied solidarity, and that nothing was to be gained by going into the rights and wrongs of the matter. When the breach in Polish-Soviet relations came about, the Foreign Office urged the press (26 April) not to get excited about it or lend it too much importance: Britain would work to bring the two sides together again, as she had done in 1941. As to the graves, no impartial investigation was possible while the Germans were in control of the area.[29]

27 PWE Central Directive, 21 April 1943, and Directive for Polish Services, 22 April, FO 371/34555, C3119/129/55; European News Directive, 17 April, BBC Written Archives, OS 137B.

28 PWE Directive, FO 371/34384, C4287/50/62; European News Directive, BBC Written Archives, OS 137E.

29 FO to Minister of State, Cairo, 26 April 1943, FO 371/34570, C4665/258/55; minute by Allen, 8 June 1943, FO 371/34578, C6424/258/55.

The War Cabinet discussed the question on 27 April, and agreed that the Minister of Information, Brendan Bracken, should ask the British press 'not to canvass the Russo-Polish quarrel or to take sides in it'. Bracken pointed out that the Soviet Ambassador was likely to influence some papers in one direction, while the Polish press took another; so it was also decided that Eden should urge restraint upon Maisky, while the Foreign Office and Ministry of Information together should prepare new rules to control foreign-language papers.[30] The British government thus resolved on a three-pronged attack on its publicity problem, dealing with the Poles, the Soviet Embassy and its satellites, and the main body of the British press.

Churchill spoke sternly about the Polish press in the War Cabinet on 27 April, and he telegraphed to Stalin in firm language:

> The Cabinet here is determined to have proper discipline in the Polish press in Great Britain. Even miserable rags attacking Sikorski can say things which the German broadcast repeats open-mouthed to the world to our joint detriment. This must be stopped and it will be stopped.[31]

This was easier said than done. Official Polish government statements could usually, though not always, be controlled – for example, Sikorski had to change a reference to the German 'revelations' about Katyn to 'allegations'.[32] An official at the British Embassy with the Polish government tried to keep an eye on the wide range of Polish papers published in Britain, of which the Foreign Office had a list of 39. Some of these were in effect private newsletters, and it was in practice almost impossible for the British to keep track of them.[33] In terms of law, the government accepted that it could not exercise more rigid control over the Polish press than over the British, which meant that there was a good deal of leeway for the papers concerned. In terms of administrative power, there was talk of using the system of licences for the distribution of newsprint to cut off supplies to a recalcitrant journal; but it was ruefully acknowledged that a small paper could always find a supplier somewhere.[34] The review of policy on the foreign-language press ordered by the War Cabinet on 27 April was not completed until 17 June, and then proved to be a very damp squib. Security censorship was already applied in the same way as to the British press, and it was not proposed to change it. Political censorship, said the report, would be an enormous task, even simply in terms of reading the material; and it would have the undesirable effect of making the British government responsible for everything that appeared – when it had no control, it could at least disclaim liability. The final recommendation was only that the foreign-language press should be warned that the government required restraint (for example, in matters likely to prejudice good relations with an ally), and that failure to practise it

---

30   CAB 65/34, WM(43)59th Conclusions.

31   Churchill to Stalin, 28 April 1943, Kimball, II, pp. 199–200.

32   FO 371/34604, C5032/1389/55, draft broadcast by Sikorski for Polish National Day.

33   FO 371/34556, C5339/129/55. One enterprising Pole in Edinburgh published two occasional newsletters, in one of which he proposed to run a competition for personal reminiscences on life under Soviet occupation.

34   FO 371/34556, C5352/129/55, minute by Allen, 8 May 1943.

might be punished by withdrawing the paper ration or the licence to publish. This was accepted by the War Cabinet on 21 June, but was a complete anti-climax after Churchill's stern talk about disciplining the Polish press.[35] In effect, the tone of the Polish papers seems to have been generally moderate in May and June; but that was due to diplomacy and self-restraint, not to new regulations.

Another object of British attention was *Soviet War News*, the weekly paper published by the Soviet Embassy, whose contents were habitually taken up by the *Daily Worker* and sometimes by other sympathetic papers. The line of *Soviet War News* was to attack the Polish government as 'accomplices of the cannibal Hitler', unrepresentative of the Polish people and unwilling to lead them in the struggle against the Germans. The *Daily Worker* reproduced and embroidered these accusations, and urged that supplies of paper to the Polish press should be cut off.[36] The Polish government complained about these articles, and found the British sympathetic – Cadogan wrote of Maisky 'disseminating poison'. First Eden, then Churchill himself, sent for the Soviet Ambassador and reproved him – Cadogan noted in his diary that 'we kicked Maisky all round the room, and it went v. well.'[37] This doubtless cheered Cadogan up temporarily, but it had little effect on the recipient. *Soviet War News* continued to publish matter which the Poles found offensive. Churchill told Eden that Maisky should be warned of the dangers of stirring up the *Daily Worker*, and that the paper itself should be told that if it did not 'lay off mischief-making' it would be suppressed again. The War Cabinet twice discussed the matter (on 10 and 17 May), and twice concluded (in the delicate wording of the minutes) that 'it would be inexpedient to offer any advice to the *Daily Worker*'.[38] The British used up a good deal of energy on this issue, but to little practical effect.

What of the response of the British press to its government's guidance? In the early stages of the crisis, between the release of the German stories about Katyn and the breach in Polish-Soviet relations, the press in general followed the lead of the Foreign Office and confined itself to printing summaries of the German claims and the various Polish and Soviet statements. There was very little comment. The *Catholic Herald* (22 April) quoted with approval opinions published in *Dziennik Polski*; the *Spectator* (23 April) wrote that, while the story looked liked a German invention, the officers had dis-appeared and needed to be accounted for. The *Scotsman* (23 April) published a letter from a Pole who had been a prisoner at Kozielsk in April 1940: his fellow-prisoners had been removed by the Soviets at that time, and never been heard of since. There was no formal editorial comment, but the

---

35 CAB 66/37, WP(43)249, 17 June 1943; CAB 65/34, WM(43)87th Conclusions, 21 June.
36 *Soviet War News*, 20 and 28 April 1943; *Daily Worker* between 20 April and 4 May, when there was a long article on 'The Polish Plot', by Ivor Montagu.
37 FO 371/34571, C4778/258/55, Eden to Kerr, 29 April 1943; FO 371/34574, C5136/258/55, minute by Churchill, 30 April; *Cadogan Diaries*, pp. 524–5.
38 PREM 3/354/9, Churchill to Eden, 16 May 1943; CAB 65/34, WM(43) 10 and 17 May 1943. Bracken did make a statement in the Commons (20 May) that the existing ban on the export of the *Daily Worker* remained in force.

very appearance of this bald and pregnant statement was comment enough. On the other hand, *Tribune* (23 April) reproved the Poles for appealing to the Red Cross – 'a slap in the face of an ally who has suffered untold agonies in a common cause'.

Given the nature of the story, this represented a success for government guidance, and indicated that the press were in sympathy with it. On 26 April, however, the breach of relations between the Soviet Union and Poland meant that comment could no longer be avoided. Foreign Office guidance was that the break was a success for German propaganda, which had set out to sow discord, and that Britain must work to heal the rift, as in 1941. Diplomatic correspondents and leader-writers reproduced these sentiments faithfully and even cheerfully. The *Daily Herald* (28 April) struck a nice balance by agreeing that the Poles had a duty to inquire into the German charges, but the Russians were right to claim that an inquiry under German control would be useless. The *Sunday Times* (2 May) produced a near-parody of earnest goodwill: we must aim at repair, not criticism; Goebbels had fished in troubled waters and got a bite from both Polish and Russian fish; we must make a fresh start. Optimism was the order of the day. On 28 April almost the whole press seized avidly on a Moscow Radio broadcast saying that relations with Poland were 'suspended', rather than severed. This proved to be of no significance, but on 6 May *The Times* found fresh hope in answers by Stalin to questions put by its special correspondent. Stalin reaffirmed that his government wished to see a strong and independent Poland after the war, in solid and neighbourly relations with the USSR. This was widely welcomed in the press, with the encouragement of official blessing – it was 'regarded in British quarters as helpful and constructive'.[39] Unhappily it was followed within a day by a harsh public statement by Vyshinsky, accusing Polish relief workers of spying for the Germans and asserting that the Polish government would not allow its troops to fight on the eastern front.[40]

There was some dissent. The Polish case attracted strong sympathy in the *Scotsman*, which on 27 April published a long leading article pointing out that some one-and-a-half million Poles had been carried off to concentration camps in Russia, because Stalin did not want them in his new territories. The whereabouts of most of them, and of 10,000 officers, remained unknown. While the article attributed no specific responsibility for Katyn, its inference was unmistakeable; and it also strongly supported the Polish case on the frontier question. The *Scotsman* published other articles in support of the Polish government, and (apparently alone among the daily press) opened its columns to letters from Poles and their friends. The *Glasgow Herald*, though in less forthright terms, also defended the Poles against charges of collusion with the Nazis and referred to the Polish deportees in Russia.[41] This sympathy north of the border was a mark of the links forged by the Polish Corps stationed in Scotland, and doubtless also a tribute to the work of the

[39] *Daily Telegraph* diplomatic correspondent, 7 May 1943.
[40] *The Times* and other papers, 8 May 1943.
[41] *Scotsman*, 28, 29 April, 3 May 1943; *Glasgow Herald*, 27 April, 7 May.

Katyn: Low encapsulates the propaganda line on 'splitting the alliance', April 1943

Scottish office of the Polish Ministry of Information, which produced a well-prepared newsletter for the Scottish press.[42]

In England, the *Manchester Guardian* was cautiously protective of the Poles: the appeal to the Red Cross was ill-advised, but had been made out of duty to the relatives of the missing men and in response to Polish opinion. The *Spectator* drew attention to the long search for the missing officers.[43] The Catholic press, while acknowledging the need to maintain Allied unity, was outspoken in its support for the Poles. The *Catholic Times* held that the Polish government had had no choice but to ask for an inquiry; *The Tablet* analysed the weaknesses of the Russian case, and emphasized the moral issue: 'We have obligations to truth and justice which must take precedence of politic calculations or the desire to say pleasant things.'[44] In *The Nineteenth Century*, F.A. Voigt produced a closely reasoned discussion of the Polish case, and emphasized that the Polish government in London did not exist 'merely to save the Foreign Office from bother or to placate the

42 A set of these newsletters (which began in April 1943) is in the Polish Institute Archives, A 9 III 2d/10. There is no sign that a similar effort was made south of the border.

43 *Manchester Guardian*, diplomatic correspondent, 1 May 1943; *Spectator*, 30 April, p. 397, 14 May, p. 441.

44 *Catholic Times*, 30 April 1943, and cf. *Universe* and *Catholic Herald*, same date; *The Tablet*, 24 April and 1 May 1943.

Russian Embassy. It exists to carry out, as far as possible, the will of the Polish nation.[45]

On the other side, the *News Chronicle* took a strong pro-Soviet line, notably in articles by A.J. Cummings, who wrote that the Poles had acted most reprehensibly by appealing to the Red Cross. The Russians were angry, and so was the British government – 'I should think so!'[46] *Tribune* wrote sympathetically of Polish suffering and heroism, but quoted Jefferson to the effect that some innocent men must fall in the cause of liberty. The *New Statesman* condemned the folly of the Poles in appealing to the Red Cross, and went on: 'this is not to say that many Polish officers may not have been shot or relegated to Siberia by the GPU. . . . the Soviet Government, often with reason, would regard the landed aristocracy and the officer class of Poland in the light of Fascists and class enemies.'[47]

This chilling comment illustrates a striking fact about the general attitude of the British press: the almost complete absence of a moral stance. This was in sharp contrast to the treatment of the deal with Admiral Darlan a few months earlier, when the press wrote freely of honour and dishonour, of the ideals for which the Allies were fighting and how they were tarnished by association with a quisling. On Katyn and Polish-Soviet relations, on the other hand, the press spoke the stern language of realism and power politics. The *News Chronicle* wrote (27 April) that 'whatever the rights and wrongs' of the dispute, the overriding consideration must be the defeat of Germany. The *News Chronicle*, the *New Statesman* and *The Times* all wrote of the necessity and the stabilizing value of a Soviet sphere of influence in eastern Europe.[48] Other papers were less forthright, but outside the *Scotsman*, the *Nineteenth Century*, and the Catholic press there was almost no concern to inquire into the truth about Katyn or to raise questions of justice. It is said that the British press is subject to periodic fits of morality, sometimes induced by stories of massacres. On this occasion there was a concentrated attack of *realpolitik*. In the midst of a long and desperate war, this may not be surprising; but it is interesting that there was so marked a contrast with the Darlan affair. The major difference appears to be that, while the Darlan deal had offered strategic gains, these were less fundamental and far-reaching than those involved in the Soviet alliance, and so allowed more scope for the play of moral scruples and political principles. In the Foreign Office, supposedly the home of *realpolitik*, there was serious discussion of the moral issues; but officials were doubtless glad to see that in the press their guidance was heeded, and the issue was damped down.

It remains to enquire how far we can trace the reactions of the British

[45] 'Poland, Russia and Great Britain', *The Nineteenth Century and After*, June 1943, pp. 241–259.
[46] *News Chronicle*, 27, 30 April, 7 May 1943.
[47] *Tribune*, leading article, 7 May 1943, article 'Bisons and Hooligans', 21 May; *New Statesman*, leading article, 1 May.
[48] *News Chronicle* and *New Statesman*, 1 May 1943. The leading articles in *The Times* by E.H. Carr, and the despatches from Moscow by Ralph Parker, who was deeply sympathetic to the Soviet point of view, consistently advocated the acceptance of a Soviet sphere in eastern Europe as the only realistic outcome of the war. On Darlan, *see* Appendix, pp. 190–202.

people to these events. Organized, or pressure group, opinion appears to have been largely pro-Soviet. The Foreign Office files retain sixty-one resolutions, letters and telegrams from trade union branches, shop stewards' committees, the Russia Today Society, and branches of the Communist Party. All castigated the Polish government for taking up the Hitlerite lies, making mischievous allegations against our Soviet allies, and so forth. Many appear to draw on a common source, though they doubtless represented the views of those who sent them. The Polish government also received similar communications (one, from a branch of the Amalgamated Engineering Union, was charitably inscribed 'Yours in unity'); and also a few letters of support from private individuals.[49] In the House of Commons there was the making of another pressure group, of MPs sympathetic to the Poles, but they made no move except in private, at a meeting of the Commons Foreign Affairs Committee on 11 May, when half-a-dozen members protested that the Poles were not being allowed to state their case about Katyn fairly.[50]

For the public at large, our best source is, as usual, the weekly Home Intelligence reports. (Gallup asked no questions about the Katyn graves.) The first report, covering the week of 13–20 April, indicated that the German stories about the Katyn graves were usually not believed, though in Scotland they were causing bitter discussion and ill-feeling. By the following week, the Katyn question was linked with the rupture of diplomatic relations, and the two issues tended to merge until interest in both died away during the last week in May. Home Intelligence made a detailed analysis of reactions, finding the most common to be that the breach in Soviet-Polish relations was a success for German propaganda, and the next the hope that the British and Americans could mediate. (These reflected precisely the line taken by the Foreign Office and most of the press.) There was criticism of the Poles for being pro-German rather than pro-Russian, and for an over-hasty appeal to the Red Cross; but also anxiety about Soviet ambitions, and unfavourable comment on Soviet speed in breaking off relations. Working-class opinion was said to favour Russia; Scotland and Northern Ireland showed strong currents of opinion supporting the Poles. The reports indicated a widespread disinclination to take sides, because people felt they did not know enough about what had happened; among those who did take sides, the balance of opinion favoured Russia, mainly on the ground that the war could not be won without her. On the issue of the graves, the reports noted specifically that it was the effects which caused most concern: 'Few people appear to worry very much about the truth or falsehood of the allegations; it is the possible results that worry them.'[51] In general, these reactions were very close to those in the press; though there appears to have been more doubt about the Soviet position among the public than in the press; in Scotland, the influence of contacts with Polish troops was clearly important.

[49] FO 371/34572, C4910/258/55; FO 371/34576, C5834/258/55; Polish Institute Archives, A 12.49/WB/Sow/4A.
[50] FO 371/34578, C6424/258/55, Wardlaw–Milne to Cadogan, 2 June 1943.
[51] INF 1/292, Home Intelligence Reports 133–9, 13 April–1 June 1943; the detailed analysis is in 135.

Reflections

The diplomatic crisis brought about by Katyn was one of publicity. The Germans, Soviets and Poles all used publicity to achieve a political end, with some measure of success. The Germans did not succeed in splitting the alliance against them, but they raised an element of friction within it. The Soviets broke off relations with the London Poles in favourable public circumstances, and so paved the way for the creation of a Polish government under their own influence. Some Polish ministers regretted their appeal to the Red Cross as a failure in foreign policy terms, but in terms of maintaining the government's reputation with its own people, in Poland and elsewhere, the move was necessary and successful.

The British government was in a different situation from these three. It found itself in a position where policy and publicity could not be separated, and where any diplomatic move behind the scenes was liable to be thwarted by a public statement or press article. Its instruments of censorship, guidance and propaganda, formidable in appearance, were of limited practical assistance. Censorship was a broken reed: nothing could stop the story of the graves being discussed, though some restrictions could be imposed where British military control was strong. Guidance was respected by those who wished to follow it, including most of the British press, which like the government wished to preserve the Soviet alliance as crucial to the winning of the war. When political commitment or powerful sentiment pulled in another direction, as in the case of the *Daily Worker*, the Polish press, and some Catholic and Scottish journals, government guidance was disregarded and editors went their own way. As for propaganda, PWE was reduced to saying almost nothing. In these circumstances, the British government could only adopt the simple and well-tried expedient of sitting tight and waiting for things to blow over. It may have been the only feasible course, but it was far removed from sophisticated theories of political warfare, and not commensurate with representations of a government controlling all the levers of publicity and the shaping of opinion.

Did the crisis affect public opinion, and did public opinion affect policy? The threat posed by the revelation of the Katyn graves to the Anglo-Soviet alliance was almost entirely averted. The episode appears to have had little effect on British opinion about the Soviet Union. There were already doubts and anxieties set against the general popularity of the USSR, which were sharpened by Katyn, but only partially brought into the open: only a few elements in the press raised public questions, and MPs remained quiet. The public impact of the story was limited, though it was not forgotten. As for British policy, that was more affected by the use of publicity by other governments than by its own public opinion. The British government was determined not to allow the main lines of its policy to be disturbed: the Soviet alliance had to be maintained, and to that end discussion of Katyn must be damped down. There was some speculation as to whether a different line would pay more dividends. From Moscow Clark Kerr telegraphed on 29 April: 'We know M. Stalin sets great store by public opinion in the United Kingdom, and that he sometimes fails to gauge it aright. . . .' Kerr thought that Stalin should be made to feel that he had gone a little too far, and had given public opinion a severe jolt. A few weeks later, Roberts wondered whether a strong press reaction against the Soviet breach of relations might not have had salutary results on Soviet policy.[52] At this stage, these remained speculations; though in the following year, during the Warsaw rising, the device of trying to bring British public opinion to bear upon Stalin was to be used. Meanwhile, damping down remained the order of the day as far as British policy was concerned. At the time, and for its immediate purposes, the policy was a success. A potentially dangerous public crisis in Anglo-Soviet affairs was muffled and indeed largely suppressed. In this process, government policy worked with the main current of public opinion, which was strongly in favour of the Soviet alliance and not disposed to see it endangered by probing too closely into the truth about Katyn.

[52] FO 371/34572, C4909/258/55, Kerr to Eden, 29 April 1943; FO 371/34578, C6424/258/55, minute by Roberts, 9 June.

5

Case Study 2: The Warsaw Rising, 1944

However revolted and indignant we may be at the callous manner in which Stalin is treating the Poles, I hope the British public will be wise enough not to lose their sense of proportion in assessing this one more horror added to the innumerable horrors of the war, in the light of the essential need with which we are faced to collaborate at all costs with the Soviet Govt. if we are to save Europe and ourselves from another world war.

(Sir Orme Sargent, 2 September 1944)

On 1 August 1944 the Polish Home Army in Warsaw, under General Bor-Komorowski, began a rising to liberate the capital from the Germans in what was hoped would be a brief interval between a German withdrawal and the arrival of the Red Army. In the event, the Germans did not withdraw and the Red Army did not arrive. For two months the Polish resistance forces, weak in numbers and desperately ill-armed, maintained an astonishing struggle against powerful German formations, including *Waffen SS* as well as *Wehrmacht* troops. The opening few days saw some Polish successes, in which important areas of the city were seized. After that, the Home Army fought a fierce defensive battle, under constant air and artillery bombardment. On 2 September the Polish forces withdrew from the Old City, and continued the struggle in various pockets of resistance until General Bor formally surrendered on 2 October. The rising lasted for 63 days. The Polish casualties were some 22,000 killed, wounded and missing from the Home Army, and somewhere between 200,000 and 250,000 dead among the civilian population. After the end of the rising, the Germans cleared the city of its remaining people, removing about 700,000 to concentration camps or forced labour. They then razed almost all that was left of

Warsaw to the ground. Only ruins remained when the Red Army finally entered what had been a city in January 1945.[1]

During these terrible events, the Polish Home Army fought almost unaided. Before the rising, on 29 July, Moscow radio had broadcast a call for insurrection – 'the hour of action has arrived', and the first tanks of Marshal Rokossovky's Army had been seen in the streets of Praga, a suburb of Warsaw on the east bank of the River Vistula. But there the Red Army halted, and did not press its attacks on Praga again until mid-September. It is still uncertain whether or not there were sound military reasons for this. But there could be no military reason for the Soviet refusal, until very late in the rising, to allow Allied aircraft to land and refuel at airfields under Russian control. Flights to drop supplies to the insurgents in Warsaw had therefore to make the round trip from Bari, in Italy – nearly 1,800 miles. Such flights were made repeatedly, sustaining very heavy losses, and with very little success in terms of drops received by the Home Army. Not until 18 September did 107 Flying Fortresses of the United States Army Air Force fly a mission from London, drop their supplies over Warsaw (though only a small proportion reached the insurgents) and go on to refuel at Soviet airfields. This was the only operation so mounted. There were a small number of Soviet drops, largely unsuccessful, and sometimes sent in without parachutes. The Poles fought alone.

These events were not the centre of publicity in the same way as the discovery of the Katyn graves, where public presentation was of the essence for all the governments concerned. However, the Warsaw rising makes a valuable case study in the detailed interplay between public opinion and foreign policy, in a number of ways. It produced a lengthy discussion in government circles as to whether public opinion could be used as an instrument of policy, offering a possible means of influencing Soviet conduct. The question was also raised of whether the Soviet inactivity during the rising, and their long refusal to allow the Americans or the British to use their airfields to aid the city, would have adverse effects on British public opinion about the Soviet Union, and so in the long term damage Anglo-Soviet relations. Finally, there was much dispute at the time as to whether the rising was being deliberately played down by the BBC and the press in response to government pressure. These questions tended to emerge in different forms during the two-month period of the rising. We must look first at the situation on the eve of Warsaw, and then divide the story of the rising itself into three phases, corresponding not to events on the ground but to stages in their presentation by the British government, press and radio.

---

[1] For accounts of the rising, see J.K. Zawodny, *Nothing but Honour: the Story of the Warsaw Uprising, 1944* (London, 1978); Jozef Garlinski, *Poland in the Second World War* (London, 1985), pp. 276–99. For the political and diplomatic aspects, as distinct from the fighting, see Jan Ciechanowski, *The Warsaw Rising of 1944* (London, 1974). For Soviet military and political actions, John Erickson, *The Road to Berlin* (London, 1983), pp. 247–90.

The background: the situation before the rising

The attitude of the British government at the start of the Warsaw rising was largely shaped by the state of Polish-Soviet relations in the middle of 1944. Since the breach in diplomatic relations between the Soviet and Polish governments over the Katyn affair, the British had been striving for a reconciliation between the two. In May and June 1944 there were secret, and apparently encouraging, conversations between Polish representatives and Lebedev, the Soviet Ambassador to the Allied governments in exile in London. But hopes of success were dashed on 23 June, when Lebedev abruptly presented a set of conditions for the resumption of diplomatic relations, including the following: the dismissal of the Polish President and the Commander-in-Chief (General Sosnkowski); the creation of a new government, to include Poles in London, the USA and USSR, and representatives of the communist resistance in Poland; the condemnation of the Polish government's attitude to the Katyn graves; and acceptance of the Curzon Line as the Soviet-Polish frontier. These terms were unacceptable to the Poles, who particularly resented the idea of accepting that the Soviet government should choose the President of Poland, and that they should be asked to swallow the Soviet version of Katyn – another example of the reverberations of that affair.

The British government, on the other hand, thought that the Poles should have made something of these negotiations. Harvey, in the Foreign Office, wrote that the Poles had wasted an opportunity – they should have got rid of Sosnkowski, and stopped prevaricating about the Curzon Line, which they should simply accept. Eden commented on 28 June: 'The Poles have made no move of any kind since these talks began. . . . They opened their mouths too wide and the Russians have turned tough.'[2] The British pressed hard for the negotiations to be resumed, and encouraged a visit to Moscow by the Polish Prime Minister, Mikolajczyk. The latter actually arrived in Moscow on 30 July, and was told by the British Ambassador that he should accept conditions not far removed from those rejected on 23 June, i.e. (1) changes in the Polish government to remove reactionary and anti-Soviet elements; (2) acceptance of the Curzon Line; (3) withdrawal of the suggestion that Katyn was the work of the Russians; and (4) reaching a working arrangement with the Polish Committee of National Liberation. This Committee had been established in Moscow on 21 July 1944; its headquarters were then set up in Lublin, and on 26 July the Soviet government recognized it as the administrative authority for all liberated Polish territory. This 'Lublin Committee' was clearly an important step by the Soviets towards the creation of a new government as a rival to that in London.[3] For the British to press for a 'working arrangement' with it was to ask the London Poles to accept relations with this rival. In short, the British government urged Mikolajczyk to accept Soviet terms; and this was the main thrust and purpose of its policy

---

[2] For the negotiations, Ciechanowski, *Warsaw Rising*, pp. 56–8, and FO 371/39403, C8836/8/55, O'Malley to Roberts, 3 July 1944, with a full account. *Ibid.* for minutes by Harvey (27 June) and Eden (28 June).

[3] Ciechanowski, p. 65; *DPSR*, vol. II, Appendix 8, pp. 652–3.

on Polish-Soviet relations on the eve of the Warsaw rising, which began just after the Polish Premier's arrival in Moscow.

The British attitude towards this particular negotiation reflected a general mood in the Foreign Office in relation to the London Poles. Eden and a number of his officials, even when they were sympathetic towards the Poles, found them difficult – intransigent, romantic, and given to what the British felt to be wild talk. The British searched repeatedly, but usually in vain, for moderate, sensible Poles who might leaven this mass of incorrigible rigidity, so alien to the British instinct for compromise. Only O'Malley, the Ambassador to the Polish government, stood out as an exception; and he clearly felt the gap between himself and Eden, to whom he wrote on 22 January 1944 that 'It will be a bad day when an Ambassador cannot speak his whole mind to his Secretary of State. It hasn't come yet. . . .' – but he obviously thought that it might.[4] In O'Malley, the Poles had a sympathetic interpreter. They often believed that they had a much more powerful supporter in the Prime Minister himself. Poles in London were wont to say that Churchill was the only man in the British government who would never let them down.[5] This confidence had some basis in fact, though not nearly as much as the Poles hoped and believed. Churchill was often deeply moved by the gallantry of the Polish forces and the remarkable achievements of the Polish Underground, not least in the realm of intelligence, on which the Prime Minister kept a close eye. But he also often shared the widespread impatience with Polish intransigence, and he sometimes subjected Mikolajczyk to extremely severe pressure. Above all, he never forgot that his first duty was to protect British interests, not Polish. Still, if there was one heart in the War Cabinet likely to be touched by Poland's sufferings, it was surely Churchill's. It was of some significance that during the two months of the Warsaw rising Churchill was out of the country for two long spells, on a visit to Italy from 10 to 29 August and at the Quebec Conference from 5 to 26 September.

Another weight which the Poles could put into the scales was the role of their forces at the battle-fronts in 1944. In Italy, General Anders's Polish Corps played a heroic part in the battles for Monte Cassino, and actually captured the famous monastery on 18 May. This Corps formed a vital part of General Alexander's armies, which were being diminished for other purposes. Most of Anders's men came originally from homes east of the Curzon Line, and British liaison officers watched anxiously over their morale as the Soviet hold on eastern Poland tightened.[6] In France, the Polish Armoured Division went into action in Normandy at the beginning of August, and played a notable part in the battle of the Falaise gap. The Polish Parachute Brigade fought with customary courage at Arnhem in late

4 FO 954/20, O'Malley to Eden, 22 Jan. 1944. O'Malley went on to argue that the truth about the Polish-Soviet crisis lay in the fundamental question of whether Polish independence was to be respected or not.

5 See Gubbins (SOE) to Roberts, 30 Dec. 1943, enclosing a report on Polish public opinion: FO 371/39447, C119/119/55.

6 FO 371/39469, C6211 and 9688/451/55 contain reports on the morale of II Corps. It was excellent as long as the Corps was in action.

September. In all three areas the Allied commanders relied heavily on the loyalty and fighting capacity of Polish troops, and were never disappointed. This was, however, only a modest element in the political calculations of the time.

Could the London Poles look for support from British public opinion? In Parliament, a group of pro-Polish MPs, mainly Conservative but including Greenwood among senior Labour figures and McGovern in the ILP, was showing increasing concern over Polish-Soviet relations. Eden tried to mollify his backbenchers when he addressed the Conservative Foreign Affairs Committee of the House of Commons on 27 January; but he told Gusev (the Soviet Ambassador, who had replaced Maisky) on 9 February that he was conscious of 'a growing feeling among many members that Poland must be given a fair deal'. He hastened to add that this did not mean maintaining the pre-war frontiers; but it was a sign of the pressure Eden was under that he raised the matter with the Soviet Ambassador at all.[7] In the House of Commons on 24 May 1944 Churchill went out of his way to appeal to members who wished to raise the question of Poland to remember the need for unity against the Germans, and tried to comfort them by saying that 'I have the impression – and it is no more than an impression – that things are not so bad as they may appear on the surface between Russia and Poland.'[8]

The Poles were also mobilizing pressure groups on their behalf. The Roman Catholic hierarchy in Scotland sent the Foreign Secretary a strongly worded protest against the setting up by the Soviet Government of the Lublin Committee, which the bishops were sure was intended to take over the government of Poland and set up a Communist system there.[9] (This was indeed what happened, though the process took some time.) There were some limited signs of uneasiness in the press. Frederick Voigt wrote in *The Nineteenth Century and After* (February 1944) that the Soviet frontier claims against Poland posed not only the question of whether Poland would continue to exist but the further question of whether Europe would exist.[10] The *Spectator* (21 January 1944) published an article by D.W. Brogan, deploring the passive attitude of most of the British press in face of brutal Soviet pronouncements about Poland, and urging that the British must 'avoid compliant acquiescence in anything that Russia may do merely because of the big battalions.' The *Spectator* warned the Soviet Union that it should take account of British and American public opinion. The same journal also published an article on the Polish troops fighting in Italy, denouncing 'the excessive discretion which prevents all reference to the suffering of the Poles in Russia'. The writer recalled that nearly all the 'Poles of the Sangro' had been in Soviet camps, and asked 'Are we to be asked to

---

[7] FO 954/20, Duncan McCallum to Eden, 31 Jan. 1944; Eden to Clark Kerr, 9 Feb. 1944.

[8] *HC Deb.*, vol. 400, cols. 778–9.

[9] FO 371/39407, C10378/8/55. The document was sent by the Archbishop of St Andrews and Edinburgh on 4 Aug., but was prepared before the outbreak of the uprising in Warsaw. A copy was sent to the Catholic hierarchy in the USA, and intercepted by the British postal censorship – *ibid.* C10347/8/55.

[10] *Nineteenth Century and After*, Feb. 1944, p. 49.

commit suicide, under the pretext that it will be for the general good?'[11] The *Economist* warned that 'no-one should know better than the Russians that peace cannot be built on the enslavement of the Poles'.[12] Even the *New Statesman* wondered what would remain of Polish independence if 'a Great Power' (meaning Russia) could dictate the composition of its government; though the journal's main line was to condemn the folly and obstinacy of the Polish government in London.[13] These expressions of anxiety were exceptions to a general diet of either optimism or resignation: there was still room for hope, but in any case the war had to be won and the fact of Russian power in eastern Europe had to be accepted.

Popular opinion in the country, as revealed in the Home Intelligence reports, still maintained a strong flow of admiration for the Soviet Union and the achievements of the Red Army, but this was tempered by increasing anxiety about the extent of Soviet ambitions.[14] During January 1944 the pro-Soviet point of view was made up of various opinions: that the Red Army had done all the fighting, and without it Poland would simply be part of Germany; that the Polish government in London was unrepresentative and reactionary; and that the Russian frontier claims were reasonable. Pro-Polish views stressed that Britain had gone to war for Poland in 1939 and should stand by her now; that the war was being fought for the rights of small nations; and that the Russians showed no sign of real discussion, but simply set out to impose their demands. The reports, though as usual not dealing in quantitative measurements, indicated widespread concern about Polish-Soviet relations. Opinion was said to be mainly pro-Russian early in January, but more evenly divided by the end of the month.[15] On 22 February 1944 Churchill reviewed the war situation in the House of Commons, giving powerful endorsement to the Soviet claim to the Curzon Line. At first, public reaction was favourable, but soon afterwards hostile comment was recorded, to the effect that the Poles were being badly treated, and that we were going too far in our desire not to offend the Russians.[16] In March and April there were consistent reports of 'minority anxiety' about Russia's ultimate aims, and of fears that Russia would dominate Europe when the war was over.[17] For some three months afterwards, the war news and public attention were dominated by events in western Europe, especially the Normandy landings; but there was clearly division and uncertainty in general opinion about the Soviet Union.

In all aspects of public opinion there were some signs of anxiety about the Polish situation. Interestingly, these were markedly stronger in opinion in the country than among the 'opinion-forming media' which are often seen as giving the lead. However, with the dramatic events in western Europe (the

11 *Spectator* leading article, 18 Feb. 1944, pp. 139–40; *ibid.* 12 May 1944, pp. 422–3, Zygmunt Litynski, 'Poles of the Sangro'.
12 *Economist*, leading article, 13 May 1944, p. 636.
13 *New Statesman*, 19 Feb. 1944, p. 117; cf. 15 Jan., p. 35, 29 July, p. 68.
14 See above, pp. 96–103
15 INF 1/292, HI Reports 170–3, 29 Dec. 1943–25 Jan. 1944.
16 *Ibid.*, HI Reports 178–9, 22 Feb.-7 March 1944.
17 *Ibid.*, HI Reports 179–185, 1 March-18 April 1944.

"WHOSE SIDE ARE YOU ON—THEIRS OR OURS ?"_____ "MINE!"

Noble Russians, selfish Poles: Low attacks Polish intransigence, January 1944

fall of Rome and D-Day at the beginning of June, the stubborn battle in Normandy and then the rapid Allied break-out at the end of July) Soviet-Polish relations were far from being at the centre of public concern.

In mid-1944 the government was much concerned about publicity policy on the Polish question. Early in May Churchill, dismayed by broadcasts from Moscow denouncing the Polish Underground as traitors, wondered whether it would pay to threaten the Russians with an appeal to British public opinion against them. On 8 May he drafted a telegram to Molotov:

> One of the greatest obstacles to Anglo-Soviet friendship and collaboration is the Soviet opinion that we will put up with anything. I have the honour to assure you this is not the case. If you want a wordy warfare to begin between our two countries on the subject of Poland, you have only to continue the present declarations of the Moscow radio broadcast on this subject. We shall start talking to our people and to the world, which will listen, not only on the broadcast but in Parliament. A series of very reasonable talks will be given by the BBC both from British and Polish sources. This will be a sad preliminary to the great operations which are pending; but the responsibility will not lie on us.[18]

Eden advised against sending this message, and it remained no more than a

[18] FO 954/20, Churchill to Eden, 8 May 1944, enclosing draft telegram to Molotov;. Gilbert, *Road to Victory*, pp. 761–2.

draft. By the end of the month, when Churchill addressed the House of Commons on 24 May, he was far from embarking on 'wordy warfare' with the Russians, and instead spoke in a soothing vein of cautious optimism. However, it is interesting to see how his mind was working, and the idea of threatening the Russians with an appeal to public opinion was to recur.

On the eve of Mikolajczyk's negotiations with Stalin in Moscow, the London Poles appealed to the British government to strengthen the Premier's hand by giving a lead to press and radio to play up the achievements of the Polish Underground forces, and to pay less attention to the Soviet-backed Committee of National Liberation. It was, they held, important for Mikolajczyk to be treated by British public opinion as the true representative of the Polish nation. O'Malley endorsed this view, commenting that both the press and the BBC were prone to take the Lublin Committee too much at the Soviet valuation. In the Foreign Office, Roberts agreed that public support would be useful to Mikolajczyk and undertook to do what he could with the press, though he was not hopeful of the effect – 'an excess of pressure may only produce contrary results', he wrote.[19] There was another difficulty. On the very same day (27 July) the Ambassador in Moscow telegraphed to London asking the Foreign Office to persuade the Poles to refrain from talking to the press while Mikolajczyk's talks were going on. Thus Kerr offered precisely the opposite advice to that coming from O'Malley. Foreign Office comment was again resigned: they would do their best to stop the Poles talking, but held out no real hope that they could do so.[20]

After Mikolajczyk arrived in Moscow on 30 July, O'Malley continued to urge the Foreign Office to persuade the BBC and the press to take a line which would support the Polish Prime Minister in his negotiations with Stalin. Raczynski, the Polish Ambassador in London, also joined in, urging Cadogan to get the press to change its tone, which was distinctly unsympathetic to the Poles. But neither Cadogan nor Roberts, who was also involved in these discussions, thought that there was anything to be done. They could not prevent journalists taking their own line, and thought they might provoke a reaction if they intervened too strongly. Roberts conceded that the editor of *The Times*, Barrington-Ward, and his deputy, E.H. Carr, were not helpful to the Poles, but he argued that this was balanced by the sympathetic attitude of Iverach MacDonald, the chief diplomatic correspondent, so that matters were about even in that quarter.[21] In fact, there was still a good deal of exasperation in the Foreign Office over what was seen as Polish intransigence. On 3 August the Polish Minister of Information, Kot, gave a press conference which seemed designed to undermine Mikolajczyk's negotiations. In the Foreign Office, Harvey commented 'I wish the Poles could keep quiet'; to which Eden added 'They are hopeless. Kot is mischievous'.[22]

19 FO 371/39406, C9958/8/55, minutes by O'Malley and Roberts, 27 July 1944.
20 FO 371/39405, C9826/8/55, Kerr to FO, 27 July 1944; minute by Allen, 29 July.
21 FO 371/39408, C10457/8/55, minutes by O'Malley and Roberts, 31 July 1944; FO 371/39407, C10148/8/55, minute by Cadogan, 2 Aug.
22 FO 371/39408, C10650/8/55.

To sum up, on the eve of the Warsaw rising the British government regarded Polish-Soviet negotiations, and especially Mikolajczyk's visit to Moscow, as the central element in British policy on Polish-Soviet relations. They were very anxious to see those negotiations pressed through to a successful conclusion, by which they meant the Poles accepting Soviet terms. Weariness and exasperation with what was seen as Polish intransigence were very plain in the attitude of Eden and some of the Foreign Office officials. Sympathy for the Poles was at a low ebb, and it is not surprising that official opinion was divided on whether it would be better to try to secure favourable publicity for the London Poles or to keep them quiet – though either way the Foreign Office had little hope that it could deliver the goods.

One final point is worth some emphasis. In June 1944 the British Chiefs of Staff, in a formal reply to an enquiry from the Polish government, had written that they could accept no responsibility in relation to a general uprising in Poland, which could only be effectively carried out in agreement with the Russians. On 27 July Raczynski asked Eden for specific forms of help to assist a rising in Warsaw: he referred to the despatch of the Polish Parachute Brigade, the bombing of German airfields, and sending fighters to airfields seized by the Polish resistance. Cadogan replied in writing on the 28th, stating that none of these three operations was feasible, mainly for reasons of distance and the necessity for Soviet co-operation.[23] So the Warsaw rising came at a time when the British government had just stated plainly that it could not be supported from Britain; when attention was concentrated on Mikolajczyk's visit to Moscow; and when Britain was giving strong support to the Soviet position in relations with Poland.

This last point was given powerful and public emphasis when Churchill spoke in the House of Commons on 2 August, before news of the Warsaw rising had reached him. He appealed for Polish understanding of the Soviet point of view; related how he and Eden had worked late into the night to bring about Mikolajczyk's journey to Moscow; and went on:

> The Russian Armies now stand before the gates of Warsaw. They bring the liberation of Poland in their hands. They offer freedom, sovereignty and independence to the Poles friendly to Russia. This seems to me very reasonable, considering the injuries which Russia has suffered through the Germans marching across Poland to attack her. The Allies would welcome any general rally or fusion of Polish Forces, both those who are working with the Western Powers and those who are working with the Soviet. We have several gallant Polish divisions fighting the Germans in our Armies now and there are others who have been fighting in Russia. Let them come together. We desire this union. . . .[24]

Nothing could be clearer. The Soviet position was reasonable, and the Polish forces in the west and those under Soviet control were regarded as being on the same level.

---

[23] Ciechanowski, *Warsaw Rising*, p. 67; FO 371/39406, C9937/8/55, Cadogan to Raczynski, 28 July 1944.
[24] *HC Deb.*, vol. 402, col. 1482.

The Warsaw rising: opening phase, 1–25 August

The Polish government in London issued a communiqué on 2 August, announcing that an uprising had begun in Warsaw on the 1st. The early treatment of the rising by the Home Service news bulletins of the BBC was plain and factual, reflecting the Polish communiqués. For example, at 6 p.m. on 4 August: 'Polish underground forces are heavily engaged in the battle for Warsaw'. Information reaching the Polish government in London referred to battles for important buildings. The 9 p.m. bulletin on 5 August included one very brief mention: 'The Polish authorities in London report that the patriot forces inside the city of Warsaw are still engaged in heavy fighting.'[25]

Such brief and straightforward presentation of the news could not be maintained for long, and problems of publicity arose for the government almost at once. On 4 August the Polish Deputy Prime Minister, Kwapinsky, called on Sargent at the Foreign Office and asked for British government recognition of the Polish Home Army as a proper fighting force, with belligerent rights. There was a recent precedent, to which the Poles appealed, in the recognition of the French *maquisards* as a force under General Eisenhower's command, to try to ensure that they would be treated by the Germans as soldiers and not as rebels or *franc-tireurs*. This request seemed a straightforward matter, but in fact it contained a serious problem for British policy. In the first instance, such recognition was directed against the Germans when they took prisoners in Warsaw; but would it also extend to Soviet forces, which were already known to be shooting and deporting members of the Home Army? Moreover, the recognition would have to be public if it were to have any effect, and dare the British publicly recognize a force in an area which came under no British or American commander, but was next door to the Soviet lines? It is not surprising that the British prevaricated on this question until the end of August.[26]

In the same interview with Sargent, Kwapinski returned to the question of press support for Mikolajczyk's mission to Moscow. Mikolajczyk would only stand a chance of success if he was seen to have full British support, but in fact most of the press criticized and belittled him. This led to further discussion of publicity policy in relation to the Poles, in which Mikolajczyk's mission was linked with the Warsaw rising. O'Malley, while accepting that the Poles often brought trouble upon themselves and that Kot, the Minister of Information, was his government's own worst enemy, urged the British government to give a stronger lead to public opinion. 'Stalin', he wrote, 'draws from the half-hearted tone of the British press the conclusion that HMG are half-hearted.' Ministers should offer public support for Mikolajczyk and praise for the Home Army in Warsaw. Roberts accepted that any intelligent reader of the British press would conclude that Stalin could do as he liked with Mikolajczyk without arousing any serious reaction in Britain. Sargent thought the Foreign Office should urge the newspapers to

---

[25] Texts of BBC news bulletins are in the BBC Written Archives.
[26] For Kwapinski's conversation with Sargent, FO 371/39408, C10529/8/55; for the problems, see minute by Sargent, 22 Aug. 1944, FO 371/39493, C11339/1077/55.

play up the Warsaw rising – 'At present they are playing this down almost ostentatiously.' The problem was that on 2 August, only three days before this exchange of views, Churchill had given a very firm lead on the question of Soviet-Polish relations – roughly, as Roberts summarized it, that the Russians were reasonable and the Poles were not, and that the Lublin Committee and the Polish government were on much the same level. Unless the Prime Minister or Foreign Secretary set a different tone, there was little to be done. But Eden was reluctant to take the lead. He agreed in principle that he would like the press to give some encouragement to Mikolajczyk and accord some words of praise to the Polish forces, but he refused to speak to editors about it personally – 'I have never spoken to the Editors and should be reluctant to start on this issue', he wrote. The upshot was that the Foreign Office News Department accepted that after Churchill's speech on 2 August it was impossible to get the press to support Mikolajczyk. The most that could be done was to try to persuade the press to put some emphasis on the rising in Warsaw and the exploits of the Polish Corps in Italy, both of which, it was agreed, had been rather ignored.[27]

There was clearly a strong impression in the Foreign Office that the Warsaw rising was being played down in the press. How accurate was this? In the first few days of the rising, it was certainly given little prominence among news items, and attracted almost no comment. This was the very time that the Allied armies broke out from the Normandy bridge-head and began their dramatic sweep across France, which naturally dominated the news for most of August. In so far as the press concentrated on Polish affairs at all during the first week of August, it was Mikolajczyk's visit to Moscow which was the subject for comment, much of it hostile to the London Poles. On 31 July the *Daily Express* produced a leader dealing with both the frontier question and the issue of a Polish government. On frontiers, the *Express* declared that Russia had every right to improve her own security; and as to a government, 'the armies of liberation' could not be expected 'to tolerate a hostile government in the Warsaw they have freed.' At the other end of the political spectrum the *New Statesman* carried a leading article (5 August) to almost exactly the same effect: that Stalin was perfectly reasonable in demanding a Polish government friendly to the Soviet Union, and that for Britain to cling to 'the discredited Polish Government in London' was a bankrupt policy.

When the press did turn from the negotiations in Moscow to events in Warsaw, the early news was scanty and its significance took time to sink in. The *Observer* on Sunday, 6 August, was one of the first papers to give the rising extended treatment, with a full-column report on the front page, sympathetic in its tone. On the 7th the mass-circulation *Daily Mirror* produced a prominent account of the rising – 'The Polish flag is flying in Warsaw again!' The report included a communiqué by General Bor, and again the presentation was generous to the Home Army. These reports were concerned solely with the fighting, but on 9 August another issue began to be

[27] FO 371/39408, C10529/8/55, minutes by O'Malley, Sargent and Roberts, 5 Aug. 1944, and Eden, 7 Aug.

mentioned: the attitude of the Soviets to the rising. As in the case of the Katyn graves, it was the *Scotsman* which took the lead, though only with a small item, placed on the Scottish news page. This reported a message from the Poles in Warsaw which had reached the Scottish Committee for Polish Freedom – which presumably passed it on to the *Scotsman*. The message claimed that the Red Army had ceased to attack on the Warsaw front when the rising began. The Russians had been asked for ammunition, but had sent none. The British had sent supplies, but only once. The chairman of the committee, Sir Patrick Dollan (the Lord Provost of Glasgow) was appealing to the Prime Minister and Foreign Secretary to send help to Warsaw. On the same day, the *Daily Herald* printed on its front page a message from General Bor: 'Warsaw in its fight receives no assistance from the Allies, just as Poland received none in 1939.' This carried the same implication as the item in the *Scotsman*, but was less explicit in pointing the finger at the Russians.

Here was the first note of criticism of the Soviet Union. The *Scotsman* followed up on 10 August with a leading article, observing that the thunder of Russian guns which could be heard in Warsaw when the rising began was heard no longer. The writer conceded that there might be sound strategic reasons for this, and agreed that the rising might have been premature; but the thought was planted in the reader's mind that perhaps the Russian reasons were *not* strategic. In any event, the article concluded, since the rising was under way, the British were in honour bound to give all the help they could. On 11 August, the *Daily Mirror* took up the accusation against the Russians, this time in more forthright language. A prominently placed leading article accepted that the rising might have been ill-advised, but pointed out that the Poles had suffered occupation for five years, without producing a single quisling, and they naturally wanted to fight for their own liberation. The *Mirror* then turned to the Soviet role in events.

> No doubt there are good reasons why the Russians paused; why no arms were sent until now, at the last minute. But they will have to be the best reasons, for the crumbling walls of Warsaw and the broken bodies of her children demand an explanation of why the help was delayed.

This article was accompanied by a long news item, filling most of the front and back pages, giving details about the fighting in Warsaw, and including an extract from a Polish newspaper:

> Russia has called, and is still calling, the Polish nation to an open uprising, and Warsaw has risen against the Germans. In spite of this, Warsaw has been fighting against the Germans for ten days, without help from anyone. . . . The only reply we have had to our blood is politics.

The same issue carried yet a third article on the rising, by Bill Greig, one of the *Mirror's* leading correspondents, emphasizing that, while help was now said to be on the way to Warsaw, it was almost too late.

This represented by far the most substantial and most prominent attention yet given to the Warsaw rising, in a Left-wing newspaper with a very large circulation. The whole content and tone of the three articles amounted to a powerful, and only slightly veiled, attack on the Soviet Union for encouraging the rising and then withholding help when it began. That the *Mirror's* readers understood the message was clear from the letters which came in – mostly defending the Russians.[28]

This strong intervention by the *Daily Mirror* stood at that point almost alone. Some of the weeklies offered criticism of the lack of aid for Warsaw, but were careful to distribute the blame evenly between Russia, the western allies, and the Poles, whose action had been over-hasty. *Tribune* (11 August) praised the heroism of the forces engaged in the rising (described as the 'Socialist workers and the Polish Home Army'); commented that the Russian advance had halted for reasons which were no doubt satisfactory to the Soviet High Command; and added that the western allies had sent little aid, for disreputable political reasons – which remained unspecified. *Time and Tide* (12 August) also admired Polish courage, but reserved its criticism for the British, who had managed to send arms by air to resistance forces in the Balkans but apparently could not get weapons to Warsaw. The *Economist*, on the same date, referred to the 'uncanny silence' on the Russian front only a few miles from Warsaw, but blamed the Polish government for its failure to co-ordinate action with the Russians, and again criticized the British for failing to send help by air. At about the same time, the serious daily press contained very little comment, and no criticism at all except of the Poles. A leading article in the *Daily Telegraph* (10 August) stated firmly that it was not to be expected that the rising, which was 'supremely gallant and natural, but strategically premature', would cause the Russian High Command to change its plans. *The Times*, in a pallid leading article on 11 August, wrote that it was unclear whether steps had been taken to co-ordinate the rising with Soviet strategy, and remarked that local resistance could only be effective as part of a general plan.

On 13 and 14 August there were press articles which bore the mark of government 'inspiration'. On the 13th the *Observer* carried a long front-page report on the rising, saluting Polish courage and emphasizing that help had now been sent from Britain, and that Stalin had promised Mikolajczyk immediate assistance from Russia. It was clear, wrote the *Observer's* correspondent, that the sudden silence on the Russian front outside Warsaw had been the result of serious military setbacks inflicted by the Germans on the Soviet forces. On 14 August the *Daily Herald* published on its front page an article by W.N. Ewer, its diplomatic correspondent, to the effect that Allied help was at length reaching Warsaw, and that its belated arrival was the result of errors, not ill-will. The Poles, in a fit of over-optimism, had ordered the rising without informing the Allies; and the Soviets for their part had underestimated the rising's importance, treating it at first as merely a propaganda gesture to support Mikolajczyk in his Moscow talks. Ewer concluded; 'This is the true story. Suggestions in some quarters that the Russians have deliberately held back so that the Polish resistance forces controlled by the London government might be weakened are the outcome of

---

[28] See the letter page in the *Mirror*, 19 Aug., which quoted from five letters supporting the Russians and two praising the paper's coverage. The editorial staff noted that this represented the rough proportions of letters received.

suspicion or hysteria.'[29] The message from both articles was the same: help was being sent to Warsaw, and the halting of the Soviet advance was not the result of deliberate policy on the part of the Russians – the *Observer* offered military defeats as the explanation, the *Herald* suggested misunderstanding.

This line of argument corresponded to the attitude adopted by Eden at the War Cabinet meeting on 14 August. The Foreign Secretary was afraid that, as a result of the difficulties of the Poles in Warsaw, something might be said in public to exacerbate Polish-Soviet relations. He hoped that Mikolajczyk (who had now returned to London) would make a 'helpful statement' at a press conference shortly.[30] Foreign Office briefing for the radio on 16 August was that both the British and the Russians wanted to send help to Warsaw by air, and that Mikolajczyk had agreed to dispel stories that the Russians were trying to suppress the Polish Underground forces. On the 17th the War Office briefing was to the effect that a pause in the Russian advance was only reasonable after their long move forward.[31]

Over the next few days, press comment tended to hold the balance between the Poles and the Soviets, and to make the case for the common ground between them. On 17 August a long and prominent article in the *News Chronicle* by Vernon Bartlett, the paper's most eminent columnist, argued that there was agreement on fundamentals between all those concerned with the Polish question. Stalin, Mikolajczyk and Churchill all wanted a strong Poland. Stalin recognized that he could not deal with Poles who were as suspicious of Russia as they were of Germany; Mikolajczyk, though he knew that the Russian occupation of eastern Poland had been ruthless, was also aware that Russia was no longer aggressively Communist; Churchill had obligations to Poland, but accepted that the Soviet armies were playing a key role in defeating Germany. All three agreed that the basic need was for a strong Poland on good terms with Russia. Similarly, on the same day, the leading article in the *Daily Herald* declared that after Mikolajczyk's visit to Moscow there was a chance for a Polish-Soviet agreement, which would require concessions on both sides. Polish elements in London which clung to their prejudices and refused to recognize the necessity of an agreement with Russia would have to be subdued, though the socialist and peasant members of the Polish government could not be expected simply to abdicate in favour of the Committee of National Liberation. 'The people of Warsaw have acted nobly', the article concluded, which made its general tenor more pro-Polish than Vernon Bartlett's; but otherwise the balance was painstakingly held.

On the same date, 17 August, almost all the British press reported that RAF supply drops were being made over Warsaw, and published a message of thanks from General Bor. Similarly on the 19th the press gave some prominence to a statement from Allied Headquarters in Italy, announcing that aircraft had been dropping supplies to Warsaw since the rising began.

---

[29] So far, suggestions like those mentioned by Ewer do not seem to have appeared in the press; but this remark is clear evidence that they were in circulation and had to be countered.

[30] CAB 65/43, WM(44)106thConclusions, 14 Aug.1944.

[31] Ryan's Background Notes, 16 and 17 Aug. 1944, BBC Written Archives, 830/17.

The communiqué pointed out that the return flight involved was 1,750 miles, and 21 aircraft had been lost on these missions, which had been flown by British, South African and Polish crews. These reports were designed to assure British readers that help was in fact being sent to Warsaw, but they left open the question of why it had to be sent from such a distance and at such heavy cost. These questions, and the general issue of Soviet policy towards the rising, continued to attract hostile comment from a small section of the press, concentrated in the pro-Polish sectors of the Scottish and Roman Catholic papers. The *Tablet* (19 August) published a translation of an article in the Vatican newspaper, the *Osservatore Romano*, claiming that there was something strange in the halting of the Russian armies before Warsaw. The *Tablet* commented, in a long article, that there might be military reasons for the Russian action, but some would always think that the Red Army had deliberately held back so that the Home Army would be crushed and the way cleared for the Soviet-created Lublin Committee. On 25 August the *Scotsman* published a substantial article headed 'The Tragedy of Warsaw'. The Poles had risen both at the command of their own military leaders and in response to broadcast calls by the Russians. 'The facts are grim: apart from supplies dropped by some British, South African and Polish planes, no help has been given to Warsaw; no supplies have come from Russia.' And the article quoted a Swedish newspaper: 'The world looks on at a tragedy in the east and keeps silent.' On the other side, the *New Statesman* (19 August) regretted the rising as an ill-judged action, and asserted as simple fact that the Russians had been driven back. The suggestions in the *Osservatore Romano* and other Catholic sources were 'a normal piece of anti-Soviet propaganda'. The two opposing views of Soviet actions were thus set out, by journals of comparatively small circulation but some influence.

During the same period (from the beginning of August to the 25th) the BBC news bulletins in the Home Service contained brief, irregular and baldly factual items on the Warsaw rising. After a brief mention on 4 August, there was nothing until the 8th and 9th, when there were reports of an appeal by General Bor for arms and ammunition, and news of hard fighting in the city. On the 10th there was one sentence in a general report on the fighting in Poland, and on the 13th a small item to the effect that German attacks on the Poles had been resumed. On 14 August the 6 p.m. bulletin reported that the Russians had 'broadened the head' of their Warsaw salient; but the bulletins of the 16th and 17th stated that SS Panzer divisions had delivered a big attack on Russian positions east of Warsaw, with some success. On 18 August the BBC gave, a day ahead of the press, the news of the supply flights from Italy. (On the 19th a few sentences adding colour to these reports by describing how the pilots had found the city on fire, and had dropped their supplies through dense smoke as well as murderous flak, were crossed out from the 9 p.m. bulletin.) After that, there were small items almost daily until the 25th, when it was reported at rather more length that the patriots, still fighting grimly, had called for Red Cross aid for the starving civilian population of Warsaw. In sum, on the BBC Home Service the rising was certainly covered, but among the other exciting news of the time it was never given either prominence or emphasis.

In the European Service, on the other hand, the rising was given much more attention. The European News Directives took up the news from Warsaw on 4 August, linking it with the successes of the French Resistance and specifically enjoining broadcasters to 'Give a good account of the Polish Underground Army's battle in Warsaw.' On the 6th the Directive gave the instruction:

Continue to play up the Poles' gallant fight in Warsaw and avoid any suggestion that the Red Army is delaying its assault for any other reasons than those which have delayed the fall of other great fortresses until they have been fully invested and their garrisons cut off.[32]

After silence until 15 August, the Directive for that date simply noted 'Allies send arms to Warsaw. Poles march to relief of Bor's army.' (This referred to the Polish forces with the Red Army, commanded by General Berling.)

The Political Warfare Executive directives, issued weekly, did not take up the Warsaw rising until 17 August, when the Central Directive gave the brief instruction:

Report factually the gallant fight of the Poles in Warsaw, and give all news of Allied assistance reaching them, but avoid comment on the timing or co-ordination of their effort.

The PWE Directive for the Polish Service elaborated on this, carefully covering the Soviet failure to press their attacks, and stressing the resistance record of Warsaw:

We must continue to report the fight of the Polish Underground in Warsaw, paying tribute to the heroism of the Polish population. We should not hint at an immediate relief of Warsaw within a matter of days but should rather point to the difficulty of such an operation, using the analogy of the German delays before Kiev and Odessa. We should be particularly careful not to hint that the early rising within Warsaw is in need of any excuse or exoneration, but we should represent it as the culmination of the five years' tradition of fighting resistance which Warsaw has established for itself.

The Directive laid down that the 'temporary hold-up' of the Soviet advance was to be represented as due to determined German resistance on the last natural line of defence before their own soil was reached.[33] The European Services thus gave much credit to Polish gallantry, but almost every directive which dealt with the question gave about half its emphasis to explaining Soviet inactivity in favourable terms.

So much for the coverage, in the press and on the radio. In general it corresponded to the cautious government response to the rising, with the main

---

32 BBC Written Archives, OS 137B. Italics in the original.
33 Central Directive, BBC Written Archives, OS 16/1, 44/1/32, week beginning 17 Aug.; Polish Directive, FO 371/39427, C9381/61/55.

emphasis on trying to promote improved Polish-Soviet relations, and on the later shift towards giving a creditable explanation of the halt in the Red Army's advance. The press showed some exceptions to this pattern, notably in the *Daily Mirror* and the *Scotsman*. The BBC Home news bulletins, which were the main source of information for most people, were uniformly brief and anodyne in dealing with Warsaw. How did the general public respond?

The first Home Intelligence Report to comment on reactions to the rising was that for the period 9–15 August. This showed a continuing admiration for the Russian advances on the eastern front as a whole. There was a minority opinion that if Warsaw had been a Russian city it would have been captured already by the Red Army, and also that the Poles in Warsaw were being deliberately let down by the Russians. (This corresponded quite closely to the reactions to the outspoken comments by the *Daily Mirror* on 11 August, which may well have influenced the opinions noted by Home Intelligence.) On the wider question of Polish-Soviet relations, there was only limited sympathy with the Polish government in London, and a strong view that the people on the spot in Poland should form their own government.[34] By the next week (15–22 August), Home Intelligence recorded a distinct shift of opinion against the Russians, despite the fact that this was the time when the government set out to circulate favourable interpretations of Soviet actions. Many people were reported as being disappointed that the Russians were not sending help, and as believing that they were holding back deliberately. People were asking why supplies had to be flown all the way from Italy, and there were stories that the Russians had refused to provide fighter protection for British planes over Warsaw. On Polish-Soviet relations, much anxiety was reported, and feeling had become sharply divided between pro-Soviet sentiment (strong among the working class) and sympathy for the Poles.[35] Not for the first time, it appeared that opinion in the country was moving independently of government guidance, and pro-Soviet feeling was already somewhat dented by the events in Warsaw.

There were also some signs of pressure group opinion being mobilized on behalf of the Poles. On 14 August the Scottish Catholic bishops wrote again to Eden, enclosing a further copy of their protest against the formation of the Lublin Committee. They asked the Foreign Secretary to say whether or not he was prepared to stand by Britain's pledge to defend the independent state of Poland against aggression; and while the bishops did not actually say so, it was clear that it was now Soviet, not German, aggression which they had in mind. Copies of the bishops' letter were sent to nearly all MPs, asking them too whether they were willing to stand by the pledge to defend Poland. (This drew a sharp letter to *The Times* from Quintin Hogg, then a Conservative MP and an officer in the Rifle Brigade, arguing that this amounted to asking whether 'we will in certain circumstances be prepared to declare war on our greatest ally.')[36] Pro-Polish opinion was well organized in Scotland, and on 22 August Sir Patrick Dollan, acting for the Scottish Committee for Polish

[34] INF 1/292, HI Report 202.
[35] *Ibid.*, HI Report 203.
[36] See Hogg's letters in *The Times*, 22 and 28 Aug. 1944.

Freedom, telegraphed to Eden to ask that Warsaw should receive the same help as the French resistance, if at all possible. (The reply to this was the obvious one that geography made any such comparison impossible.)[37] From the other end of the country the Plymouth Anglo-Polish Society also wrote to urge that all possible help should be sent to Warsaw, and to point out the failure of the Russians to do anything to assist the Poles.[38] Sir Richard Wells, a Conservative MP, wrote to the Foreign Office to pass on a reproach from a Polish airman about the failure to send help to Warsaw; and Wells added on his own behalf that the BBC never mentioned the rising.[39]

These approaches were made privately. The Labour Party, on the other hand, intervened publicly on 23 August, when the National Council of Labour and the General Council of the Trades Union Congress issued a joint statement sending greetings to 'the valiant defenders of Warsaw', recording appreciation of the help given by the British and American governments (the Soviet government was pointedly omitted), and urging that all possible help should be sent by all the Allies. This statement was given wide coverage in the press, and was accompanied by a leading article in the *Daily Herald* on the theme of reconciling Soviet-Polish difficulties by 'common sense and honourable compromise' – a very British approach to a matter which was well beyond the reach of such solutions. But the support for the Home Army was strongly expressed, and since Labour formed part of the coalition government this had the force of a semi-official pronouncement.[40]

In mid-August there were two important developments behind the scenes. One was that Churchill (who left London for Italy on 10 August) began to show anxiety about the reasons for Soviet inactivity on the Warsaw front, and to urge Eden to do something about it. On 14 August the Prime Minister telegraphed that it was 'very curious' that the advance of the Russian armies should have ceased at the moment when the rising began, and that for the Russians to drop supplies to the city required a flight of a mere hundred miles. He suggested that Eden might send a message to Molotov 'drawing attention to the implications which are on foot in many quarters' – a vague phrase, but presumably implying a return to Churchill's earlier idea of using public anxieties as a lever to influence Soviet policy.[41] The second development was that on 15 August the Soviet government told the British and Americans in the plainest terms that they would not be associated in any way with the 'adventure' in Warsaw, which was a change from earlier statements which had at least held out the possibility of assistance. On the 15th and 16th, Vyshinski (by word of mouth) and Molotov (in writing) refused to allow landing facilities at Soviet airfields to Allied planes on flights to

---

37 FO 371/39492, C11134/1077/55. One Foreign Office official proposed simply to ignore Dollan's telegram, but Roberts explained that they could not ignore the Lord Provost of Glasgow.

38 FO 371/39495, C11692/1077/55, letter of 22 Aug. 1944.

39 FO 371/39495, C11789/1077/55, Wells to Richard Law, 25 Aug. 1944.

40 Text of statement and leading article, *Daily Herald*, 24 Aug. 1944. Readers could not know that on 23 August Stalin had described the 'valiant defenders of Warsaw' as 'a group of criminals'.

41 Churchill to Eden, 14 Aug. 1944, PREM 3/352/12, f. 617.

supply the Warsaw rising.[42] This was absolutely categorical. The Soviets would neither help the rising themselves nor, so far as it was in their power, allow others to do so.

In London, Eden's reaction to this Soviet refusal was to try to keep the news from the Poles and from the public in general. He sought to conceal the harsh reality by asking General Spaatz, the American Air Force commander, to tell the Poles that they were still waiting for clearance from the Russians to use their airfields.[43] The Foreign Office briefing for the BBC on 16 August was that both the British and the Russians wanted to send help by air to the Poles in Warsaw, which was at that stage a deliberate attempt to mislead public opinion by giving an account of Soviet policy which was the opposite of the truth.[44]

At the same time, however, Eden took up Churchill's suggestion, and telegraphed to Kerr about the danger of a movement of public opinion against the Soviet Union.

> Important sections of British Parliamentary and public opinion of all political parties are already showing grave anxiety over the Warsaw situation and apparent Soviet inaction. We have hitherto done our best to present the facts' in the most favourable possible light. If, however, the present negative Soviet attitude is maintained suspicions concerning Soviet good faith and future Soviet intentions will be confirmed and may well receive public expression with result useful only to the enemy and highly damaging to Anglo-Soviet relations.[45]

Eden tried this line of argument on the Soviet Ambassador in London, Gusev, on 18 August. Eden expressed grave concern over the Soviet refusal to allow American aircraft to use the airfields, and went on to say that the British people felt sympathy for the people of Warsaw in their fight. If the Soviet government persisted in its refusal, and when the facts became known, 'opinion here would judge that it was because they did not wish to send help to the people in Warsaw.' Gusev denied this; though he also argued that the object of the rising was political, not military.[46] So Eden got little out of the exchange, and on the same day he heard from Kerr in Moscow that he and the American Ambassador, Harriman, had already tried the tack of warning Vyshinski and Molotov of the dangers of public opinion. They had told Vyshinski on 15 August that 'hostile voices would be raised and colour would be lent to the false story that the Red Army were holding back from Warsaw for reasons of policy.' Vyshinski's reply was that the Red Army was already being slandered in this way, but 'such stuff did not scare him' – the Red Army proved itself by killing Germans. When they tried the same line on Molotov, he merely replied that the Soviet government would judge who

---

[42] PREM 3/352/12, ff. 599–604; FO 371/39499, C12613/1077/55, Molotov to Clark Kerr, 16 Aug. 1944.

[43] CAB 65/43, WM(44) 107th Conclusions, 16 Aug. 1944; CAB 65/47, Confidential Annex.

[44] BBC Written Archives, 830/17.

[45] Eden to Kerr, 16 Aug. 1944, PREM 3/352/12. ff. 585–91.

[46] Eden to Kerr, 18 Aug. 1944, *ibid.* ff. 545–7.

were its friends.[47] There was no sign that the Russians were in the least susceptible to an appeal to public opinion.

Nonetheless, the idea persisted. Roosevelt took it up in a telegram to Churchill on 19 August, proposing that they should send a joint message to Stalin telling him that they were 'thinking of world opinion if the anti-Nazis in Warsaw are abandoned', and asking him to send immediate supplies or to help Allied planes to do so. This message was in fact sent on the 20th.[48] In Italy, Churchill remained anxious, and formed the impression from what he saw of the British press that the Warsaw rising was being very much played down. He telegraphed to Bracken, the Minister of Information, on 23 August:

> I see from the papers that the agony of Warsaw has been practically suppressed. There is no need to mention the Soviet behaviour but surely the facts should be given publicity. Is there any stop on this matter? Is there any reason why the consequences of the strange and sinister behaviour of the Russians should not be made public? It is not for us to cast reproaches on the Soviet Government but surely the facts should be allowed to speak for themselves.[49]

It is not absolutely clear how Churchill thought the facts could be given publicity without mentioning Soviet behaviour, or without casting reproaches at least by implication; but he plainly thought that the press was concealing important parts of the truth about Warsaw, and that this was at government instigation.

Bracken replied with characteristic vigour on 24 August. He began forthrightly: 'There is nothing to prevent the British Press publishing anything they like about Warsaw.' But, he went on, there was an abundance of good war news, and the press was not very interested in Warsaw among everything else that was happening. Moreover, the press was not well informed about the rising, and distrusted Polish sources in London, especially the Polish Minister of Information, who was regarded in Fleet Street as 'an incompetent hypocrite'. He concluded:

> If the Government are willing to release the reports we have received from Ward [an RAF Flight Sergeant in Warsaw] I think I can persuade the newspapers to publish them. I know not what effect they will have on our public who regard the Poles as a feckless race. Uncle Joe's newspaper friends will certainly be spurred on to attack the Poles. And when newspaper polemics cease relationships between the Russians and Poles will not be improved.
> The Russian Polish controversy is the only black cloud in the horizon. I greatly doubt if newspaper publicity will be helpful in clearing it.

Eden noted that this was 'A pretty good message.'[50] It is not clear to which

---

47 Kerr to Eden, 15 and 18 Aug. 1944, PREM 3/352/12, ff. 599–604, 545–7.

48 Kimball, III, p. 283.

49 Churchill to Bracken, 23 Aug. 1944, FO 371/39493, C11400/1077/55. The version printed in Churchill, *Second World War*, vol. VI, p. 122, is heavily paraphrased.

50 Bracken to Churchill, 24 Aug. 1944, FO 371/39494, C11444/1077/55.

aspect of the telegram Eden was directing his approval. The first part was certainly somewhat misleading. It was true that there was no formal censorship stop on news from Warsaw, which as we have seen appeared in the press throughout August. It was also very much the case that the press was full of other news, all of it good – victories in Normandy and Italy, and very recently the liberation of Paris. Newspapers had very little space, and simply in terms of news value Warsaw was not at the top of their list of priorities. But it was also true that news of Soviet refusal to allow Allied planes to use their airfields had been withheld, and that optimistic briefings about Soviet intentions had been given to the news media. It is doubtful whether Bracken could have got away with this misrepresentation if Churchill had been in London.

Bracken's concluding advice was against encouraging the press to publish matter which would give offence to the Russians, on the ground that it would do more harm than good. It was probably this passage which drew Eden's particular approval, and it certainly coincided with his views so far. But the question of publicity policy in relation to the Warsaw rising had been sharply posed by Churchill himself. How was it to be answered?

The Warsaw rising: middle phase, 26 August–13 September

The fighting in Warsaw continued, against all expectation. No-one outside the city, or perhaps within it, had believed that the Home Army could hold out for so long without support from outside or relief from the Red Army. As the struggle went on, Churchill's emotional involvement increased, especially when on 26 August he visited General Anders, commanding the II Polish Corps in Italy. On that visit, Churchill told Anders that he realized that the Russians were trying to kill all the 'strong and responsible' people in Poland, and expressed his heartfelt sympathy with Anders himself, whose wife and family were in Warsaw. He declared, with great emphasis, that neither Britain nor the USA would abandon Poland.[51] Churchill had proposed to Roosevelt, on 25 August, that they should send a joint message to Stalin urging him once again to allow the use of Soviet airfields by Allied aircraft carrying supplies to Warsaw; but on the 26th Roosevelt rejected this proposal, cutting off the Prime Minister's main hope of influencing Soviet policy.

This exchange between Churchill and Roosevelt became the starting-point for an extensive discussion in the Foreign Office on the role of the press and public opinion in the Warsaw crisis and Soviet-Polish relations, a question which had already been raised by Churchill's telegram to Bracken on 23 August. In a long minute on 28 August, Harrison argued that the effect of Clark Kerr's and Eden's warnings about British public opinion had been diminished by the fact that there had actually been little criticism of the Soviet attitude in the British press, and that the public knew very little about what the Russians were doing – or not doing. This meant that Gusev was

[51] Record of conversation between Churchill and Anders, 26 Aug. 1944, FO 371/39411, C12441/8/55.

doubtless able to report to his government that there was little evidence of anti-Soviet feeling over Warsaw. Harrison concluded from this that 'if we really wish to turn on the heat', the government should allow some of the facts to become generally known, and not discourage press comment upon them. 'Only then will Marshal Stalin really take note of warnings that the Warsaw incident may have serious implications for the future of Anglo-Russian relations.' The Prime Minister would then be able, in perhaps a week's time, to go back to Stalin and say that, to defend himself against charges of abandoning the Poles, he would have to reveal that the Russians, who were the only people who could provide help, had refused to do so. Roberts agreed with this diagnosis. 'It seems to me useless', he wrote, 'to make any further representations to Stalin until British public opinion has in fact begun to manifest itself.' From recent Home Intelligence reports, and from comments by Newsome at the BBC and Vernon Bartlett at the *News Chronicle* (whom Roberts described as 'notable pinks'), he thought that there was already great uneasiness abroad about Warsaw; and he concluded: 'I shall be surprised if some indiscretion does not touch things off soon.'[52]

On the same day, Eden met Mikolajczyk and explained to him that neither the British nor the United States air forces could carry out a large-scale air drop over Warsaw. It was plain that Mikolajczyk's position as Prime Minister was extremely precarious. and that he would probably have to resign unless he could secure help for Warsaw. Roberts thought that it was urgent, if Mikolajczyk was to be saved, for the British government to state publicly 'what has been done to help Warsaw and why more could not be done.' He proposed that a declaration on the rights of the Home Army as a duly organized force (which was still delayed) should be issued, accompanied by a factual statement about aid to Warsaw, drafted 'so as to avoid directly incriminating the Russians'. (He did not say how such a feat of drafting could be achieved.) At the War Cabinet that day, Eden referred to the danger that the Polish government would fall; and Bracken said that the press would not keep silent much longer about the Russian refusal to allow the use of their airfields. The result, he prophesied, would be damaging to Allied unity.[53]

It was clear from these discussions that opinion in the Foreign Office was moving towards an attempt to use the press to influence Soviet policy on Warsaw, but Bracken remained opposed to such a move. There was also a general expectation that someone in the press was about to accuse the Russians of obstructing British and American attempts to send help to Warsaw. Indeed, this had already been done. We have noted the *Daily Mirror*'s articles on 11 August; and on the 26th *The Economist* published a remarkable leading article, headed 'A Tale of Two Cities', which drew a bleak contrast between the liberation of Paris and the agony of Warsaw. For three weeks the Poles had been fighting a battle far bloodier than the brief rising in Paris, without material or even moral support from the

52 Minutes by Harrison and Roberts, 28 Aug. 1944, FO 371/39410, C1127/8/55.
53 FO 371/39493, C11434/1077/55, record of meeting between Eden and Mikolajczyk, 28 Aug.; minute by Roberts, same date; CAB 65/47 WM(44) 111th Conclusions, Minute 7, Secretary's standard file.

Allies – instead, they had been rebuked for acting prematurely. In cold calculation, this might be correct; but it was not the fighting Poles who had made the rising a forlorn hope. The next passage is worth extensive quotation.

> It is not the people of Warsaw who have done nothing to co-operate. The Russian armies are still engaged in heavy battles at the gates of Warsaw; but still no contact has been made between them and the men who fight on their side within the city. Only from the West, far-off, sporadically, inadequately and at a high cost to Polish and Allied fliers, does any help come by air. Yet there are Allied airfields within easy distance behind the Russian lines, and Allied aircraft and pilots who have already bombed remote enemy oilfields and factories from Russian bases. This state of affairs is intolerable. The Russians are undoubtedly now doing their utmost to take Warsaw. . . . But this battle still hangs in the balance; and meanwhile it is sheer casuistry to withhold other forms of aid which might save many thousands of Poles – and perhaps Warsaw itself. . . . It is known that the British . . . and the Americans have pressed for Russian assistance to Warsaw.

Talks were said to be going on for aid to be sent to Warsaw from Russian sources near the city. 'But, incredibly, the present prospect is said to be precisely the opposite. To our joy in victory it seems that the Allies may still have to add the ultimate shame of desertion.' The article stopped short of saying that the Russians had actually refused the use of their bases, but there was no other conclusion to be drawn. On the same day (26 August) the *Tablet* too drew attention to the contrast between the acclamation surrounding the liberation of Paris and 'the conspiracy of silence about Warsaw', to which city the Russians had so far sent no supplies. The line of comment was clear, but it had not yet become general. This was about to change.

On 29 August the *News Chronicle* carried on its front page an article by Vernon Bartlett which was all the more striking because the paper was normally extremely sympathetic to the Soviet Union. Bartlett began:

> A situation has arisen over the Poles in Warsaw which may have even graver consequences than the massacre of several thousand Polish patriots. The British and Americans have recently made urgent requests that the air shuttle service between Italy and Russia which has enabled them to give such valuable and timely aid to the Soviet armies should be developed so that they could send supplies to Warsaw. Their request was refused by Moscow.

In consequence, he went on, the British and Americans were in fact sending help to Warsaw, but without the use of Russian airfields the amounts dropped were small and the risks to the pilots great. Meanwhile, the Russians were broadcasting promises of help to the insurgents, but also threats to court-martial their leaders. Unless this situation was cleared up, Bartlett prophesied dire results: heavy casualties for the Poles in Warsaw, an immeasurable increase in Polish distrust of the Russians, and severe strain on relations between the three great Allies. This article was given particular prominence in the European News services that same day, on specific instructions by Newsome.[54]

As soon as this lead was given, other papers joined in. Significantly, two of the most important were on the Left. On 30 August the *Daily Herald* carried a front-page story by W.N. Ewer, telling a very different tale from his reassuring article on the 14th. This time Ewer wrote: 'It is, unhappily, a fact that the Soviet Government has refused to allow British or American planes bringing supplies to Warsaw to fly over and land in Soviet-occupied territory.' Whatever the Soviet reasons for this refusal, the effect was to diminish the help reaching Warsaw and to increase RAF casualties in flights to the city. Ewer described the effect on Polish feelings towards the Soviet Union as 'unfortunate', which must count as understatement of a high order. The *Daily Mirror*, which had after all been the first to raise the issue in plain language, returned to the charge with a front-page article by Bill Greig. 'It can now be revealed that the use of Russian bases has been refused to British or American planes attempting to supply the patriots in Warsaw with food and arms.' In consequence, good relations between Britain and Russia were seriously threatened. An accompanying leading article pointed out that the Russians could have made a serious effort to supply the Poles but had not done so. If they had good reasons, it would be best to publish them. There followed strong criticism of the Soviet attitude in the *Scotsman*, the *Spectator* and the *Tablet*.[55] Very surprisingly, A.J. Cummings, whose articles in the *News Chronicle* were always glowingly pro-Soviet (one journalist called him 'Tovarish Cummings'), offered a mild reproof. He wrote on 1 September that the Soviet failure to co-operate in sending supplies to Warsaw was 'an ungenerous attitude which is not understood here'.

A striking addition to this outburst of criticism came from George Orwell in *Tribune* on 1 September, protesting against 'the mean and cowardly attitude adopted by the British press towards the recent rising in Warsaw.' (Orwell's article was written before Bartlett's piece appeared in the *News Chronicle*.) The Poles were condemned for acting 'prematurely', and no-one even suggested that the Russians should drop supplies, though they were only twenty miles away. Orwell concentrated his fire on the Left-wing intelligentsia:

> The enormous majority of left-wingers who swallow the policy put out by the *News Chronicle* etc. know no more about Poland than I do. All they know is that the Russians object to the London Government and have set up a rival organization, and as far as they are concerned that settles the matter. If tomorrow Stalin were to drop the Committee of National Liberation and recognize the London Government, the whole British intelligentsia would flock after him like a troop of parrots.

He had a message for Left-wing journalists and intellectuals:

[54] BBC Written Archives, OS 137B. It is interesting to see that Roberts's pair of 'notable pinks' seem to have been working together.
[55] *D. Herald* and *D. Mirror*, 20 Aug. 1944; *Scotsman* and *Spectator*, 1 Sept. 1944, *Tablet*, 2 Sept.

'Do remember that dishonesty and cowardice always have to be paid for. Don't imagine that for years on end you can make yourself the boot-licking propagandist of the Soviet regime, or any other regime, and then suddenly return to mental decency. Once a whore, always a whore.'

Orwell's conclusion was that Anglo-Soviet friendship was of vital impor-tance, but that it would not be attained without plain speaking and genuine criticism.[56]

On the other hand, support for the Soviet Union emerged in some force, ignoring the specific question of the use of airfields to concentrate on other issues. On 31 August the *News Chronicle*, balancing its account, carried a long article from Paul Winterton in Lublin, explaining in fulsome terms how the Russians were respecting the independence of the Lublin Committee, and how the Polish divisions in the Soviet forces were winning over volunteers from the Home Army. According to this article, all was rosy in eastern Poland. The *Daily Express*, which had been absolutely silent on Warsaw for the whole of August, produced a leader-page article on Poland on the 31st, still ignoring Warsaw but supporting the Committee of National Liberation and describing Lublin as the provisional capital of Poland. *The Times*, again on 31 August, produced a tortuous leading article by E.H. Carr who wrote of a 'malicious and unfounded rumour' that the Russian forces had deliber-ately held back outside Warsaw – they had probably simply outrun their supplies. The question of the airfields was ignored, except in a convoluted double negative: it was 'difficult also not to understand' Russian reluctance to help those who were opposed to them. Carr fell back on his usual position about spheres of influence: Britain and the USA were sensitive to inter-vention by other powers in certain regions, and they must recognize Soviet sensitivity in their sphere of interest. It was an article in which occasional guarded acknowledgements of the Polish point of view were heavily outweighed by defences of Soviet policy.[57]

This outbreak of discussion, almost recrimination, in the press came, as we have seen, at a time when the Foreign Office was examining the possibi-lity of using public opinion as lever with the Russians. It might have been expected to lead to a more definite government line being taken with press and radio; but for some time this was not the case. Indeed, the Foreign Office seems to have been uncertain both as to what it was actually doing and what it wanted to do. On 31 August a letter from Guy Lloyd, a Conser-vative MP and a member of the pro-Polish lobby in the House of Com-

[56] This article is reprinted in *The Collected Essays, Journalism and Letters of George Orwell*, vol. III (Penguin ed., London 1980), pp. 260–4. It is of some interest to historians to note that Orwell directed a considerable part of his attack against a letter in the previous week's *Tribune* by a certain G. Barraclough.

[57] One of Carr's claims drew heavy fire in the Foreign Office, where the whole article was unpopular. Carr wrote that the Russians had only denounced the Warsaw rising as the work of traitors *after* Polish broadcasts from Warsaw had reasserted the Polish claim to Lwow and Vilna. Roberts pointed out that these broadcasts were on 29 Aug., after the Soviet denuncia-tions; Ridsdale added that Carr had actually telephoned to check the date of the broadcasts, and so had no excuse for his inaccuracy. FO 371/39495, C11718/1077/55, minutes by Sargent and Roberts, 31 Aug. 1944, and Ridsdale, 1 Sept.

[58] Guy Lloyd to Eden, 31 Aug 1944, FO 371/39427, C9381/61/55.

mons, asked whether more could be done 'to show more sympathy for, and give more publicity to, the gallant Poles in Warsaw'. He claimed there was a sharp contrast between 'our BBC boosting of the *Maquis* in France with the comparative silence about our Polish Allies in Warsaw.'[58] This aroused some discussion as to how best to frame an answer. One official, Gatehouse, was inclined to accept that the BBC was not giving Warsaw its due, even since the issue had been opened up in the press. She thought there was still too much in the press which would give the Russians the impression that the British did not care about Warsaw. The BBC might well give more prominence to Warsaw, and so give the public and the press 'something to bite on'. But this line was sharply countered by Bruce Lockhart, the head of the Political Warfare Executive, who argued strongly that the treatment of the rising in the European Services had been pro-Polish, using material mainly taken from Polish sources. Vernon Bartlett's article of 29 August had been given prominence, and had drawn a harsh response from Moscow radio. Lockhart was not responsible for Home Service broadcasts, but he claimed that they too had given Warsaw sympathetic treatment, and had emphasized the help given by the British to the insurgents. He believed that for the British people 'the siege of Warsaw has become a conflict of conscience in which emotion strongly overrides reason. The latest reports on home morale show that on this issue emotional indignation is widespread. These reports are proof that both on the BBC and in the Press the Polish case has not been understated and has assuredly not been suppressed.' In any case, he concluded, the broadcasting services were bound to reflect in their news priorities the actual state of affairs, and especially the Allied victories and 'the approaching defeat of Germany'.[59]

Lockhart's views, and his evidence from the PWE Directives and Moscow radio, carried the day, and were embodied in the reply sent to Lloyd. For the European Service, where Lockhart's responsibility lay, he was correct. The Home Service news bulletins of the BBC, however, gave a different picture. As we have seen, the coverage in the earlier part of August was sparse and far from prominent.[60] The 6 p.m. and 9 p.m. bulletins on 27, 29 and 30 August said nothing about Warsaw. On the 28th there was a reference to fierce fighting in Warsaw, and to the Russians edging a little closer to Praga. On 31 August and 2 and 3 September there were brief references to Home Army reports; and after the 6 p.m. news on 1 September there was a broadcast by Raczynski to mark the fifth anniversary of the German attack on Poland in 1939. This broadcast was particularly mentioned by Lockhart as showing that the Poles were getting fair treatment on the Home Service, and it is interesting to see that when Roberts vetted the Ambassador's script he cut out the following sentence: 'To us Poles this hour which we have awaited so long and for which we have never ceased to fight has become an hour of uncertainty and deep anxiety.'[61] This was not an excessively fiery or provocative remark, and its deletion must support the view that BBC coverage of

59 Minute by Lockhart, 12 Sept. 1944, *ibid.*
60 See above, pp. 137, 142.
61 Minute by Roberts, 31 Aug. 1944, FO 371/39430, C11726/61/55.

Polish affairs in the Home Service was being kept very low-key. If there was widespread indignation in the country about Warsaw, it certainly did not arise from the BBC Home Service news bulletins.

Internal Foreign Office discussion had got no further than the suggestion of a policy of encouraging public denunciation of Soviet actions in order to be able to use the argument of public opinion. This had not reached the point of action, and the forthright comments in *The Economist*, *News Chronicle*, *Daily Herald* and *Daily Mirror* appear to have been spontaneous. Despite much sympathy for the Poles, there was no clear government line of publicity to support them. In fact, on 2 September one of the most senior and influential officials in the Foreign Office, Sargent, made a powerful statement of the opposite case. Sargent considered whether the government should send a message to Stalin, using the argument of the effects on British public opinion of the Warsaw rising, but came down firmly against such an idea. His argument needs extensive quotation, beginning with his view that the government should not overdo the picture of a British public enraged at Stalin's inhuman behaviour.

> We have I think said all that is necessary and wise on that subject until and unless there is an uncontrollable outburst of public indignation in this country. I still hope that this will not happen. Indeed we ought I suggest to do all that we can to prevent public opinion from getting out of hand over this Polish issue, for if it does it may well distort and endanger the whole of our relations with Russia on which our post-war policy in Europe is necessarily based, and we cannot afford to quarrel with Russia in present circumstances. . . . Such a quarrel might well endanger the security of this country in the coming years, either by driving the Soviet Union back into isolation or, still worse, forcing her into collaboration with Germany as soon as occasion offers. However revolted and indignant we may be at the callous manner in which Stalin is treating the Poles, I hope the British public will be wise enough not to lose their sense of proportion in assessing this one more horror added to the innumerable horrors of the war, in the light of the essential need with which we are faced to collaborate at all costs with the Soviet Govt. if we are to save Europe and ourselves from another world war.

If another approach were to be made to Stalin, Sargent concluded, it should not be on the grounds of public clamour and press polemics, but on the ground of common Anglo-Soviet interest during the war and at the peace settlement.[62]

This was a clear statement of a plain proposition: that the need for co-operation with the Soviet Union to secure a solid post-war settlement was so great that issues of morality and indignation must be firmly subordinated to it. The possible short-term advantage of exploiting public opinion on the Warsaw question was minor in comparison with the wider and deeper issues of Anglo-Soviet relations in post-war Europe. It was rather strange, and symptomatic of the government's difficulty in arriving at a

[62] Minute by Sargent, 2 Sept. 1944, FO 371/39410, C11277/8/55.

policy on this question, that this powerful argument was followed almost at once by a War Cabinet decision to take exactly the opposite line.

On 4 September the War Cabinet met, with Churchill rising from his sickbed to take the chair. The Prime Minister had returned from Italy on 29 August, and at once went down with a high temperature which kept him out of action for some days; but his return, full of sympathy for the gallant Polish struggle in Warsaw, seems to have been the decisive factor at this point. According to the minutes, the War Cabinet felt that Stalin 'might well not realize how deeply stirred public opinion was in this country about the sufferings of Warsaw and what a shock it would be to public opinion if the Poles fighting in Warsaw were overwhelmed by the Germans, without material help having been sent to them from outside.' Ministers also noted that the Russian refusal to allow the use of their airfields was 'becoming known'. (It had in fact been blazoned across the pages of the *News Chronicle* and the *Daily Mirror* a week before this meeting.) It was agreed that the Prime Minister should send a message to Stalin, in the name of the War Cabinet, as follows:

> The War Cabinet wish the Soviet Government to know that the public opinion in this country is deeply moved by the events in Warsaw and by the terrible sufferings of the Poles there. . . . Our people cannot understand why no material help has been sent from outside to the Poles in Warsaw. The fact that such help could not be sent on account of your government's refusal to allow United States aircraft to land on aerodromes in Russian hands is now becoming publicly known. If on top of all this the Poles in Warsaw should now be overwhelmed by the Germans, as we are told they must be within two or three days, the shock to public opinion here will be incalculable.[63]

(In the event, the telegram was sent to Molotov rather than Stalin.) At the same meeting, the War Cabinet agreed also on a further message from Churchill to Roosevelt, appealing to him to send aircraft to Warsaw, and if need be to 'gate-crash' Soviet airfields by landing without consent.

Roosevelt's reply came almost at once. The President wrote that he was informed by his Military Intelligence that the fighting in Warsaw had ended and the Germans were in full control. 'The problem of relief for the Poles in Warsaw has therefore unfortunately been solved by delay and by German action, and there now appears to be nothing we can do to assist them.'[64] This was quite untrue, and fighting in Warsaw was to go on for another month; but for the time it meant very plainly that the British were on their own in trying to deal with Stalin about Warsaw. Of the two lines of approach decided on by the War Cabinet on 4 September, only that which relied on the threat of public opinion remained. From the Russians, no reply was received until 9 September.

At this point, the War Cabinet, after a good deal of hesitation and with contradictory advice from the Foreign Office, had decided on an appeal to

63 CAB 65/43, WM(44) 115th Conclusions, and CAB 65/47, Confidential Annex. Cf. Gilbert, *Road to Victory*, pp. 928–9.

public opinion as its best – perhaps its only – card. What was the public opinion which was to be appealed to? We have already seen that various parts of the press had taken up the cause of the insurgents in Warsaw, and criticized the Russians for their refusal to allow use of their airfields, and sometimes more widely for their failure to pursue their offensive. The newspapers and periodicals involved were much more diverse than those which took a similar stance at the time of Katyn. The Catholic press and the *Scotsman* were now joined by the Left-wing *Mirror*, *Herald* and *News Chronicle*, making a strange but impressive combination. The circulation and readership of these papers was extensive, and a considerable proportion of the reading public was exposed to these views critical of Soviet policy.

At the same time, there was considerable activity of a 'pressure group' kind. A number of MPs who formed a small 'Polish group' in the House of Commons wrote to Eden to press their views. Sir Kenneth Pickthorne, MP for Cambridge University, wrote on 29 August telling Eden that on Polish questions the government was 'excessively deferential to Russia', and asking for Parliament to be recalled. He thought this would strengthen the British hand, because Stalin might behave better if he knew of Parliamentary feelings about Warsaw. Victor Raikes wrote to the Foreign Secretary with the same request on 30 August, giving much the same reasons – if those who were conducting British foreign policy could show that Parliament was determined to support the principles of the Atlantic Charter, it would 'clear the air' and encourage some hope of a just European settlement. Colonel H.P. Mitchell wrote (29 August) to express his amazement that the Russians would not allow the use of their airfields to supply Warsaw, and to urge the recognition of the Home Army's belligerent status.[65] Major Guy Lloyd wrote on 31 August to express his 'disgust and distress' at Russia's behaviour in allowing the Poles in Warsaw to be liquidated when they could send help from so close at hand; and also to make the complaints about the BBC's coverage which we have already noted.[66] On 4 September Lord Vansittart joined in, sending Eden a leaflet published by the Help Warsaw Committee, demanding to know what was really being done to help the Poles, and proposing to put down a motion in the House of Lords when Parliament reassembled.[67] Sir Alfred Knox wrote on 6 September to tell Eden that there was much anxiety about Warsaw, and a widespread suspicion that the Russians were deliberately sacrificing the Home Army because it was loyal to the London government.[68]

At the same time there were a number of letters and telegrams to the Foreign Secretary and Prime Minister, mainly from individuals but

[64] Roosevelt to Churchill, 5 Sept. 1944, Kimball, vol. III, p. 313.

[65] Pickthorne to Eden, 29 Aug. 1944, FO 371/39495, C11629/1077/55; Raikes to Eden, 30 Aug., FO 954/20, cf. Barker, *Churchill and Eden at War*, pp. 255–6; Mitchell to Eden, 29 Aug., FO 371/39495, C11693/1077/55.

[66] Lloyd to Eden, 31 Aug. 1944, FO 371/39495, C11817/1077/55; pp. 152–3, above. Lloyd also made a speech in his constituency (East Renfrewshire) on 5 September, asking why the Russians refused supplies for Warsaw. (*Scotsman*, 6 Sept.)

[67] Vansittart to Eden, 4 Sept. 1944, FO 371/39496, C11943/1077/55.

[68] Knox to Eden, 6 Sept. 1944, FO 371/39496, C12086/1077/55.

sometimes from groups, and for the most part from Scotland. There are something over 50 preserved in the Foreign Office files: they are impressive in content, in no way contrived or standardized, and often forceful in their expression. A lady from Edinburgh wrote that she was ashamed of her own country, which was apparently terrified of Russia. The wife of a Polish sergeant, writing from Blairgowrie, asked why her husband and his comrades should fight on when their homeland was being wiped out, and added: 'this Empire has fallen low indeed to take orders from any foreign power, let alone savages'. There was a simple telegram from Duns: 'For God's sake help Warsaw and save Britain's honour.' Two hundred and ninety-eight women from Kirkcaldy appealed to Eden to send medical supplies at once in response to the SOS from the women of Warsaw to the Pope. Lord Elgin, President of the Scottish Polish Society, wrote on the Society's behalf to ask for immediate help to Warsaw and the restoration of Polish sovereignty.[69] From England, the Archbishop of Westminister (Griffin) wrote to Eden that he did not want to embarrass the government by writing to the press, but sought private assurance that everything possible was being done to help Warsaw. The President of the Newman Society wrote to emphasize that there was widespread anxiety, both about Poland and about the British government's silence on the subject.[70] But it was not only a Catholic affair. The Moderator of the General Assembly of the Church of Scotland wrote to the *Scotsman* on 7 September calling on the people of Scotland to pray for Poland, and for the establishment of a government acceptable to its people and with complete independence.

There is normally no certainty that those who write to the Foreign Secretary or to the newspapers represent wider opinion in the country as a whole; but on this occasion the Home Intelligence reports indicated a distinct movement of opinion in sympathy with the Warsaw Poles. The first three weeks in August had already seen growing anxiety about Warsaw.[71] The week of 22–29 August was naturally dominated by other events – the liberation of Paris and other victories in France produced a wave of euphoria and a belief that the war was almost over. In this atmosphere, interest in the eastern front was muted, but the comments which did emerge showed some slackening in admiration for the Russian advance, and widespread concern about Warsaw. There was bewilderment that the RAF had to fly supplies all the way from Italy when the Russians were only a few miles away. As to the Russians' motives, some said they were political, others that the Red Army had simply met a setback; others again 'just don't know what to think'.[72] It is interesting that all these opinions were formed and expressed before the *News Chronicle* and *Daily Mirror* raised these issues on 29 and 30 August. The next week's report (for 29 August–5 September) recorded widespread

---

69 The letters and telegrams are in FO 371/39495, C11724, 11743, 11691/1077/55. I counted the signatures on the petition from Kirkcaldy.

70 Archbishop of Westminster to Eden, 6 Sept. 1944, and President of the Newman Society to Eden, same date, FO 371/39496, C11845, 12062/1077/55.

71 See above p. 144.

72 INF 1/292, HI Report 204.

public pleasure at continued Russian advances in the east, tempered by increasing anxiety and bewilderment about Russo-Polish relations. As before, opinion on Russian motives for refusing to help the rising was divided, with a growing number believing that the delay was deliberate, to allow the Russians to impose their own rulers on Poland and to get the Home Army killed off. Only a few blamed the Poles for premature action.[73] As usual, the Home Intelligence reports did not quantify these reactions; but it is clear that there was increasing uneasiness about Soviet policy, and a tendency to criticize the Russians much more seriously than at any previous time. These changes were noticed in the Foreign Office and by Lockhart at PWE; but there is no indication that they owed anything to government guidance of public opinion. The BBC radio bulletins, which were most people's source of news, said little about Warsaw, and that little was factual and unemotional, and certainly not critical of the Russians. The press, or part of it, intervened with strong opinions, but there is every sign that general opinion was ahead of it.

All in all, there is ample evidence that public opinion, in different forms, was concerned about the Warsaw rising, and that substantial sections of it were critical of Soviet policy. If there was any chance for the government's policy of appealing to public opinion, this seemed an excellent opportunity to do so. But at this precise moment the Polish Commander-in-Chief in London, General Sosnkowski, intervened with an Order of the Day addressed to the Home Army, which was deeply emotional, wholly understandable, but as far as British opinion was concerned badly misjudged. In language which was almost desperate as well as despairing, he declared that the people of Warsaw and the Home Army were alone and abandoned, for reasons which were 'a tragic mystery which we Poles cannot fathom, particularly in view of the technical preponderance of the Allied forces. . . .' Warsaw was waiting, not for empty words of recognition, appreciation or compassion, but for arms and ammunition. If the population of Warsaw had to perish through 'lack of assistance, passive indifference, or cold calculation, it will be a sin of unbelievable magnitude and without precedent. . . .' Sosnkowski left no doubt that he blamed Britain, as well as Russia, for leaving Warsaw without help.[74] This Order of the Day was issued on 1 September, but was reported in the British press only on 5 September. On the 5th Eden saw Mikolajczyk and told him that Sosnkowski's intervention had made a very bad impression on the British government, and especially on Churchill.[75] (This may well have been so but it is by no means clear. Churchill left London that morning by train on the first stage of his journey to meet Roosevelt in Quebec. His absence over the next three weeks removed what had been for the Poles a sympathetic influence.)

Certainly the Order of the Day checked, though it did not entirely stifle, the pro-Polish current which had been running in the press. Even the

[73] INF 1/292, HI Report 205.

[74] For a translation of Sosnkowski's Order of the Day, of 1 September 1944 (the anniversary of the German attack and Poland's entry into the war), Zawodny, *Nothing But Honour*, pp. 127–8.

[75] *DPSR*, vol. II, Doc. No. 223, pp. 384–7.

Scotsman, very sympathetic to the Poles, reported in its 'London Letter' on 6 September that the Order of the Day had created a most unfavourable impression; and the writer pointed out that the RAF had made brave and costly efforts to drop supplies to Warsaw. In the *News Chronicle* Vernon Bartlett made a sharp attack on Sosnkowski, claiming that he was deliberately trying to wreck any attempt to improve Polish relations with the Russians; though at the same time Bartlett stuck to his guns about the Soviet failure to help Warsaw, and defended himself vigorously against attacks by *Pravda*.[76] In general, however, Sosnkowski's despairing cry brought about a revival of anti-Polish feeling in the press. It was characteristic that A.J. Cummings, who had been showing signs of embarrassment over Warsaw, was at once revived in his pro-Soviet ardour, and pitched into Sosnkowski for making a 'monstrous attack' upon the Allies.[77] Comment was generally unfavourable, mainly on the lines that the RAF had been doing its best to aid Warsaw, and sustaining heavy casualties in the process. Sosnkowski's criticisms were not deserved. Interestingly, the *Tablet* (8 September) tried to argue that the Sosnkowski incident had been wilfully built up, with the BBC news bulletins giving it special prominence. It is true that the 9 p.m. bulletin on 5 September mentioned that there had been considerable criticism in London of Sosnkowski's remarks, and that Eden had told Mikolajczyk of the bad impression which they had created. This was certainly a Foreign Office release, but it was given no special prominence – it figured only on the ninth out of thirteen pages of text, and was a short item.

The press was much more prickly about this incident than was opinion in the country, on which it made little impact. There was some resentment noted in the Home Intelligence Report for 5–12 September, but the main impression remained one of widespread concern about Warsaw, with what was now plainly described as a majority expressing suspicion of Russian policy. There were comments about the Russians letting the Poles down, and great sympathy for the Polish patriots in Warsaw.[78]

The most significant event, which was to affect government policy on the Warsaw affair and bring about a considerable change of emphasis in the press, occurred on 9 September. This was Molotov's reply to Churchill's and the War Cabinet's telegram of 4 September, drawing attention to the dismay of British opinion about Warsaw. For the most part this was an uncompromising document. Molotov referred to the Polish 'émigré' government, which was a term of disrespect if not abuse; and he again described the Warsaw rising as an adventure, for which the Soviet government was in no way responsible. As to the War Cabinet's attempt to alarm him by raising the issue of public opinion, his language was scornful:

. . . the Soviet Government express their complete confidence in the fact that true statement of the facts regarding events in Warsaw will give public opinion every reason unconditionally to condemn the authors of Warsaw adventure and correctly to understand the position of the Soviet

76 *News Chronicle.* 6 Sept. 1944.
77 *Ibid.*, 8 Sept. 1944.
78 INF 1/292, HI Report 206.

Government. It would only be necessary to try to enlighten public opinion thoroughly about the truth of events in Warsaw.

In short, if the British Cabinet wanted a propaganda battle with the Russians, it could have one. All this was stern stuff, in authentic Molotov style. Yet in the middle of his message there was a statement that the Soviet had several times attempted air drops into Warsaw, only to lose the material to the Germans; but despite this they would be willing to let the British and Americans try again. If the British were convinced that an air-drop would be an effective form of assistance, and insisted on the Soviet Command organizing it in conjunction with the British and Americans, then the Soviet government was prepared to agree. The one condition was that the operation should be in accordance with a pre-arranged plan. Kerr, having transmitted this on 9 September, commented on the 10th that this was an unexpected and remarkable climb-down, tucked away in the middle of what he called 'a preposterous pi-jaw'.[79]

This was seen as a distinct success in London. On 13 September Eden telegraphed to Churchill (now in Quebec for his conference with Roosevelt) with the news that the Russians had given clearance for an American operation to fly supplies into Warsaw. Eden's comments were enthusiastic:

This is really a great triumph for our persistence in hammering at the Russians where we had a good case. . . . Your judgement was correct when you said that Stalin had not understood the significance of his refusal on world opinion. The violence of our representations has made him understand it and he has now come round.

This was the time, Eden went on, to press on with an improvement in Polish-Soviet relations. He would urge Mikolajczyk to get rid of Sosnkowski (who was regarded as a great stumbling-block for the Russians), and try to persuade the Poles to resume contacts with the Russians and the Lublin Committee.[80] In Eden's view the crisis was over, and the next step was to get back to the position at the beginning of August, when the main item on the agenda was to get Mikolajczyk to come to terms with the Russians. To this end, the government returned rapidly to its earlier line of doing nothing to offend the Russians. Hope springs eternal!

Publicity policy was at once taken in hand. On 12 September there was a meeting of officials in the Foreign Office to discuss the wording of a Polish communiqué to be published in the press the following day on the question of supplies to Warsaw. The British wanted the Poles to say outright that Britain had done everything possible to help Warsaw; and for their part the Foreign Office would brief the 'reliable press' to the effect that the Russians were willing to give way to a limited extent. Meanwhile, the note of this meeting concluded, 'nothing should be done to antagonize the Russians'.[81] It was a motto which had been heard before, and brought to a close the period during

[79] Kerr to Eden, 9 Sept. 1944, FO 371/39496, C11965/1077/55, and 10 Sept., *ibid.*, C12010/1077/55.

[80] Eden to Churchill, 13 Sept. 1944, FO 371/39499, C12788/1077/55.

[81] Memorandum, 12 Sept. 1944, FO 371/39497, C12246/1077/55.

which the British government had contemplated exploiting public opinion in favour of the Poles. They were now back on an earlier course; though it was by no means certain that public opinion would follow them.

The Warsaw rising: the end, 14 September–4 October

It was on 9 September that Molotov indicated Soviet willingness to allow the use of their airfields for a shuttle flight to drop supplies into Warsaw. It took until 18 September for the operation to be mounted. On that date there was a daylight flight by 107 B-17s (Flying Fortresses) of the American Eighth Air Force, with long-range fighter escort. The aircraft flew on to refuel at Soviet bases, and then returned to England via Italy. The flight was accomplished successfully and with only light casualties, but the drop was largely a failure. By then, the Germans held most of the city, and from a drop of 1,284 containers the Home Army received at the most 288, and perhaps as few as 130.[82] Another flight was prepared by the Americans at the end of the month. Clearance was received from the Soviets; the operation was planned for 2 October, but it was cancelled on the 1st because at that stage the Russians withdrew permission, on the false grounds that the Home Army had withdrawn from Warsaw.[83]

In the event, therefore, only one large-scale operation using Soviet airfields was undertaken. However, the Russian permission for this attempt, and the flight itself, were made the basis for an optimistic line in British publicity policy. The actual communiqué was issued by General Spaatz, commanding the Eighth Air Force, but the Foreign Office urged on the Americans the need for the earliest possible announcement that the aircraft had used Russian bases, as well as publicity for the fact that while the aircraft were American nearly all the supplies were British.[84] The press carried the news of the air-drop on 19 September, the day after it was made; the coverage was generally prominent and distinctly over-optimistic. Also on the 19th, Mikolajczyk broadcast on the Polish Service of the BBC, welcoming the air drop. He referred to earlier flights by Polish, British and South African airmen, but claimed that Warsaw had finally become the symbol of united effort by Britain, the United States and the Soviet Union. He ended by asserting the role of public opinion in these events – the conscience of the world had been awakened by the cries of the dying in Warsaw, and public opinion had helped to bring about co-operation for the relief of the city. The text of this broadcast was submitted to the Foreign Office in advance. There were no changes, and on 20 September the European News Directive instructed broadcasters to make much of Mikolajczyk's comment that Warsaw was now a symbol of Allied unity.[85] Significantly, the Soviet refusal to permit a

---

82 See descriptions of the operation in Garlinski, *Poland in the Second World War*, pp. 292–3; Zawodny, *Nothing But Honour*, pp. 133–5; W.F. Craven and J.L. Cate, *The Army Air Forces in World War II*, vol. III (Chicago, 1951), pp. 316–17.
83 Zawodny, *Nothing But Honour*, p. 136; Craven and Cate, vol. III, p. 317.
84 Minute by Harrison, 18 Sept. 1944, FO 371/39498, C12538/1077/55.
85 BBC Written Archives, OS137B.

second operation was not released to the press. The picture of unity was not to be spoiled at that stage.

Churchill too gave an optimistic lead. The Prime Minister reached London on the last leg of his long journey from Quebec on 26 September, and on the same day he appeared in the House of Commons to answer questions about Warsaw. He spoke warmly of 'the heroism and tenacity of the Polish Home Army and population of Warsaw', but at the same time gave a favourable account of Soviet actions during the rising.[86] On 28 September Churchill made a long speech, reviewing the whole war situation and the state of foreign affairs. He made no direct reference to Warsaw, but expounded British policy on the whole Polish-Soviet situation. He emphasized that all three great Allies wanted a strong Poland, and he warned the House against the use of 'intemperate language' which might diminish the chances of a satisfactory settlement. 'We recognize our special responsibilities towards Poland, and I am confident that I can trust the House not to engage in language which would make our task harder.' He went on:

> I cannot conceive that it is not possible to make a good solution whereby Russia gets the security which she is entitled to have, and which I have resolved that we shall do our utmost to secure for her, on her Western frontier, and, at the same time, the Polish nation have restored to them that national sovereignty and independence, for which, across centuries of oppression and struggle, they have never ceased to strive.

He hoped that the 'unhappy spectacle' of rival Polish governments could be avoided, and that Mikolajczyk would soon resume his talks in Moscow.[87] This speech reverted to the long-standing British theme of an independent Poland friendly to the Soviet Union, and put the emphasis on negotiation to bring together the London Poles and the Soviet government. Churchill's fears of Russian intentions, expressed so strongly during his visit to General Anders in Italy, were now forgotten or suppressed.

Between these two statements by the Prime Minister, Eden had a difficult time replying to questions on 27 September. Sir Alfred Knox asked what reason had been given by the Soviet government for refusing permission for RAF aircraft to land in Soviet territory after dropping supplies to Warsaw. The phrasing allowed Eden to reply truthfully that there had been no question of RAF planes making shuttle flights (this had throughout been a matter for the Americans). He added that the Soviet government had now agreed to the use of its bases, and referred to the operations which had actually been carried out on 18 September. Knox then asked a supplementary question: was it not a fact that the Soviet government had refused to give permission to use their airfields until 14 September? Eden's reply was evasive:

> My Hon. and gallant Friend is asking me why one of our Allies did not give assistance to another of our Allies. That is a question which might

---

[86] *HC Deb.*, 5th series, vol. 403, col. 26.
[87] *Ibid.*, vol. 403, cols. 489–91.

well be discussed in this House, but I would rather give consideration to my answer.

Knox then put a further question, asking Eden to make representations to the Soviet government on the arrest and deportation of members of the Polish resistance by the Soviet authorities. The Foreign Office had tried to persuade Knox to withdraw this question, but he had refused to do so. Eden's reply was that he had brought the reports of these events to the attention of the Soviet government, which did not consider that they gave a true picture. At that point McGovern, of the Independent Labour Party, intervened to ask whether there was anything to be gained by covering up the fact that one of our Allies was deporting and shooting nationalists and socialists. Eden replied that these were delicate and difficult matters, requiring caution and reserve – an unhappy answer, indicating that he did indeed think that there was something to be covered up.[88] It was an uncomfortable and unconvincing peformance by the Foreign Secretary, but he did his best for the Russians, and was clearly determined not to rock the boat.

The key to the attitudes of both Churchill and Eden lay in the fact that they were expecting to go to Moscow in the very near future, to try to settle a whole range of questions, including the Polish problem. Churchill had already got to work on the travel arrangements as early as 27 September, before Stalin had agreed to the visit taking place.[89] In that context, Eden's stone-walling in the Commons was perfectly comprehensible: it was indeed a time for caution and reserve, not for giving honest answers to dangerous questions about shootings and deportations. The sensible line was to say nothing to antagonize the Russians, and both Churchill and Eden followed it. So did the BBC and PWE, which prepared a special script to greet what was expected to be the imminent relief of Warsaw. This paid tribute to both the people of Warsaw and the Red Army which had come to their help, and was to finish with the playing of both the Polish and the Soviet national anthems. It was designed as a fitting public tribute to Allied unity, but alas the day for its transmission never came.[90]

At home, the BBC news bulletins were able to present a picture of Soviet-Polish co-operation. Between 15 and 22 September, the main bulletins at 6 p.m. and 9 p.m. referred to the Warsaw rising on six out of the eight days, and on each occasion they mentioned Soviet aid for the Poles or Polish contact with the Red Army. For example, Russian aircraft had dropped supplies to Warsaw (15 September); General Bor had reported contact with Rokossovsky's headquarters (the 17th); and Soviet aircraft were protecting the Poles from German air attack (20th and 21st). It was altogether an edifying representation.

[88] *Ibid.*, vol. 403, col. 218; see FO 371/39500, C13074/1077/55 for FO minutes on Knox's questions.

[89] Gilbert, *Road to Victory*, p. 976.

[90] BBC Written Archives, OS 137B. The special Warsaw script was written by Moray McLaren, head of the Polish Section of PWE. After the war, McLaren came to believe that he had shared in a betrayal of the Poles, and he suffered a nervous breakdown – see Christopher Sykes, *Evelyn Waugh* (London, 1975), pp. 289–90.

For some time, between 14 and 19 September, views in the press continued to be divided. The *Tablet* continued its stern comments in an article on 16 September:

> The Warsaw episode has brought home to the Western public the ominous truth about the Soviet attitude to their neighbour. . . . the Russians did not really want to help the Warsaw Poles, because these Poles are genuinely independent, and do not accept the authority of the Poles selected and nominated by the Soviets to be the future Government.

At the other end of the ideological spectrum, *Tribune* published on 15 September a letter from Arthur Koestler declaring that the Russian attitude towards the Warsaw rising was 'one of the major infamies of this war which, though committed by different methods, will rank for the future historian on the same ethical level with Lidice.' This was then a household name: the village wiped out by the Germans after Czech resisters had assassinated Heydrich in 1942. The parallel was in other minds. A trade union official wrote to George Hall, the Labour junior minister at the Foreign Office giving details of Soviet arrests and deportations in Poland, and adding: 'Many Lidices are taking place on the orders of our embarrassing ally.'[91]

On 14 September the *Scotsman* carried reports of meetings held by the Scottish-Polish Society in Glasgow and London, with spirited speeches by the Duchess of Atholl and Captain Graham, one of the pro-Polish group in the House of Commons. These meetings sent letters and telegrams to the Foreign Secretary. On the 15th sixteen Conservative MPs (including four from Scottish constituencies) published in the *Scotsman* an appeal for all possible help to be given to the Poles in Warsaw, and for the government to publish the facts about obstructions which prevented aid from reaching the city:

> We believe that what our Government has done and is doing should be made abundantly clear. It should be known beyond any doubt what limitations, if any, have been imposed upon its activities and by whom. Where such limitations arise from the actions of other Governments the public should be assured that our Government has made crystal clear what it thought right and desirable. We are convinced that the British people fully understands that fidelity to all its Allies is the basis of its power.

The *Scotsman* published an approving article about this statement, which also appeared in some English newspapers on 16 September.[92]

An opportunity for favourable comment on the Russians came when, on 16 September, most newspapers carried reports of a statement by General Bor that the Russians had dropped small amounts of food and ammunition

---

[91] Millar to Hall, 21 Sept. 1944, FO 371/39412, C13022/8/55.

[92] The 16 MPs were: Lionel Berry, Henry Brooke, J.D. Campbell, Edward Cobb, A.G. Erskine-Hill, T.D. Galbraith, E.G.R. Lloyd, R.E. Manningham-Buller, Joseph Nall, Kenneth Pickthorne, Donald Scott, Archibald Southby, H.G. Studholme, Spencer Summers, Douglas Thomas, and Herbert Williams. See *Manchester Guardian*, 16 Sept. 1944.

into Warsaw. Bor's communiqué noted that this assistance had arrived on the 45th day of the fighting, and was understandably sparing in expressions of gratitude. The *News Chronicle*, however, seized the opportunity which it offered. A long article by E.P. Montgomery linked Bor's statement with a new communiqué from the Lublin Committee, which praised the defenders of Warsaw instead of condemning them, and recognized their patriotism. These two developments, wrote Montgomery, marked a change in attitude which would improve the whole Polish-Soviet situation. Much of the credit for this should go to Eden, who had worked so hard to improve relations.

A great turning-point in the attitude of the press came with the American air-drop on 18 September, widely and often fulsomely covered in the press on the 19th. The *Spectator*, usually guarded in its comments on Russia, produced a leading article on 22 September declaring that Soviet permission for the Americans to use their airfields was 'to be hailed with profound satisfaction.' Further improvement in Soviet-Polish relations could now be expected. On the 23rd a leader in the *Daily Telegraph* observed that the venom had gone from the public utterances of both the Polish and the Soviet governments, and expressed confidence that the Russians had 'dispelled any idea that they were indifferent to the garrison's fate.' Even the *Tablet* (23 September) recognized some improvement in the situation. The Poles had received some Soviet help, and the Russians had allowed the use of their airfields. The reason for this was the intensity of feeling which had been shown in Britain, and also in the United States. The British press had played a part in this, with only some papers being willing to support the whole Soviet position – the writer hoped that the episode might have had some educational value even for the editor of *The Times*. So the normally stern and unbending *Tablet*, whether knowingly or not, endorsed the government line.

In the country as a whole, the Home Intelligence Reports showed something of the same pattern, but with a significant difference in the underlying trend of opinion. The report for 12–19 September indicated that Russian activity on the Warsaw front had done something to reassure people, but the majority remained suspicious of the Russian attitude on Warsaw, 'for familiar reasons' – an interesting phrase, showing that the compilers were now dealing with a regular phenomenon, no longer requiring explanation. For the week of 19–26 September the report registered marked public relief at the improvement in the situation (the news of the American air-drop made a clear impact); yet at the same time an increasing number of people were reported as believing that the Russian motive for their delay had been political. Anxiety about the future of British relations with the Russians was said to be widespread and increasing. Both these reports indicated some continuing criticism of the Polish government in London, but the general trend was one of increasing concern about Soviet intentions, despite relief at immediate events.[93]

Opinion in the country, therefore, was far from reassured by the change in the Soviet attitude., Similarly, pro-Polish sentiment in the House of Commons still ran strongly among the twenty or so MPs who had taken up

93 INF 1/292, HI Reports 207, 208.

the Polish cause. This was shown by the questions to Eden which were pressed home on 27 September, to the Foreign Secretary's obvious discomfort; and by the fact that, even after Churchill's appeal for restraint, seven MPs spoke on the 28th in support of the Poles and in criticism of the Soviets – though their tone was moderate, in deference to the Prime Minister's wishes.[94]

The desperate struggle in Warsaw was now drawing to an end. At its close, two events made an impact on British public opinion: the dismissal and replacement of General Sosnkowski, the Polish Commander-in-Chief; and the formal capitulation of the Home Army in Warsaw. These two events came to be closely linked with one another, but will be best dealt with separately.

On 30 September the Polish President, after long pressure from the British, finally gave way and dismissed Sosnkowski from the post of Commander-in-Chief. The British wanted this as a measure to appease the Russians, who correctly regarded Sosnkowski as anti-Soviet; and the general had weakened his own position by his Order of the Day at the beginning of September, which had been so critical of Britain as well as of Russia. When Sosnkowski was removed, it was at the same time announced that he was to be replaced by General Bor, the commander of the Home Army in Warsaw, who would take up his duties when he was able to do so. This appointment was at once attacked by the Committee of National Liberation in Lublin, which denounced Bor as a criminal, and a man more hated even than Sosnkowski. The CNL chairman, Morawski, also claimed that Bor had been outside the city, and that he had not been in any contact with the Russian forces.[95]

The Polish Foreign Minister, Romer, denied these accusations against General Bor in an interview with O'Malley on 2 October, and asked the British government to request the press to react strongly against them. Romer still believed – or at least professed to believe – that the Russians were watching the British press and Parliament, and would be impressed by critical comment. O'Malley agreed, and hoped that the press might be induced to act accordingly.[96]

However, it is clear that Eden had no sympathy with this point of view. He was in fact disposed to accept the accusations against Bor, commenting that there was no proof that he had been in Warsaw – the reports from Ward (the RAF sergeant whose signals from the city had been so valuable) had never mentioned seeing him, and the mere fact of radio messages offered no evidence as to his whereabouts. In any case, Eden wrote, Bor's appointment as C-in-C was controversial, and therefore unwise, and he added: 'I had no easy task in defending the Poles at Cabinet tonight.' (i.e. 2 October) In fact, the minutes of that meeting of the War Cabinet give no indication that the Poles were attacked or that Eden defended them. The only comment

[94] *HC Deb.*, 5th series, vol. 403, cols. 505–683, for the debate on 28 September. The speakers were six Conservatives (Graham, Dunglass, Southby, Thorneycroft, Headlam and Mitchell) and one ILP (McGovern).

[95] Garlinski, *Poland in the Second World War*, p. 298.

[96] FO 371/39412, C13360/8/55, note by O'Malley, 2 Oct. 1944.

recorded on the question of Bor's appointment was in support of the London Poles, complaining that the BBC had given undue prominence to the accusations against Bor. The Cabinet endorsed this view, and Bracken was asked to instruct the BBC accordingly.[97] But this had nothing to do with Eden, who seems to have been weary of the London Poles and suspicious about Bor. In any case, he was preparing for his Moscow visit, now imminent.

There is no sign that guidance of the kind requested by Romer and O'Malley was given to the press, whose reactions to the CNL's denunciation of General Bor were mixed. The *Scotsman* had a leading article on 2 October, condemning the CNL's action, and contemplating the tragedy inherent in the growing likelihood that the German domination of Poland would simply be replaced by Russian mastery. The *News Chronicle* on this occasion hedged its bets, with a leading article suspending judgement until more was known, but also a front-page article by Stefan Litauer critical of the CNL. (Litauer was himself a Pole, who had often been in disagreement with the London government, so his comments carried weight.) The *Daily Herald* (3 October) published a leading article which began by explaining carefully that of course the working people of Britain honoured the military and industrial feats of the Soviet Union, and were devoted to the Anglo-Soviet treaty of 1942, but then went on to say that the British public – including socialists – were deeply anxious about the attacks on General Bor. The CNL should think again about its attitude, and the Soviet government should exert a moderating influence upon them. This fell a good way short of the whole-hearted support that Romer and O'Malley had been looking for. Other papers contented themselves with simply reporting the events of Bor's appointment and the Lublin Committee's attack on him, without comment.

The second event, and the last act of the Warsaw rising, was the formal capitulation of the Home Army in the city, ordered by General Bor on 2 October. This news was broadcast by the BBC on the 3rd, when the 9 p.m. bulletin included one of the longest single items devoted to the rising. It opened by announcing that: 'The epic struggle by the Poles in Warsaw is at an end', and went on to quote Mikolajczyk's tribute to both the Home Army and the population, who had 'fulfilled their soldierly duty beyond the limits of human endurance and gallantry'. On the question of outside help, the account went on to say that 'What help *could* be flown from Italy, Britain and the Soviet Union was flown to Warsaw in response to urgent appeals.' The Red Army had fought its way into Praga (across the Vistula from Warsaw); Russian planes and anti-aircraft fire had helped to ward off German air attacks against the insurgents. In this account of the surrender, therefore, the BBC still went out of its way to stress that the Russians had helped the rising.

The CNL's response to the news was to condemn Bor for not trying to break out from Warsaw, and for giving up arms and ammunition to the Germans. The BBC European News Directive for 3 October instructed

---

[97] *Ibid.*, marginal notes by Eden; CAB 65/44, WM(44)130th Conclusions, Minute 3, Confidential Annex.

broadcasters to ignore these comments, and instead to repeat Bor's own final address to his troops. The PWE Directive for the week beginning 5 October laid down that the bare fact of the CNL attacks on Bor should be reported, but without prominence and without repeating their content. Broadcasts should pay tribute to the courage of the people of Warsaw, and should associate General Bor with that tribute. It should be emphasized that Britain still wanted a unified Poland with a fully representative administration, and also that the future of Poland must rest on the basis of friendly relations with the USSR. This would not be easy, but 'our general tone should continue optimistic . . . with good will on both sides a fair and acceptable solution is not impossible.'[98]

There was by now little comment in the press, other than a general sad head-shaking over 'the tragedy of Warsaw' which was a common, correct, yet inadequate phrase. The *Scotsman* (4 October), having stood by the Poles throughout, devoted a leading article to 'one of the most tragic and glorious episodes of the war', and continued to maintain that the Russian grounds for refusing help to the uprising were political, not military. The *Tablet* (7 October), individual as ever, reflected particularly on the destruction of Polish intellectual life, which during the occupation had flourished underground in Warsaw. The leader-writer had some hope that the CNL's tactics were continuing the 'education of public opinion' in the facts of life in eastern Europe – he again saw signs of hope even in *The Times*. The *Economist* (7 October), which had been the first to raise the question of the Soviet refusal to aid Warsaw, commented that the denial of landing facilities to the Americans had been inexcusable. Observing that the CNL had now threatened Bor with court-martial, the *Economist* asked whether the Soviet government endorsed this or not. The *News Chronicle* (4 October) carefully faced both ways, reproving the Poles for their divisions, but going on to say that British opinion had been deeply moved by the struggle, and did not understand the attitude of the Lublin Committee, which had first condemned the Warsaw insurgents for rising in revolt, and then damned them again for giving up the fight. However, inability to understand seemed to be as far as the writer was willing to go. The *Daily Express* (4 October) which had offered no comment on the rising at any stage, and provided very little in terms of news items, suddenly produced, apparently *à propos* of nothing, a leading article headed 'These Grand People', meaning the Russians, who had borne heavy burdens, won the admiration of the British people, and carried out every undertaking they had given to their allies. It was a remarkable encomium, and it is hard to believe that its timing was fortuitous.

The general trend of the limited comment which marked the closing stages of the rising was elegiac rather than bitter. The press remained divided in its views, but even papers critical of the Soviet Union's policies did not pursue the matter far. The BBC, as we have seen, did all it could do emphasize such Russian help as there had been for the rising. Finally Churchill, in his valedictory tribute to the Warsaw insurgents in the House of Commons on 5 October, struck a calming and conciliatory note. He praised the heroism of

[98] FO 371/39427, C9381/61/55.

the Home Army and lamented the sufferings of the population, 'unsurpassed even among the miseries of this war.' He then went on to say that Soviet succour for the city could not come in time. British, American, Polish and Soviet airmen had done all they could, but to no avail.[99] He thus let it be clearly understood that the Russians had tried to help the rising; and he avoided any reference to their holding back their advance or refusal to co-operate with the western air forces.

Again, this speech must be seen in the context of Churchill's impending visit to Moscow, for which Stalin's agreement had been received on 1 October. Churchill and Eden were due to set off on the 7th, and their words and actions were governed by this coming event, on the success of which, as Churchill told Mikolajczyk, 'he had set his heart'.[100]

Aftermath

Churchill and Eden arrived in Moscow on 9 October 1944, and stayed there for ten days. It was the conference at which the extraordinary 'percentages agreement' about proportions of influence in five south-eastern European countries was produced by Churchill and accepted by Stalin.[101] Power politics were in the ascendant, and Churchill was trying to reach a realistic settlement of eastern European questions before the war came to an end. Speaking to Stalin, he referred to the London Poles in harsh terms, even saying that 'as for General Bor, the Germans were looking after him.'[102] Mikolajczyk was virtually compelled to fly to Moscow, and was there put under the most severe pressure to accept the Curzon Line as the Polish frontier in the east, and to come to terms with the Lublin Committee. These efforts failed; but the point here is that they were made. The Warsaw rising had not marked any significant change in British policy on the Polish question, which was essentially to persuade (or even coerce) the London Poles into accepting Soviet territorial terms, and a large role for the Lublin Committee, in the hope of salvaging for them some real part in the future government of Poland. This is not the place to discuss the soundness or morality of that policy, or whether there was any alternative: only to emphasize that Warsaw had not changed it. Nor had Warsaw quenched the hope which sprang repeatedly in Churchill's breast when he met Stalin face to face, and believed that he had made a personal contact which could be translated into political advantage.

As for British public opinion, at dinner on 11 October Stalin was at pains to assure Churchill that failure to relieve Warsaw had not been due to any lack of effort by the Red Army, and Churchill was equally earnest in his affirmation that no-one who mattered had ever believed otherwise.

The Prime Minister said he accepted this (i.e. Stalin's) view absolutely and

99 *HC Deb.*, 5th series, vol. 403, cols. 1139–40.
100 Gilbert, *Road to Victory*, p. 979.
101 The countries concerned were: Greece (Britain 90%, Russia 10%); Rumania (Russia 90%, others 10%); Bulgaria (Russia 80%, others 20%); Yugoslavia and Hungary (50–50).
102 Gilbert, *Road to Victory*, p. 990.

he assured Marshal Stalin that no serious persons in the United Kingdom had credited reports that failure had been deliberate. Criticism had only referred to the apparent unwillingness of the Soviet Government to send aeroplanes. Mr Harriman who was present said that the same was true of the people in America.

However, public opinion as a means of influencing Soviet policy was not quite a dead duck. In that same conversation, Churchill and Eden went on to try to persuade Stalin that, in the interests of Anglo-Soviet relations, there must be a settlement of the Polish question 'which would seem reasonable to the British people'. Britain had entered the war for the sake of Poland, and 'The British people would not understand that she should be let down.'[103] In short, Stalin was assured almost in the same breath that British public opinion had not been at all perturbed by the Soviet action (or lack of it) over Warsaw, and yet that the same public opinion 'would not understand' some future failure to reach agreement on the Polish question. It is hard to believe that there was any point at all in this gambit.

At home in Britain, the evidence was that Churchill's account of public opinion as given to Stalin was well wide of the mark. The Home Intelligence Report for the week of 3–10 October – the week before Churchill's dinner with Stalin – recorded that the tragedy of Warsaw had caused deep regret throughout the country. 'Feeling appears to have crystallized against the Russians, who are now chiefly blamed for the city's fall.' The Russians were accused of not giving all the help they could, for reasons which were often thought to be political. There was widespread concern that Russian-Polish relations were going to be an obstacle on the way to a secure peace.[104] In Moscow, Churchill was following a line dictated by one kind of realism. In Britain, the general public had apprehended another sort of reality in regard to the fundamentals of Soviet-Polish relations. It is of some interest that the public proved to be more perceptive than the Prime Minister. It is also very striking that this grasp was achieved with little help from the mass media of the day. The BBC Home Service coverage of the Warsaw rising was not, as was sometimes said, hostile to the Poles, but it was small in quantity and colourless in character. Moreover, in September it went out of its way to emphasize Soviet help for the rising, and to that extent was pro-Soviet. For the newsreels, the rising scarcely existed. No footage was shown, and in all probability none was available; references in commentaries on film about the eastern front to difficulties in Soviet-Polish relations were very few in number and oblique in wording. Only the press offered some criticism of Soviet actions; and then it was only some newspapers, and for a limited time. How considerable numbers of the British people came to make up their minds, so that feeling crystallized against the Russians, remains a mystery.

How much did public opinion matter? It is clear that public opinion, in all its forms, was much more affected by the Warsaw rising than by the discovery of the Katyn graves. The rising was long-drawn-out; it was forlorn

---

[103] Eden to Sargent, 12 Oct. 1944, FO 371/39414, C14115/8/55; cf. Gilbert, *Road to Victory*, p. 1002, where these passages are quoted in part.
[104] INF 1/292, HI Report 210.

and painfully heroic, even as depicted in the limited reports which reached the British press and radio; and it came at a time of victory in the west, so that the contrast between Paris and Warsaw – *The Economist*'s 'Tale of Two Cities' – stood out starkly and harshly. MPs were active, in the House of Commons and in public meetings, in a way far exceeding their cautious private interventions about Katyn. Pressure groups (the Scottish-Polish Society and the Scottish Catholic hierarchy) tried to work on both the government and the press. Individuals – especially those married to Polish servicemen, or who had other close connections with the exiled Poles – were deeply distressed. The people at large were affected by events, and the substantial pro-Soviet consensus which was so obvious in the spring of 1943, just after Stalingrad, was badly shaken, so that general opinion blamed the Russians for the fall of Warsaw. The rising certainly made an impact on British public opinion.

It was also true that government expected public opinion to matter in relation to the issues raised by the rising. At different times, both ministers and Foreign Office officials either hoped for advantages from developments in public opinion or were afraid of their consequences. Hope concentrated on the belief that public opinion could be brandished at the Soviet government to bring about a change in policy. Look! they could say to the Russians, the British press and British people are so dismayed about the Soviet failure (or even refusal) to help Warsaw that the future of Anglo-Soviet relations is in jeopardy. We are sure you don't want that, so please do something to help. At one point (4 September) the War Cabinet actually took this course, and believed that it worked. Yet fear was aroused by the same set of possibilities. Suppose that public opinion 'got out of hand' (a favourite Foreign Office phrase), and caused such offence to the Russians that it endangered the Anglo-Soviet alliance. This was very reasonably regarded as a potential disaster. The war against Germany was not yet won; that against Japan loomed ahead for what was then an unknown period, threatening a heavy cost in lives. The peace settlement to follow both these wars demanded co-operation between the victors, and if there was serious dispute with the Soviet Union there could be no true post-war stability. Surely, then, public antipathy towards the USSR should not be used or encouraged for the sake of securing short-term advantage over Warsaw? Both sets of arguments were used; both made some sense. Public opinion was, either way, seen as an element in foreign policy.

No evidence has come to light that the Foreign Office actually tried to activate anti-Soviet opinion. Officials may have done so, in ways that have left no trace; but so far it appears that the outbreak of criticism in the *News Chronicle* and *Daily Mirror* at the end of August was spontaneous. There is, on the other hand, plenty of evidence of government attempts to damp down opinion, especially after the Soviet government had agreed to allow the use of its airfields for a shuttle flight. After that, all the emphasis was on not rocking the boat; and on the whole the press followed suit.

In substance, government policy remained unaffected by public opinion. There was some uneasiness about Soviet policy towards the Warsaw rising, and Churchill was sometimes deeply and genuinely moved by the desperate fight of the Home Army – it was, after all, a romantic gesture, and Churchill was in many ways a romantic. But his consistent policy was to make the Soviet alliance work, an objective shared with even greater conviction by Eden and fully accepted in the Foreign Office. To this policy the interests of Poland and the Polish people were subordinated. Churchill would do his best to salvage something for the London Poles, but not at the expense of a breach with Stalin. Even the idea of using public opinion as a bargaining counter was intended to make the alliance with the Soviet Union work better, not to endanger it.

So public opinion, in its various forms, was affected by the Warsaw rising. It was moved to a considerable extent in an anti-Soviet direction, largely in defiance of government guidance and the slant of the mass media. But foreign policy remained on its existing course.

6

The Yalta debate and some reflections

'*Let us hear the conclusion of the whole matter.*

(Ecclesiastes, XII, 13).

Man propounds negotiations, Man accepts the compromise,
Very rarely will he squarely push the logic of a fact
To its ultimate conclusion in unmitigated act.

(Kipling)

Kipling's lines are more appropriate to the tenor of this chapter than the forthright exhortation of the Preacher. In this particular matter there are no ultimate conclusions, and indeed no obvious point at which to halt the exploration. The war in Europe continued until May 1945, and the last meeting of the Big Three took place at Potsdam, 17 July–3 August 1945. Public opinion in Britain continued to be concerned with the Soviet Union when the war was over, and its interest has shown little sign of flagging since then.

However, the conference at Yalta in February 1945 is a good place to call a halt. In retrospect it has come to seem a watershed in the affairs of the wartime alliance. It has appeared to some as the apogee of co-operation; to others as the time when things went badly awry and the outlines of what came to be called the 'cold war' began to appear. In any case, it was in simple fact the last of the allied conferences held during the European war. The agreements reached at Yalta were also the occasion for a full-dress debate in the House of Commons, focusing Parliamentary attention on the government's conduct of relations with the Soviet Union and ending in a vote of confidence. This vote, and the importance of the issues involved, naturally commanded the attentive scrutiny of the press, so that there was a 'Yalta debate' in print as well as in the speeches of Members of Parliament. It was a time when contemporaries tried to sum up the state of Anglo-Soviet relations after some three-and-a-half years of a working alliance. Let us see what conclusions they had reached at that time, before seeing what reflections may bring this enquiry to a close.

The Yalta debate

The House of Commons was slow to voice any open disquiet about Anglo-Soviet relations. There was a group of MPs, mainly but not exclusively Conservatives, who were in close and sympathetic touch with the Polish government in London, and for whom the Polish question was a focus for anxiety about Soviet intentions in eastern Europe. But as we saw during the crisis over the Katyn graves, these MPs for a long time confined themselves to writing private letters to the Foreign Secretary, and to pressure exerted through back-bench committees. Later, they put down questions in the House, and sometimes pursued them closely and severely, as in the late stages of the Warsaw Rising. In mid-December 1944 there was a short debate in which members were severely critical of the Lublin Committee (described variously as unrepresentative and bogus) without encountering any serious opposition to their views. However, the critics stopped well short of an outright attack on government policy on the Polish question or towards the Soviet Union, and there was no question of demanding a vote.[1] It was not until the Yalta debate that the government's critics went to such lengths.

The Yalta Conference of the Big Three (often referred to at the time as the Crimea Conference) was held from 4 to 11 February 1945. It was keenly awaited by the British press, which had been highly conscious, and often critical, of the long period which had elapsed since the great men had met at Teheran at the end of November 1943. Anticipation built up when it was announced in Washington that President Roosevelt's annual message to the Congress on the State of the Union was to be read on his behalf, not delivered in person, and then it was observed that Churchill and Eden were both absent from an important session of the House of Commons on 30 January. A three-power conference was clearly imminent, and the tenor of British press comment was that it came not a moment too soon. All agreed that it would be the most important meeting of the war, and that it was above all necessary for the allies to demonstrate their solidarity. In the words of a *Sunday Times* leading article (4 Feb.), 'Any beginnings of separation at this stage would be dangerous: Europe needs unity, and still more unity.'

News of a meeting 'in the Black Sea area' was published in the press on 8 February, and on the 13th all the newspapers carried the communiqué issued at the end of the conference.

This dealt with several important issues, including the establishment of a new international organization (the United Nations), the future of Germany, and a general declaration on liberated Europe. On the question of Poland, the communiqué accepted the Curzon Line as the Soviet-Polish frontier, and agreed that the Lublin government should be reorganized by the inclusion of

---

1 *HC Deb.*, 5th series, vol. 406, cols. 1478–578; see, e.g., Price (1493), Pickthorn (1508).

other members from within Poland and from 'Poles abroad' (the Polish government in London was not specifically mentioned), and would thus become a Provisional Government of National Unity. This government would then hold free elections as soon as possible. The immediate reaction was a chorus of praise from the press, with very few jarring notes. To some extent this reflected a particularly emphatic government briefing to the press, which was very apparent in the reports by diplomatic correspondents. *The Times* reported on its news page that 'Unbounded satisfaction was expressed in London last night with the results of the Crimea Conference. . . .' Specifically, the proposals on Poland 'are regarded as one of the greatest achievements of the conference.' (13 Feb.) Leading articles followed suit with impressive similarity. *The Times* (13 Feb.) was delighted to find the 'remarkable harmony of policy over a wide and most controversial range', and welcomed the 'sacred obligation of unity' proclaimed in the conference declaration. Its leading article on the 14th, after a further day for reflection, was equally emphatic, and went out of its way to commend the main decisions on Poland (on the frontier with the USSR and a new government) as 'firmly rooted in both common sense and equity'. The *Manchester Guardian* (14 February) wrote that Stalin had made 'generous concessions' on the issues of liberated Europe and free elections; the Polish settlement was 'by no means a bad one'. The *News Chronicle* (13 February) found cause for 'profound satisfaction' in the Yalta communiqué, and held that the Polish section set 'a happy precedent' for the future. In the same paper Vernon Bartlett, who six months earlier had expressed his anxiety so sharply over Warsaw, acknowledged that there were still problems in the ruthless behaviour of the Soviet forces in Poland, but concluded that the Yalta decisions were 'the best that could have been reached in the circumstances' (14 February). The *Daily Telegraph* was also rather guarded in its comments, but held that the Polish compromise provided a basis for a settlement, as long as there was a will for peace on both sides (13 February). The *Daily Herald* wondered hesitantly whether close examination of the Yalta agreements might reveal problems, but still concluded that the Poles had now received a signal to make a supreme effort to achieve unity.

A few days later, as Churchill and Eden returned home from their long journey, their welcome in the press was warm, both on personal grounds and because they had achieved a great success at Yalta. From this general chorus there was little dissent. The *Scotsman* continued its sceptical course: 'Russia has had her way, and the new Poland can hardly be regarded as a really independent state' (13 February). The *Observer* noted cautiously that judgement on the Polish settlement depended heavily on the interpretation to be given to the word 'democratic' (18 February). In the *Daily Mail* (20 February) Alastair Forbes took this point further, claiming that the Yalta documents might need the total redefinition of a number of English words, including 'democratic' and 'freedom-loving'. 'Compromise' was another word which, though frequently used to describe the Polish settlement, was in fact wholly inapplicable. But such doubts were rare.

In general, therefore, Parliament met to debate Yalta against a background of warm approval of the Conference, sometimes amounting almost to euphoria, and of Churchill's actions. But despite this atmosphere, there was a current of uneasiness, mainly but not entirely on the Conservative benches. On 15 February the Government Chief Whip telegraphed to Eden (who was then in Athens) warning him of anxiety among Conservative MPs, and recommending the avoidance of an open display of disunity. It would be best if the government were not to seek a vote of confidence on the Yalta agreements, which might lead to a damaging division. Eden replied that he and the Prime Minister would prefer a debate to be followed by a division, because otherwise there might well be a preponderance of critical speeches without the weight of a vote to put them in the right perspective.[2] Whatever happened, there was bound to be a debate of some kind, because Churchill, alone among the Big Three, had to report to his country's legislature. Stalin was a dictator, and an American President is not responsible to Congress in the way that the Prime Minister is answerable to Parliament. On other occasions, Churchill had often used the device of making a wide-ranging speech on the war situation, inviting questions and discussion but not a division. This time, however, it was made known to political correspondents and others by 20 February that the Prime Minister intended to ask for a vote endorsing the Crimea agreements, which would amount to a vote of confidence in the government. About twenty Conservative MPs met to discuss what they should do, and the press reported that a number of Labour members were also in doubt about their vote. Arthur Greenwood, a senior figure in the Labour Party known to be sympathetic to the Poles, was reported to have called on the Polish Prime Minister. Churchill was aware of the potential opposition, and addressed a meeting of non-Cabinet ministers, including Under-Secretaries, to impress his views upon them before the debate began. The Parliamentary correspondent of *The Times* wrote that 'everybody expects the forthcoming debate to prove quite the most important held since the war began'; and the *Daily Telegraph's* political correspondent noted that an exceptional number of MPs wanted to speak.[3]

There was thus a real sense of occasion when Churchill rose to speak on 27 February. A division on a question of foreign policy was a rarity, and there was much speculation as to the result. To vote against the government, or even to abstain, was a serious matter, and a large number of defections would endanger the standing of the Prime Minister and the Cabinet at a crucial stage of the war. How many members would risk such a course?

Churchill opened by moving:

> That this House approves the declaration of joint policy agreed to by the three great Powers at the Crimea Conference and, in particular, welcomes their determination to maintain unity of action not only in achieving the final defeat of the common enemy, but thereafter, in peace as in war.

It would be hard to vote against such wording. The Prime Minister went on to appeal outright for the support of the House in order to strengthen

---

[2] FO 954/20, Chief Whip to Eden, 15 Feb. 1945; Eden to Chief Whip, 17 Feb.

[3] See articles by political or Parliamentary correspondents in *Manchester Guardian*, 21, 22 Feb. 1945; *News Chronicle*, 21 Feb.; *Daily Herald*, 21, 24 Feb.; *The Times*, 23 Feb.; *Daily Telegraph*, 26 Feb.

Britain's position among her allies – an appeal hard to resist. His speech dwelt upon the theme of unity: 'The Crimea Conference finds the Allies more closely united than ever before. . . .' The Germans must have impressed upon them the lesson that it was futile to hope for division among their enemies. Churchill tackled the Polish issue boldly and vigorously, acknowledging that it had been the most difficult problem at Yalta, but conceding nothing to his critics. On the frontier question, he defended the Soviet claim to the Curzon Line, not on grounds of expediency, still less on those of *force majeure*, but because it was 'just and right'. On the central question of Polish independence ('Are they to be masters in their own house?') he emphasized that Britain would try to ensure that consultations for the formation of a new government would be as wide as possible, and that free elections would be fairly carried out. He chastised the Polish government in London for casting aside chances of agreement with Russia as recently as the previous October. But above all he expressed his trust in Stalin, and appealed to the House to share it:

> Marshal Stalin and the Soviet leaders wish to live in honourable friendship and equality with the Western democracies. I feel also that their word is their bond. I know of no Government which stands to its obligations, even in its own despite, more solidly than the Russian Soviet Government. . . .
> It is quite evident that these matters touch the whole future of the world. Sombre indeed would be the fortunes of mankind if some awful schism arose between the Western democracies and the Russian Soviet Union. . . .

He followed this ringing assertion with the slightly lame hope that members of the Polish forces would return to Poland, and a proposal to offer British citizenship to those who did not wish to go. As later speakers were quick to point out, this detracted somewhat from the persuasiveness of his argument; but as to his main message there could be no doubt. The Soviets both must and could be trusted.[4]

The remainder of Churchill's speech dealt with other issues and problems in Italy, Greece, Turkey and the Middle East. He paid a handsome tribute to Eden for his work at the Yalta Conference, pre-empting any attempt to draw out differences between himself and the Foreign Secretary. He ended on the note of unity, with an echo of his rallying-cry earlier in the war: 'Let us walk forward together.' The speech was wide-ranging, but it was on the Polish issue that he threw down the gauntlet to the government's critics, and it was on Poland that much of the ensuing debate concentrated.

It was at the beginning of the second day of the debate (28 February) that the critics put down their formal challenge, in the shape of an amendment to the government motion, regretting 'the decision to transfer to another power the territory of an ally', and the failure to ensure to liberated nations 'the full right to choose their own government free from the influence of any other power'. This amendment was moved by two Conservative members,

---

4 Churchill's speech is in *HC Deb.*, 5th series, vol. 408, cols. 1267–95. The opening passages and those on Poland are at cols. 1267–84.

Petherick and Sir Archibald Southby. Conscious of the power of Churchill's appeal to trust Russia, both went out of their way to disclaim anti-Soviet sentiments. Petherick declared his firm belief that Britain could and should work with Russia (though co-operation was not 'a one-way street'). Southby made a point of referring to 'that very great man, Marshal Stalin'.[5] Three MPs (Guy Lloyd, Lord Willoughby de Eresby and Raikes) spoke in support of the amendment; three others (Lord Dunglass, McEwen and Graham) had already made speeches to the same effect on the previous day. All concentrated on the two issues raised in the amendment: Polish borders and Polish independence. They saw the frontier settlement not as an act of justice, but as an act of force and naked annexation – as Petherick put it, the Poles were said to be difficult, but 'so should we be, if half our country were to be given away to somebody else.' As to independence and free choice of government, the Yalta agreement amounted to a complete acceptance of the new government of Poland, and would not allow free elections. It amounted, Lloyd said, to the supersession of the legal Polish government by a 'prefabricated, Lublinized Government'.[6]

Those who spoke in support of the government included two of those who were absolutely committed to the Soviet Union (Gallacher, the Communist member, and Pritt, a fellow-traveller). Pritt declared that the Soviet Union could not possibly want a puppet Poland, because she had never wanted puppets round her. Gallacher attacked those who supported the amendment as mere representatives of the Polish gentry, and made a fierce attack on General Anders for refusing to march with the Red Army to liberate his own country.[7] But as well as such extreme remarks, Gallacher struck a more acceptable note, which was echoed by a number of other members: that the government's opponents were motivated not by love of Poland but by hatred of the Soviet Union. A Labour member, Haden Guest, held that the amendment arose from 'the muddle and obscurity of anti-Soviet prejudice'; and another, Emanuel Shinwell, said that it recalled the era of Chamberlain, the Anglo-German Fellowship and the friends of Franco.[8] Other speakers shifted the argument to the question of practicalities: what could reasonably be expected in the circumstances? W.J. Brown, an Independent member, said that the real question was whether the Prime Minister had secured at Yalta the maximum that the situation allowed. His answer was that Stalin held most of the cards ('It was not the British Army that liberated Warsaw'), and that Churchill had done better than could be expected. Harold Nicolson, recalling his diplomatic experience at the end of the previous war, thought it remarkable that Russia had not simply gone back to the old Tsarist frontiers; Yalta was an attempt to save something for Poland by means of negotiation.[9] There was also some criticism of Polish territorial claims on historical grounds, with members arguing that the Treaty of Riga was based on Polish

5 Speeches by Petherick and Southby, cols. 1421–37.

6 Speeches by Dunglass (1304–8), McEwan (1325–8), Graham (1332–4), Lloyd (1450–2), de Eresby (1466–8), and Raikes, winding up for the amendment (1490–7).

7 Pritt (1319–29), Gallacher (1449–72).

8 Guest (1439), Shinwell (1484).

9 Brown (1446–8), Nicolson (1477–83).

military victory and a sort of imperialism, and that the Poles who now complained of partition had done some partitioning themselves in the past.[10]

However, the dominant theme on the government side, picked up and repeated from Churchill's speech opening the debate, was the need to trust the Russians. This spanned party boundaries and wide political differences. Manningham-Buller, a right-wing Conservative who was associated with the 'Polish group' in the Commons, argued that the amendment was based on the assumption that the Yalta agreement on the Polish government and free elections would not be carried out. But that remained to be seen: 'I myself am not prepared to say that the signature of Marshal Stalin is not worth the paper it is written on.' Shinwell, who was on the Left wing of the Labour Party, declared that 'if we question the good faith of the Soviet Government, there is no hope of unity in Europe.' The British must accept Stalin's good faith and try it out; they could then complain if they were let down. Harold Nicolson, who as a National Labour member was somewhere in the middle, pointed out that the Yalta agreement itself would ensure the independence of Poland. 'What we are discussing is therefore a matter of some impertinence; namely, whether you can trust Russia.' He went on to claim that Stalin had made many promises during the war, and kept every one; only recently he had shown his loyalty to Churchill during the Greek crisis, when British forces had been in conflict with the Greek Communists.[11]

Eden wound up for the government, arguing that Poland, accepting the Curzon Line in the east and making teritorial gains in the west, would emerge stronger for the changes. (He also pointed out that at no time had Britain guaranteed Poland's pre-war frontiers.) On the issue of Polish independence and government, he emphasized that it was Britain's wish that the country should be truly free, and claimed that 'We would not recognize a Government which we did not think representative.' He concluded with an appeal for Allied unity and a warning against anti-Soviet sentiment. 'If any life is to be restored to Europe, if it is to be saved from anarchy and chaos, it can only be done by the three powers working together.' Some speakers had seemed to fear that Russia, in the flush of victory, was 'dreaming dreams of European domination'. That was the theme of German propaganda, as it had been before the war, and it should not be heeded.[12]

The House then divided on the amendment, which was defeated by 396 votes to 25, the latter all Conservatives save for McGovern, of the ILP. There were a number of abstentions, including a few Labour members. One junior minister, H.G. Strauss, Parliamentary Secretary in the Ministry of Town and Country Planning, resigned his office.[13] On 1 March the House of Commons approved the original government motion approving the declaration of policy agreed on at Yalta by 413 votes to nil: the ILP, which forced a division, mustered two tellers but no voters.[14]

10 Price (1329), Ward (1344).
11 Manningham-Buller (1475), Shinwell (1489), Nicolson (1481).
12 Eden (1498–1516).
13 Letter of resignation, *The Times*, 2 March 1945.
14 *HC Deb.*, 5th series, vol. 408, cols. 1517–20. For abstentions, see reports by the political correspondents of the *D. Telegraph* and *Manchester Guardian*, 1 March 1945.

The press reaction to the debate and votes was in general very favourable to the government and to the Yalta agreements. *The Times's* leading article on 28 February singled out the section of Churchill's speech dealing with Poland for its confidence and cogency. The *Daily Express* on the same day found nothing in the Prime Minister's speech more heartening than his outright affirmation of his confidence in Stalin. 'Speak as you find is a good maxim. For the people of Britain it means Trust Russia.' In the *Daily Telegraph*, a more orthodox organ of Conservatism, the leader-writer thought that the government had been wise to allow its critics on Poland scope to express themselves, because the debate had revealed their weakness. 'Substantially, the criticisms consisted of distrust of Russia, but contained nothing practical.' The Yalta agreement offered the only chance of an independent Poland and the hope of a truly representative Polish government (1 March). The *Sunday Times* (4 March) argued that the amendment, even if carried, would have done nothing to advance Polish independence. Its supporters seemed to think that Poland could be detached from the crucial problems of winning the war and the wider relations between the great powers; but this was not so. The *Sunday Times* leader-writer put his faith in Churchill and Roosevelt: both were friends of Poland, and both believed that the Yalta agreement was the best that could be done. Among Conservative papers in the provinces, the *Yorkshire Post* emphasized Churchill's insistence on Russian good faith, and claimed that the verdict of the future would be that the Prime Minister, by his vision and sincerity, 'broke down the barriers of distrust which had so long impeded the full co-operation of Russia and the Western democracies' (28 February). The *Glasgow Herald* wrote that the Poles had obtained promises of independence more valuable than any territory: 'the assurances of Britain and the United States are guarantees of their liberties' (28 February).

The *Manchester Guardian* supported the government, and its language on the London Poles and those who spoke in their favour was very severe. Its leader-writer was weary of special pleading to justify Polish claims to 'stolen territory in the east'. On Polish independence, it was necessary to take things on trust, and hope that the conditions for freedom would be fulfilled. But even if they were not wholly met, 'we in this country must be careful where we let our sentiments carry us.' Notably, people should not follow Tories who had previously been appeasers of Hitler in their old anti-Soviet paths. It would be wrong to assume that in any quarrel between a great nation and a small one 'right must be on the side of the weak'. The paper's political correspondent summed up the debate thus: 'If the result is to be interpreted in a sentence, it is a pledge of faith in Russia.'[15] The *News Chronicle* carried two articles by A.J. Cummings (1 and 2 March) attacking the supporters of the amendments for their past record as backers of Chamberlain and Franco, and commending Eden for making it plain that those who professed fear of Russian domination of Europe were playing the German game. The common-sense view of the vast majority of the British people was that peace in Europe depended on sincere co-operation between Britain, the United

---

[15] *Manchester Guardian*, leading articles, 28 Feb. and 1 March 1945.

States and Russia. The *Daily Herald* (28 February) was more cautious, choosing not to mention Poland at all, but finding encouragement in Churchill's confidence in the close unity of the Big Three.

There were some notes of doubt, and others of outright opposition. The *Observer* (4 March) thought that anxiety over Poland had not been confined to those who voted for the amendment, and that everything would depend on how the Yalta statements of principle on Polish independence and government were put into practice. The *Scotsman* too claimed that the number of votes for the amendment was not a fair reflection of the uneasiness either in the House of Commons or in the country, and was sceptical as to how far representative government in Poland could be assured (1 March). In the *Daily Mail* (6 March), Alastair Forbes agreed that the vote did not truly reflect feeling in the House: in the circumstances it could not do so, because no-one wanted to endanger the government. 'Not since Munich', he wrote, 'has the House seen so much heart-searching.' And he thought that the taunt of 'Munich', used freely against the government's opponents, was a sign that the case for Yalta was felt to be shaky: it was noticeable, for example, that no-one had been willing to say much about what was actually happening in Poland and Rumania.

But despite such occasional dissent, the government case was sustained, in the House of Commons and in the press. At the time, the Yalta agreements won enthusiastic support, and the general view was that we must put our trust in the Russians – to some extent in order to test their good intentions, but much more because trust was the only basis for a lasting peace.

The Yalta debate and its accompanying commentary in the press provide valuable indicators as to public opinion and policy as the war in Europe drew to an end. It was of considerable importance that the debate was pressed to a division – the first time that the House voted on an issue of confidence in the government related to its policy towards the Soviet Union. The current of doubt and opposition which had run underground since at least the time of the Katyn revelations had come into the open. But when it did so, its limitations were sharply revealed. This was not just a matter of numerical strength, though the vote went heavily against the critics. It was also a matter of the arguments which they chose to present. If, as was frequently said, their real motive was dislike of the Soviet Union, it is clear that they did not dare openly to declare their hostility. Both the proposer of the amendment (Petherick) and the seconder (Southby) declared their belief in co-operation with Russia, and denied that to be pro-British meant being anti-Russian. The full case that the Soviet Union was out to dominate eastern Europe and would not permit any true measure of Polish independence could not be made while these professions of faith were sustained.

There were two very solid reasons for this limitation on the scope of the argument. The first was that the government, with Churchill giving the clearest possible lead, made plain its commitment to the Soviet alliance. Churchill and Eden had both been at the Yalta Conference, and shared responsibility for its conclusions. Each had his private doubts as to what would actually follow, but both still hoped for an outcome which would save something for an independent Poland; and in any case neither could see any other way forward. The situation was very similar to that in June and early July 1941, when there had been all kinds of doubts about the Soviet Union, but a firm lead from Churchill and the practical necessity for a Soviet alliance had combined to smother all disquiet. After Yalta, Churchill's authority was still powerful, and the case for maintaining the alliance remained overwhelming. The second reason lay in the general state of opinion concerning the Soviet Union. The high tide of Russomania was over, but a climate of opinion favourable to the Soviet Union was still prevalent. In that climate, though there were doubts, there persisted a strong inclination to give the benefit of such doubts to the Russians. The combination of these two forces – government leadership and a strong current of opinion – was powerful enough to restrict the opposition to small numerical proportions and limited types of argument.

What impact did the Yalta Conference and the subsequent debate have upon general opinion in the country? At the end of 1944 the Home Intelligence reports were brought to an end, and the only direct evidence available is that of a Gallup poll held in March 1945. The following questions were put.

> At the Crimea Conference the Allies said that they would continue to co-operate during peace, as they have during war. Do you think that they will or will not be able to work together after the war?
>   Will 58   Will not 21   Don't Know 21
> Churchill, Roosevelt and Stalin have agreed that Poland's boundary with Russia should be roughly the same as the Allies laid down after the last war. Do you approve or disapprove?
> Approve 61   Disapprove 15   Don't Know 24[16]

The phrasing of the second question was, of course, heavily loaded. (It might, though it is highly unlikely, have referred to the Molotov-Ribbentrop line; or it might have asked whether respondents approved of Russia taking half the territory of pre-war Poland – two other possible ways of loading the dice). But the first question, on post-war co-operation, was fairly put, and produced an answer very similar to those given over the two previous years.[17] A solid, though not overwhelming majority still expected that allied co-operation would continue.

This was surely very natural. The war had gone on for five and a half years. The Grand Alliance had been in existence for three of those years, and was on the verge of defeating Germany. How many people, in those circumstances, were likely to be looking for further trouble, or even expecting it, when the war was over? The Yalta debate, in the House of Commons and in the country, held out the prospect of real difficulty for the government. Churchill and Eden both nursed private doubts about the Polish settlement and about Soviet objectives in eastern Europe. There was a serious case to be made on both these issues, if a powerful opposition in Parliament or the press had cared to do so. But in the event, as we have seen, the opposition was

---

[16] Gallup archive, BIPO Survey 117, March 1945.
[17] See above, pp. 102–3.

limited both in quantity and in the lines of its argument. The position which we have seen emerging in earlier chapters – growing doubts as to Soviet intentions, accompanied by support and admiration for the Soviet Union – still prevailed after Yalta. Government policy, meanwhile, could continue on its course, which was still to work towards post-war co-operation with both the United States and the Soviet Union. Whatever was to be said about Yalta in the future – and there was to be plenty – the contemporary debate was extremely limited in its effects.

Reflections

At the end of the introductory chapter, three questions were set out as the main guidelines for this venture into the difficult but fascinating terrain of public opinion and foreign policy. First, what policy did the British government adopt towards public opinion in relation to the Soviet Union? Second, how did public opinion towards the Soviet Union in fact develop? (This includes the further question of how far it conformed to government wishes and how far it moved in its own ways.) Third, how much interaction was there between policy and opinion – did policy make use of public opinion, and did opinion affect policy? How far has this study taken us towards answering these questions?

The British government adopted in 1941 a two-pronged policy on the issue of public opinion and the Soviet Union. Churchill's first act, his broadcast on the evening of 22 June 1941, was a *coup de théâtre,* a brilliant piece of publicity as well as an act of policy. Amid shoals of difficulties which might well have given even the boldest leader cause to hesitate, he took a course, and struck a note, which rallied almost everyone in the country. The course was towards alliance with the Soviet Union, though he did not use the word and the terms of an alliance had yet to be worked out; the note was one of solidarity with a fellow-victim of German aggression while yielding nothing to the claims of Communist ideology. This double line was the basis of all that followed.

A publicity policy was elaborated by the Ministry of Information during the next few months, emerging as a similar double line of combatting anti-Soviet feeling which might jeopardize Churchill's policy and hinder the alliance, and curbing excessive pro-Soviet propaganda which might work to the advantage of Communism. Of these two aims, the second has tended to attract more attention. The phrase 'stealing the thunder of the Left' was a striking one, and the attempt to put this line of policy into practice makes a fascinating study in the strategy and tactics of propaganda. At the same time, the nervousness of the government in face of what was a numerically small British Communist Party can appear somewhat strange, and has invited caricature.[18] This combination of attractions is powerful, and it is not

---

[18] Ian McLaine's book on the Ministry of Information, *Ministry of Morale*, skilfully used 'stealing the thunder of the Left' as the theme of one of its chapters, and gave an excellent account of propaganda strategy. A caricature of government policy appeared in a Channel Four television programme, 'Arm in Arm Together', 16 Sept. 1988.

surprising that this aspect of government policy has aroused much interest. It was, of course, important. It was half of the government's publicity-cum-propaganda policy relating to the Soviet Union. But it was only half. When the policy was formulated, it appeared as number 2, not number 1; and as time went on it became increasingly the less important half. Number 1 was, from the beginning, to ensure that public reactions against Communism or the Soviet Union did not impede the working of the alliance. This appeared in the skilful recruitment of religious leaders to preclude a hostile reaction to the alliance from the churches, and especially Roman Catholics. More important, both our case studies have shown the predominant part played in government policy by the desire to prevent or damp down public indignation or protest against the Soviet Union in the episodes of the Katyn graves and the Warsaw rising. It is salutary to recall Sir Orme Sargent's views on 2 September 1944: '. . . we ought I suggest to do all that we can to prevent public opinion from getting out of hand over this Polish issue, for if it does it may well distort and endanger the whole of our relations with Russia on which our post-war policy in Europe is necessarily based . . . However revolted and indignant we may be at the callous manner in which Stalin is treating the Poles, I hope the British public will be wise enough not to lose their sense of proportion in assessing this one more horror added to the innumerable horrors of the war, in the light of the essential need with which we are faced to collaborate at all costs with the Soviet Govt. if we are to save Europe and ourselves from another world war.'[19] Let us also remember the attitude of Churchill, who could be deeply moved by the plight of the Poles, and could assure General Anders that Britain would never let Poland down, but still appeal to MPs not to use language which might cause difficulties between Britain and the Soviet Union. Much later, on his return from the Yalta Conference, Churchill made his greatest effort along these lines, which is worth repeating here: 'I decline absolutely to embark here on a discussion about Russian good faith. It is quite evident that these matters touch the whole future of the world. Sombre indeed would be the fortunes of mankind if some awful schism arose between the Western democracies and the Russian Soviet Union.'[20]

The alliance with the Soviet Union, once it had been brought into being by the German assault and Churchill's speech, both on 22 June 1941, became for Britain both a military necessity in war and a political hope for the peace which would follow. It should cause no surprise that publicity and propaganda policy, and on occasion censorship, were directed primarily to the end of ensuring that public revulsion against Soviet ideology, or tyranny, or brutality, however appalling, should not interfere with the creation or the working of that alliance. Almost certainly, it was the changed perspective introduced by the development of the 'cold war' which has led observers to place the lesser concern of the British government with the danger of Communism at home above the greater interest in promoting the smooth working of the alliance. While the Second World War itself was in progress, the perspective was very different.

[19] See p. 154, above.   [20] *HC Deb.*, 5th series, vol. 408, col. 1283–4.

The British government therefore had a policy on public opinion and the Soviet Union, to which it attached much importance. How did public opinion respond, and how did public opinion towards the Soviet Union develop?

Public opinion was not one entity but several. In Parliament, there was a slow growth of disquiet and opposition after a remarkably smooth passage for the Anglo-Soviet alliance in the early part of its existence. In 1943, over Katyn, the small number of MPs who were uneasy confined themselves to private expressions of their disquiet. In 1944 over Warsaw they came out into the open, making speeches in the country and giving Eden (though not Churchill) a difficult passage in the House of Commons. In the debate on Yalta, they spoke in terms of sober criticism rather than denunciation, and they were careful to make no outright attack on Stalin or the Soviet Union, but they chose to divide the House. In the division they summoned up 25 votes, plus two tellers. It was not many. Considering that this was the House of Commons which was elected in 1935, with only the few changes brought about in by-elections, what is striking is not that opposition to the government's policy towards the Soviet Union developed, but that it grew so slowly and attained such limited dimensions.

As for the press, the picture was broadly similar. The press as a whole approved of the Anglo-Soviet alliance. There were various degrees of zeal and commitment. *The Times*, following the line laid down in E.H. Carr's ruthlessly logical leading articles, went the whole hog in accepting Soviet control of eastern Europe. The *Daily Express*, following whatever spirit moved Lord Beaverbrook at the time, never ceased to proclaim that the Russians were splendid people, to be helped and trusted so that all would turn out for the best. The *News Chronicle*, with occasional exceptions from the pen of Vernon Bartlett, was fervently fellow-travelling, and for A.J. Cummings the Russians could do no wrong. These papers tended to go further than the government wanted, even though it was down the same road. *The Times* was occasionally particularly embarassing to the Foreign Office, because of the semi-official status which was still frequently attributed to it. But even when they went too far, these papers generally reinforced the government line. There were few who went against it. Among the Catholic press, the *Tablet* was courageous, consistent and acute, but very limited in its circulation and appeal. The *Scotsman*, repeatedly telling home truths about the Soviet Union and Poland, was only a national paper north of the Border. The *Nineteenth Century and After* was a periodical with a very small circulation, and F.A. Voigt a sort of John the Baptist crying in a very large wilderness. Among the middle-of-the-road weeklies, the *Spectator* published some sceptical articles about Russia, and the *Economist* occasionally intervened with some weighty leading articles, as it did at the time of Warsaw. So, with few exceptions, there was a consensus in favour of the Soviet alliance. Of the papers which diverged from this on either side, those which were highly favourable to the Soviet Union were much more important than those which were against. It is not possible to tell with certainty how much this consensus owed to government guidance, which was undoubtedly provided; but the strong inference from particular case studies is that editors were most amenable to guidance when it led in a direction which they already wished to follow. When it did not, then the Ministry of Information could issue its guidance memoranda in vain. It is highly likely that the majority of the press and the government simply wanted the same thing, if not always for the same reasons.

General opinion, or popular opinion in the country as a whole, was also given government guidance, not least in the news which was presented on the radio and in the press. Naturally, opinion often (indeed mostly) responded to this flow of news, and to the general slant put on it by the mass media of the day. There were occasional crises of confidence, and in 1941 and 1942 a kind of gloomy scepticism about any good news; but in general British reliance on the basic accuracy of the news, especially that given by the BBC, remained high. This was surely one of the most important elements influencing general opinion. It is all the more significant to note the substantial signs of independence shown by this opinion. During 1941 and 1942 people developed a much greater degree of admiration for Russia than the government wanted, or than was encouraged by the guarded line officially adopted by the Ministry of Information and the BBC. Of course, the press and the newsreels went beyond the Ministry's restrictions, and presented a glowing picture of the Soviet struggle; but this left people free to form their own judgement. They did; and it was favourable. Moreover, the public followed the course of some of the battles on the eastern front, notably those for Moscow in the winter of 1941–42 and Stalingrad in 1942–43, with an intensity which was quite remarkable, and beyond the call of either duty or propaganda. Naturally, some of the admiration for Russian courage and fighting power rubbed off on the regime, its ideology and its leaders, to an extent which was presumably a disappointment to those who framed the original Ministry of Information policy. Eventually, the government was impelled against its will to stage an apotheosis of this admiration on Red Army Day, 1943. But then general opinion began to change again, and for the rest of 1943 and 1944 showed an increasing anxiety about Soviet intentions, and doubts about Russian reliabilty as an ally in peacetime, which went beyond anything they were offered except in very limited sections of the press. On the radio the same *couleur de rose* prevailed. The newsreels were unabating in their praise for the Russians and their liberation of eastern Europe. Yet the Home Intelligence reports showed a steady and growing note of doubt, with an occasional sharp, humorous stab – 'Will Joe stop at the Channel?' Here the case of Warsaw is particularly interesting. For most of September 1944 government, radio and most of the press united in presenting a favourable interpretation of Soviet actions. But by the first week in October Home Intelligence was categorical: 'Feeling appears to have crystallized against the Russians, who are now chiefly blamed for the city's fall.'[21]

In relation to specific episodes, it is striking that sometimes the general public would react favourably to something which was little more than a stunt. This was clearly the case with 'Tanks for Russia Week' at the end of

---

[21] See p. 170, above.

September 1941, which caught the popular imagination even though there were wiseacres who pointed out that not all the tanks produced that week either could or should go to Russia – which, on a moment's reflection, was obviously true. At that moment, people *wanted* to help the Russians, and they willingly suspended their disbelief and accepted what Lord Beaverbrook told them with such impassioned fervour. The Stalingrad Sword, which so many queued to see, was surely another example of an ardent public response to something which, if not quite a stunt, was certainly a propaganda exploit. On the other hand, popular opinion sometimes moved quickly and largely of its own volition, as in the case of the Dieppe raid, when the public swiftly grasped what had happened – probably starting, as Home Intelligence indicated, with the troops and men of the RAF who came back, or those who treated them in hospitals. In Britain during the Second World War, army and population were closely linked, and word of mouth is the most powerful of all means of communication.

There is little sign that opinion in the country could be moulded at the government's will, though much evidence that it could be encouraged to move in a direction which it already wished to follow. And of course it was often possible for government to withhold information; though even this sometimes made little difference. No-one told the British people that the Russians had refused to allow a second shuttle flight to Warsaw. They simply made up their minds on what they knew already.

Public opinion certainly had a life of its own, and was not merely a reflection of what the government wanted it to be. It is therefore proper to ask the next question, about the interaction between policy and opinion, which in the broadest sense amounts to asking how much public opinion mattered. It is clear that government believed that it mattered, from the sheer amount of time and effort that was put into matters relating to public opinion. This was true both on the large scale, in the devising of a broad propaganda policy on the Soviet Union, and perhaps even more so on the small scale, in the day-to-day concern of the Foreign Office with the press, and with particular articles in the newspapers. (It is worth adding that this concern was shown by Foreign Office officials who were hard pressed by the constant demands of wartime diplomacy, and who would surely have let such matters slide if they had not thought them really important). At both levels, the government set out to influence opinion, trying to limit the appeal of communism on the one hand and to restrain anti-Soviet feeling on the other. There were also deliberate attempts to make use of public opinion, sometimes against the government, as in the 'second front' campaign, and sometimes by the government, as in the War Cabinet's telegram of 4 September 1944 threatening Molotov with the danger of alienating British opinion. So public opinion was *thought* to be important, and there was a widespread assumption that it could or did influence policy. How far can such an influence be discerned?

Such influence can certainly be found at the level of incidents and irritants, where individual newspaper articles, even in quite obscure publications, could bring the Soviet Ambassador round to the Foreign Office and throw some grit into the workings of Anglo-Soviet relations. Similarly, public displays of esteem and recognition were used as lubricating oil in the same workings, or – to change the metaphor – as emollients for hurt feelings. Such matters are the small change of diplomacy, but they were quite significant enough to demand attention at the time, and we should not underrate them now. On a wider issue, it is clear that a consensus of support was necessary for the waging of the war and the smooth working of the 'Grand Alliance'. The maintenance of such a consensus had some effect on the conduct of policy and diplomacy. All conferences had to be seen to succeed, and serious difficulties (for example, over Soviet frontiers during Molotov's visit to Britain in 1942) had to be concealed or glossed over. This was not just a matter of deception, though deception was sometimes involved. It was more a question of statesmen accepting ambiguities and obscurities for the sake of a communiqué which had to display unity and success. The classic case is surely the Yalta communiqué, with its references to democracy and free elections, which a purely secret diplomacy might not have troubled itself with.

Such forms of influence must not be discounted. But is it possible to be more explicit, and to point to specific examples of the fundamentals of government foreign policy being changed by public opinion? Within the range of this study, the answer must be No. The government did not change its mind about the Second Front. Public anxiety about the Soviet Union and the Warsaw Rising did not affect the line which Churchill took when he went to Moscow in October 1944; indeed, he simply told Stalin that such anxiety was not serious. It was of course true that the fundamental question was never put. What would have happened if a strong and deep public revulsion against Soviet methods and objects had developed, perhaps in 1941 before the alliance was confirmed, or perhaps in 1944 when Warsaw was on the rack? We do not know, because it did not happen. But even to put the question shows why the government could never afford to neglect public opinion.

May we now approach the conclusion of the matter, bearing in mind that this refers not to the whole matter of public opinion and foreign policy, but only this particular enquiry? First, despite the wartime conditions of censorship and propaganda, public opinion had an autonomous life of its own, and was sometimes fully capable of following its own path. Second, and this time probably *because* of wartime conditions, which gave foreign affairs a dramatic immediacy, public opinion was much concerned with foreign policy issues, sometimes in a remarkable degree of detail. But third, the actual formulation and conduct of foreign policy remained in the hands of a small group: the Prime Minister and Foreign Secretary, the War Cabinet, Foreign Office officials and diplomats. Public opinion was one of the elements which this group took into account, often to avoid potential dangers, sometimes to seek useful support. When tensions arose between movements of opinion and the conduct of policy, the government's usual tendency was to try to guide or to damp down public opinion rather than to follow it or to adjust the course of policy to meet it. If the government was seriously attempting, in its foreign policy and general conduct of the war, to advance and defend the national interest, it is hard to see that it could do anything else. Nonetheless, tensions between opinion and policy certainly arose. To observe the nature and development of these tensions adds to our understanding of both public opinion and foreign policy, as well as having a fascination of its own – a fascination which will continue as long as men deal in the art of politics.

Appendix
Public Opinion And The Darlan Deal, November–December 1942*

The affair of the deal made by the British and Americans with Admiral Darlan in French North Africa at the end of 1942 is not directly connected with Anglo-Soviet relations. However, it is referred to in Chapter 4 of this book, on Katyn, and offers some interesting points of comparison with the way in which British public opinion reacted to the Katyn graves. To provide a short study of public opinion in relation to the Darlan deal will help to clarify those points of comparison, and perhaps be of some general interest as an addition and counterpoint to the main argument of the book.

American and British forces landed in French North Africa in the early morning of 8 November 1942.[1] The operation presented serious military difficulties. Neither the troops involved nor the Supreme Commander, the American General Eisenhower, were experienced in combat. Success depended on speed in getting ashore, in coping with French resistance, and in moving from the landing zones in Morocco and Algeria to Tunisia to prevent the Axis powers from moving forces in from Sicily. It was recognized in advance that to secure speed the Allies must seize every possible political advantage in North Africa, to minimize or even avoid opposition from the French forces there, which were under the authority of the French government at Vichy under Marshal Pétain. To this end, the Americans promoted a conspiracy for a *coup* in Algiers, and also brought in from France General Giraud, to rally support to their side. They failed: the *coup* went off at half-

---

* The substance of this Appendix appeared as an article on 'War, Foreign Policy and Public Opinion: Britain and the Darlan Affair, November–December 1942', in *Journal of Strategic Studies*, vol. 5, No. 3, 1982. I am grateful to the Joint Editor, Professor John Gooch, for permission to use this material again here.

[1] For accounts of the landings, the campaign and the politics of French North Africa see Keith Sainsbury, *The North African Landings, 1942* (London, 1976); Michael Howard, *Grand Strategy*, vol. IV (London, 1972), chapters X and XVIII; Arthur L. Funk, *The Politics of TORCH: The Allied landings and the Algiers putsch* (Lawrence, 1974).

cock, and Giraud proved a damp squib. In their urgent need for co-operation from the French in North Africa, the Allied (primarily American) commanders turned to Admiral Darlan, Minister of Marine in the Vichy government and (after Laval) its most important member, who was in Algiers at the time of the landings. They lost little time in coming to this decision. On 10 November General Clark (Eisenhower's deputy) met Darlan and arranged a cease-fire for Algeria and Morocco. On the 13th Clark and Darlan signed an agreement accepting Darlan as head of the civil administration in North Africa in return for his co-operation with the Allied forces; and on the 22nd this arrangement was formally embodied in a lengthy written agreement. In all these steps, Clark's actions were ratified by Eisenhower as Supreme Allied Commander. This was the 'Darlan deal'.

At the time, the deal appeared to be an improvised affair, springing from the initiative of the men on the spot; and in part this was the case, for the actual circumstances of Darlan's presence were not foreseen. But it was also true that the possibility of an arrangement with Darlan was considered at a meeting in London on 17 October 1942, at which Churchill, Eden and Smuts (the South African Prime Minister) were present, as well as Eisenhower and Clark; and it was not rejected – Smuts remarked that Darlan 'would be a big fish to land if it could be done'. On the same day, Admiral Leahy, Roosevelt's Chief of Staff, authorized Robert Murphy, the President's diplomatic representative in Algiers, to initiate any agreement with Darlan which might assist military operations.[2] In principle, therefore, the highest members of the British and American governments were prepared to consider a deal with Darlan if the price was right. There was no reason why Eisenhower and Clark should think that such a deal was ruled out on the grounds of Darlan's record as a Vichy minister, a collaborator, a fascist – or a rat.[3]

It was at this point that public opinion came in. The news of the cease-fire agreement of 10 November was published in Britain on the 11th; and a broadcast by Darlan on Algiers radio on 13 November announcing that he had resumed responsibility for French interests in Africa with the approval of the American authorities was reported in BBC news bulletins and the press on the 14th. As early as 13 November the Left-wing weekly *Tribune*, edited by Aneurin Bevan, noted the armistice agreement with Darlan, wondered what the French Résistance made of it, and asked: 'What kind of a Europe have we in mind? One built by rats for rats?' *Tribune*'s circulation was small, and Bevan usually ploughed a lone furrow in the House of Commons. What

[2] Arthur L. Funk, 'Negotiating the "Deal with Darlan"', *Journal of Contemporary History*, vol. 8, No. 2 (April 1973), especially pp. 94–7; R. T. Thomas, *Britain and Vichy. The dilemma of Anglo-French relations 1940–42* (London, 1979), pp. 146–8. CAB 79/87, COS(42)151st meeting (O) contains the British record of the meeting. At that stage, what was contemplated was that Darlan might hold a military post under Giraud's political authority. This position was later reversed, so that Giraud held a post under Darlan; but it would be hard to elevate this into an issue of principle.

[3] A document prepared for American troops taking part in the landings included the sentence: 'For each Nazi rat like Laval, or Déat, Darlan, Doriot, there are hundreds of thousands of brave Frenchman who have shown they are really and truly our allies.' FO 954/18B.

was striking on this occasion was the range of support which rallied to this point of view. There was a note of doubt in a leading article in the Conservative *Daily Telegraph* on 11 November. The Diplomatic Correspondent of *The Times* wrote on the 16th that 'few people at the present stage like the granting of status to a man who . . . has often proclaimed the need to collaborate with the enemies of Britain, America and France itself.' An impulse came from outside when Ed Murrow, one of the most influential of American radio correspondents, broadcast on the BBC for American listeners on 15 November, claiming that the issue at stake was whether Britain and America were to stand dishonoured in the eyes of the conquered peoples of Europe. Would the Allies, he asked, be prepared to occupy Norway and turn it over to Quisling on grounds of military expediency? Murrow's attack on the Darlan deal was prominently reported in the British press on 17 November; and on the same day the main news pages carried a statement from General de Gaulle's headquarters declaring that de Gaulle and the French National Committee had no part in, and assumed no responsibility for, the negotiations in North Africa – if these negotiations confirmed Vichy's authority in that territory, this would not be accepted by the Fighting French. This statement attracted much favourable comment, not least from the Conservative *Telegraph* and *Yorkshire Post*.

These anxieties were widely shared by opinion in the country, Foreign Office officials and government ministers. The Home Intelligence report for the week of 10–17 November noted that the public were puzzled and cynical about Darlan's change of sides. No-one had a good word for him, and it was widely held that 'General Eisenhower had better not trust Darlan further than he can throw a piano'.[4] Foreign Office officials feared trouble with public opinion, and blamed the Americans for blundering into a difficult situation. Cadogan (the Permanent Under-Secretary) wrote in his diary: 'An awful tangle in N. Africa . . . The Americans and naval officers are letting us in for a *pot* of trouble'. Harvey, Eden's Principal Private Secretary, wrote in similar vein: 'I fear our blind self-effacement before America over this whole business. . . . What will Parliament and the British public say? It may be a Hoare-Laval over again'. Among ministers, Bracken (Minister of Information) wrote to Eden that Darlan was 'as treacherous and tricky as Laval. If the British Government assents to his being given any authority in North Africa a great storm will blow up in Parliament and the Press.' Attlee was approached by a member of de Gaulle's headquarters (which knew how to use private contacts as well as public statements), and passed on to Eden a warning about the dangers of a breach between a Vichy administration in North Africa and democratic movements in metropolitan France.[5]

Eden's own position was equivocal, because he had been a party to the October discussion of a deal with Darlan; but he too grew uneasy as events developed. On 16 November he argued in the War Cabinet that Roosevelt should be told formally that 'we thought it would be disastrous if we were to

[4] INF 1/292, HI Report 111.
[5] *Cadogan Diaries*, p. 492, cf. p. 494; Harvey, *War Diaries*, pp. 183–4; Bracken to Eden, 13 Nov. 1942, FO 954/8A; Attlee to Eden, 12 Nov. 1942, *ibid*.

make any permanent arrangements with Admiral Darlan'. Churchill deferred this approach for a day, but then telegraphed on the 17th:

> I ought to let you know that very deep currents of feeling are stirred by the arrangement with Darlan. The more I reflect upon it the more convinced I become that it can only be a temporary expedient, justifiable solely by the stress of battle. . . . A permanent arrangement with Darlan or the formation of a Darlan government in French North Africa would not be understood by the great masses of ordinary people, whose simple loyalties are our strength.[6]

On the same day, Eden telegraphed to the British Ambassador in Washington, Halifax, telling him that de Gaulle had made it plain that he would not work with Darlan; that British public opinion would not tolerate the abandonment of de Gaulle in favour of Darlan; and that 'We are fighting for international decency, and Darlan is the antithesis of this.'[7]

Roosevelt was himself under pressure from American newspapers and radio commentators; and on 17 November he was obliged to meet his critics by making a public statement that he understood and approved the feeling that no permanent arrangement could be made with Darlan, 'We are opposed to Frenchmen who support Hitler and the Axis.' The future government of France would be settled by the French people themselves after their liberation. 'The present arrangement in North and West Africa is only a temporary expedient, justified solely by the stress of battle.' Commenting in his memoirs on Roosevelt's statement, Churchill wrote; 'This met my view and the public need.'[8] Perhaps it did; but only in part, and only briefly.

The trouble was that Roosevelt's statement was rapidly belied by news from Africa. On 19 November Darlan made a broadcast from Algiers stating that he had assumed the post of High Commissioner in North Africa, in agreement with the American authorities and in execution of orders issued by Marshal Pétain when he was still at liberty to act. On 23 November Darlan announced (again on the radio) that French West Africa had placed itself under his orders, showing that it remained faithful to its oath to the Marshal. On 2 December he proclaimed that he was forming an Imperial Council, with himself at the head; and that he was exercising the functions of chief of state. All these items of news were quickly and prominently reported on the BBC and in the press, and they gave Roosevelt's claim that the arrangement with Darlan was only temporary a very hollow ring. A cartoon by Philip Zec in the *Daily Mirror* (9 December) caught the point exactly. It showed Darlan arriving at Allied headquarters with an invitation for the week-end, but carrying an immense pile of suitcases. 'A lot of luggage for a short stay', ran the caption.

The anxieties aroused by Darlan's position were obvious enough; that he

---

[6] Avon, *The Reckoning*, pp. 348–9; Churchill, *Second World War*, vol. IV, pp. 566–8; CAB 65/28, WM(42)153rd conclusions.

[7] E. L. Woodward, *British Foreign Policy in the Second World War*, vol. II (London, 1971), p. 370.

[8] Churchill, IV, pp. 568–9; cf. James McGregor Burns, *Roosevelt; The Soldier of Freedom* (London, 1971), p. 297.

remained a collaborator; that he intended to make his authority in North Africa permanent, and perhaps impose it on France; that the precedent once set could be followed by any quisling in Europe; that the resistance movements in occupied countries were being set at nought; and that all this was happening with the connivance or worse of the British and American governments. All these views were strongly expressed across the whole range of public opinions. In the House of Commons, the matter was first raised by Bevan on 11 November; and the pressure increased instead of diminishing after Roosevelt's statement on the 17th. Cripps, then Leader of the House and a Labour member of the War Cabinet, parried questions on 18 November by quoting the President. On the 24th a maverick Labour member, Richard Stokes, revealed that Churchill had stopped a proposed broadcast by de Gaulle, and put Eden in difficulties by saying that the latter had earlier found the script acceptable. A motion was put down asserting that British relations with Darlan were inconsistent with the ideals for which the country was fighting the war. It attracted only eleven signatures (mostly Labour, though including Robert Boothby from the Conservatives); but lobby correspondents expected that in time it would gain more. Eden (who had just become Leader of the House as well as Foreign Secretary) thought feeling in the Commons was very strong, and he was given a rough passage by questioners on 26 November. The War Cabinet, while not expecting the critical motion to win much support, recognized that 'there was an undercurrent of anxiety among a number of persons well-disposed to the Government but who were not in possession of the full facts.'[9]

Pressure groups were also active, not least the Fighting French and the governments in exile who felt that their integrity and political prospects were alike under threat. The publicity work of de Gaulle's headquarters was masterly. On 18 November, when Roosevelt's statement about the temporary nature of the Darlan deal appeared in the British press, it was accompanied by reports of a press conference given by French officers, who had escaped from North Africa up to three months earlier, expressing their surprise and bitterness at seeing Darlan and the men of Vichy profiting from their work for resistance. The following day a trade union leader recently arrived from France told the press how the recognition of Darlan had cooled the early enthusiasm for the North African landings among the French people. On 7 December General Catroux (always the smoothest and most statesmanlike of de Gaulle's senior associates) gave a press conference, at which he denied that Darlan's help was even militarily expedient – he would personally not like to fight with such a dubious friend in his rear.[10] The Dutch and Norwegians, well known as the least touchy and most gentlemanly among the exiled governments, conveyed their anxieties privately to the Foreign Office; and Eden took care that the Dutch concern was drawn to

---

[9] *HC Deb.*, 5th series, vol. 385, cols. 689–90, 692–4, 730-1, 882–6. Cf. *Manchester Guardian*, 26, 27 Nov., *Scotsman*, 27 Nov. 1942; Barker, pp. 65–7; Harvey Diaries, British Library, Add. Mss., 56389, entry for 25 Nov. 1942; CAB 65/28, WM(42)161st Conclusions. Vansittart threatened to put down a critical motion in the House of Lords, but was dissuaded.

[10] See the press for 18, 20 Nov. and 8 Dec. 1942. The BBC news bulletins also gave prominence to the trade unionist (Morandat) and to Catroux.

the attention of the War Cabinet.[11] A number of protests from Labour constituency parties and trade unions also reached the Foreign Office.[12]

Much press comment continued to be hostile to the Darlan deal. Roosevelt's 'temporary expedient' statement received a widespread but qualified welcome. Among the more enthusiastic comments were that it had 'removed most of the anxiety' (*Telegraph*, 19 November), and that it had 'gone far to clear the air' (*The Times*, 20 November). Among the least welcoming was that of *Tribune* (20 November), that the deal was not an expedient at all but the natural extension of the policy of the American government, which had 'played ball with Vichy since 1940'. In between, *The Economist* (21 November) followed a cursory nod of approval with long paragraphs of closely reasoned criticism, concluding that actions spoke louder than words and that Darlan's actual position meant that the Allies were undertaking 'the unsavoury task of making France free for Vichy'. As the evidence of Darlan's permanence accumulated, Roosevelt's statement ceased to carry even limited conviction. What had Darlan's Imperial Council to do with military expediency? Was it not clear that for Darlan 'temporary' meant at least for the duration of the war? Such comments spanned the political spectrum; and again in the centre *The Economist* offered some striking reflections. Its leading article on 28 November accepted that the deal with Darlan had brought great benefits, but argued that the manoeuvre had been in the old style, from military weakness. In future, with military strength, there must be no such bargains – the days of appeasement were over:

> Total victory, unconditional surrender, no compromise – these are the banners which the United Nations can freely fly . . . which they must fly if their aim of a better and safer world is to be achieved . . . To seek a speedier peace by making terms with the men, Germans, Italians, or of whatever country, whose creeds and habits brought war about would be a betrayal of all that has been worked and fought for . . . The deal with Darlan must be no precedent.

As well as the press, the BBC news bulletins, which were wholly subject to government control, gave considerable coverage to criticisms of the Darlan deal, notably in the House of Commons and by spokesmen for de Gaulle.

At the level of general opinion in the country, the Home Intelligence reports for the three weeks between 17 November and 8 December showed keen and widespread public interest in the Darlan affair. Darlan was reported to be 'the most discussed figure of the week' of 17–24 November. There was some evidence of differing views, with a minority feeling that the deal might be justified if it was only temporary, or that the Allies should get what they could out of Darlan and then ditch him; but all reports indicated that the majority were both perplexed by the deal and hostile to it. Roosevelt's explanation on 17 November did something to blunt the

---

11 FO 371/32144, Z9874–5/8325/17 for Norway (27 Nov., 2 Dec. 1942); CAB 66/32, WP(42)576 for the Netherlands (memo. by Eden, 11 Dec., with a note of 9 Dec.).
12 FO 371/32144, Z9708/8325/17.

criticism, but its effect was temporary, and there were even signs of a decline in trust in the President, who was normally much respected and admired. On the other hand, there was much sympathy for de Gaulle: he had stuck by us when times were hard, and we should stick by him now. Distrust of Darlan; dissatisfaction with the deal; dislike of the Americans, who were held responsible for it; and support for de Gaulle – these were the main trends which emerged from the regional reports and from the postal censorship.[13]

In face of this public outcry, the War Cabinet sought to restore confidence by appealing to the House of Commons, but to do so in secret session so that reference could be made to confidential information. The belief was that if anxiety was allayed in Parliament this would have an indirect effect on the press and the public. The date was fixed for 10 December. Churchill opened the debate, and wrote in his memoirs that 'The speech which I then made was conceived with the sole purpose of changing the prevailing opinion, and I chose with the greatest care the points to make.' He began with understated humour. 'Since 1776 we have not been in the position of being able to decide the policy of the United States' – which contrived to put the Americans in the centre of the stage. He disclaimed any such intention: 'I do not want to shelter myself in any way behind the Americans', he said; and of course Churchill rarely gave the impression of sheltering behind anyone. Yet he managed to imply that Britain had not been consulted at all about Darlan, which was not the case. He also made full use of the argument of military expediency, quoting from various secret telegrams. In his memoirs, he claimed complete success: 'The Commons were convinced, and the fact that all further Parliamentary opposition stopped after the Secret Session quenched the hostile Press and reassured the country.' Harold Nicolson noted in his diary that he had never heard Churchill more forceful or effective. 'He convinces us (a) that we were never consulted about the Darlan move; (b) that when it happened, he himself realized at once what trouble would be caused, and warned Roosevelt accordingly; (c) that it is purely temporary.' It is of some interest to note that (a) stretched the truth, (b) was exaggerated, and (c) involved a prediction of doubtful certainty.[14]

The effects of the speech, indeed, were by no means so clear-cut as Churchill stated in his memoirs. Bevan and his friends were not convinced; and Harvey heard that they had declared their intention of continuing to attack the government about Darlan both in and out of the House of Commons. On the opposite political wing, Lord Cranborne (Colonial Secretary, and a long-standing associate of Eden's) thought that the secret session had demonstrated the deep cause of uneasiness in the public mind over the Darlan affair; the fear that it was a precedent which would be followed in the future. In a memorandum which he sent to Eden on 11 December (the day after the debate), Cranborne wrote that the long-term

---

[13] INF 1/292, HI Reports 112, 113, 114; cf. 115 for an analysis of letters by the postal censorship during November.

[14] The text of Churchill's speech may be found in Robert Rhodes James, (ed.), *Winston S. Churchill: His Complete Speeches, 1897–1963*, vol. IV (New York and London, 1974), pp. 6718–30. Churchill, IV, pp. 573–6; Nigel Nicolson (ed.), *Harold Nicolson; Diaries and Letters, 1939–45* (London, 1970), p. 267.

effect of such deals would be disastrous: 'It would take the heart out of the British people. Their present resolute, heroic mood would give way to one of cynicism. They would feel that they had been sold a pup by their leaders. . . .' In a personal covering note, he wrote simply: '. . . I am *not* repeat not happy about the situation that is developing.' Cranborne himself was plainly not convinced by Churchill's case; and he thought there was still some uneasiness in the Commons. Harvey too, picking up impressions of the debate, wrote that there had been 'extreme disquiet' about Darlan's continuing to hold power in North Africa.[15]

Outside the House, the press was less quenched than Churchill indicated. Concern over the Darlan affair came in waves. The first wave was partially stilled by Roosevelt's statement on 17 November; but then another wave built up, which had to be calmed by the secret session. Disquiet began to develop again almost at once. On 14 December the *Manchester Guardian* noted in a leading article that Darlan's forces in North Africa were being used more to defend the Vichy system there than to fight the Germans. On the 16th the *Daily Mirror* put on its front page a report from de Gaulle's headquarters that Darlan was still holding 25,000 political prisoners in North Africa, all opponents of the Vichy regime. On 16 December Darlan declared at a press conference his intention to save French Africa, help to free France, and then retire to private life. (In the Foreign Office, Strang commented bitterly that this statement had been dictated by Roosevelt and was sponsored by him, without consultation with the British. 'The Americans are quite determined to go ahead on their own lines in North Africa.')[16] The BBC's midnight news on 16/17 December reported Darlan's remarks, and followed them at once with comments by a Fighting French spokesman, who declared that Darlan's real intention was to impose his dictatorship on the French people with the aid of an army from North Africa. The Admiral's offer of an amnesty for political prisoners, made during the press conference, was dismissed with contempt; patriotic Frenchmen did not accept amnesty from traitors. The American Admiral Stark, who heard the bulletin, told a Foreign Office official the next day that 'It came over pretty bum'. The official explained that British feeling was 'by no means favourable to Admiral Darlan', and the government had to take this into account in arranging for the news and comment put out by the BBC.[17] Press comment made clear that there was a general welcome for Darlan's intention to retire into private life, with equally general scepticism about the time he would take to do so.[18]

Once again, Darlan's own statements had revived anxiety about his position, and about the morality (or even the expediency) of co-operating with him. On this occasion, the press and radio appear to have found less of

15 Harvey, *War Diaries*, p. 198, cf. British Library, Add. Mss., 53689, entry for 11 Dec. 1942; FO 954/16A, Cranborne to Eden, 11 Dec. 1942, and attached memo.

16 FO 954/16A, minute by Strang, 16 Dec. 1942.

17 Text of BBC news, midnight, 16/17 Dec. 1942, BBC Written Archives; FO 371/32148, Z10595/8325/17, note by Peake of conversation with Stark, 17 Dec. 1942.

18 For example, *Yorkshire Post*, *Daily Telegraph*, *Manchester Guardian*, *The Times*, 17 Dec. 1942; *Spectator*, 18 Dec.

an echo in the country at large. The Home Intelligence report for the week of 15–22 December noted a decrease in the amount of comment about the Darlan affair, together with some increase in the proportion of those who were willing to accept the position. These changes may have owed something to Churchill's intervention, but doubtless also something to the passage of time and the approach of Christmas. In any case, Gallup Poll evidence from December 1942 and February 1943 showed only limited support for the arrangements with Darlan, and considerable disapproval.

December 1942.
Do you approve of Admiral Darlan becoming Head of the Government in French North Africa?
Approve 18%   Disapprove 51%   Don't Know 31%
February 1943.
Do you approve of the Allies working with men who have collaborated with the Axis?
Approve 18%   Disapprove 62%   Don't Know 20%[19]

The secret session had some effect in calming opinion; but that effect was far from complete, and there were signs that another wave of anxiety and criticism was building up. No-one can say how this would have developed, because on Christmas Eve 1942 Darlan was assassinated. This was the only war news to make much impact on the British public over the holiday period: and it was received with relief as the best way out of an unpleasant situation. People seem to have felt that they ought not to approve of assassination, but Home Intelligence reported that 'the majority are inclined to make an exception in this case'.[20]

A number of reflections are prompted by these events. It is clear that public opinion, in all its various manifestations, was much concerned over the Darlan affair. Parliament, pressure groups, the press and the public at large were all involved. It distracted a good deal of attention from spectacular military events involving British forces (the pursuit of Rommel after El Alamein, the Tunisian campaign); and Home Intelligence reported that in the week of 8–15 December it appeared to have supplanted the Beveridge report, published at the beginning of the month, as the main topic of public discussion.[21] The general tone of public comment was moral and ideological; in favour of decent conduct and loyalty to one's friends (especially de Gaulle), and against compromise with fascists and collaborators. The episode brought out in concentrated form the belief that the war was not simply a conflict between states, to be conducted in terms of power politics and military expediency, but involved also ideals and loyalties which cut across state boundaries. (In this aspect, the contrast with the treatment of Katyn is very marked.)

In the face of such widespread public concern, what role was played by

[19] INF 1/292, HI Report 116; Gallup Archive, BIPO Surveys 94 (Dec. 1942), 96 (Feb. 1943).
[20] INF 1/292, HI Reports 117, 118, 119.
[21] *Ibid.*, HI Report 115.

government influence on opinion? Censorship was certainly applied on a number of occasions. De Gaulle was prevented from using the BBC to broadcast 'exactly what he thinks of Darlan'.[22] Newsreel film showing Darlan in friendly association with Allied commanders in North Africa was held up until 17 December.[23] The main line of guidance for the press was that of military expediency: the arrangement with Darlan was necessary to help operations and save lives. Roosevelt's statement of 17 November ('a temporary expedient, justified solely by the stress of battle') became the staple defence. The government also claimed to be shielding the Americans: Eden assured Halifax on 10 December that he was being careful not to throw disproportionate blame on the Americans – for example, he made a point of referring to the Allied (not American) Commander-in-Chief in North Africa.[24] But the government was singularly unsuccessful in damping down press criticism of the Darlan deal, and especially of the Americans, who were commonly blamed for it. Even the BBC, which could not broadcast a word which had not been submitted to censorship, reflected much of the criticism, especially by the Fighting French.

One reason for this failure was the strength and widespread nature of the feelings which were aroused. On one occasion, when the American Ambassador complained about the publicity given by both press and radio to remarks by General Catroux, Eden telegraphed to Washington:

> Given the state of feeling in the country about Darlan, it would have been useless to persuade the press to play down the interview. The BBC Home Service were in fact advised not to make too much of it, but felt compelled to report it fairly fully, since they knew that it was bound to feature prominently in the press.[25]

This was true enough. However closely the government controlled the radio, the BBC would lose credibility if it ignored something which was on the front page of every newspaper; and the press, though normally amenable to government guidance, was during the Darlan episode very sympathetic to the Fighting French. With the best will in the world, the British government could not have damped down the anxiety over the Darlan deal, or the way in which criticism was directed against the Americans, without altering the whole way in which it conducted its censorship policy. The standing warning in D Notices about 'matters prejudicial to the good relations between ourselves and any . . . allied country' carried little weight.

All this was true; but it was not the whole story. It must be doubted whether the British government in practice showed the best will in the world, particularly with regard to criticism of the United States. Some government guidance was designed not so much to damp down indignation over the Darlan affair as to deflect it upon the Americans. When the BBC News

22 The words were Harvey's, *War Diaries*, p. 191, entry for 22 Nov. 1942.
23 British Paramount News, 1231, 17 Dec. 1942; Gaumont British News, 934, same date.
24 Eden to Halifax, 10 Dec. 1942, FO 371/32144, Z9765/8325/17.
25 Eden to Halifax, 18 Dec. 1942, FO 371/32145, Z9978/8325/17.

Controller attended his daily 'background guidance' meeting at the Ministry of Information on 14 November he noted the following:

> Darlan's appointment has been received with consternation . . . the official line here is that Eisenhower's political education began and ended on the prairies and that for the sake of a short-term and extremely hypothetical advantage he is running into much longer-term trouble. If you say 'any Frenchman' will do provided he can keep order in North Africa, then when we enter Metropolitan France Laval will do, and a Quisling will do in Norway.[26]

It was not only a matter of background briefing. In the House of Commons Eden drew attention to American responsibility in a way which belied his assurance about not throwing disproportionate blame on the Americans. 'It must be remembered that this expedition is under United States command. The 1st British Army is subordinated to the Allied Commander-in-Chief' (25 November). The matter was 'not entirely or even mainly a British subject. The United States are the principal party' (26 November).[27] The Prime Minister too gave, in secret session, the impression that North African policy was primarily an American responsibility. It is doubtless true that the government would in any case have been hard pressed to damp down public anxiety and criticism about the Darlan affair; but it is also true that, at least as regards criticism of the Americans, its attempts to do so were half-hearted.

There was, then, a substantial movement of public opinion, which the government did not suppress. How far was government policy affected by this movement? It is clear that the public outcry against the Darlan deal caused some tactical manoeuvring which would not otherwise have taken place. The secret session of the House of Commons was necessitated by the pressure of opinion, and Churchill's speech was a deliberate effort to change public opinion. The government was pushed into a number of shifts and discords in its relations with the Americans which the Prime Minister at least would have preferred to avoid. But the central elements in government policy were not affected. The deal with Darlan was not abrogated, nor did the British government press that it should be. The quisling admiral was not dismissed from his posts. In the short run, all the public agitation went for nothing: it was the assassin's bullet, not leading articles or questions in the House, that got rid of Darlan. This is not surprising. The main arguments for the deal with Darlan were military and strategic, and it is hard to see how the government could have sacrificed the immediate practical advantages to placate public opinion, however vociferous. But the short run was not everything; and in the long run public reaction to the Darlan deal produced some significant effects.

The most important was on the position of de Gaulle in Britain. The Darlan affair demonstrated beyond a peradventure that de Gaulle and the Fighting French commanded strong and widespread public support, and also that they had the skill to make full use of publicity. From June 1940 to the

---

[26] BBC Written Archives, 830/16: Background Notes by A. P. Ryan. These views were similar to those which Bracken put to Eden on 13 Nov. – FO 954/8A.

[27] *HC Deb.*, 5th series, vol. 385, cols. 730–1, 882–6.

end of 1942 de Gaulle and his followers had been the only Frenchmen fighting on Britain's side; and at the moment when that monopoly was broken and others emerged as rivals to de Gaulle his position in British public esteem was emphatically confirmed. This stood him in good stead when, in May and June 1943, Churchill (under Roosevelt's influence) tried to eliminate de Gaulle as a political force. The War Cabinet, Eden and the Foreign Office argued against this, despite the fact that de Gaulle was always difficult to work with and sometimes quite insufferable; and a powerful reason for their opposition was the general's standing with the British public. Harvey thought that the storm over Darlan would be as nothing to that which would be aroused by an attempt to break de Gaulle: 'We would not break him but make him. . . . What fools these Americans are.' And Cadogan wrote: 'I don't know what case there was against St John the Baptist, but public opinion was less formed – and less formidable in those days.'[28] Another argument, equally powerful, was the accumulating evidence that de Gaulle commanded widespread public support in France, especially among the Resistance groups – another manifestation of public opinion. De Gaulle could not be got rid of except at the cost of public reactions which were thought to be unacceptable; and it was the Darlan affair which made this clear.

There were also serious, though more diffuse, consequences for Anglo-American relations. The North African landings were the first great Anglo-American operation. In strategic terms they were a remarkable success; but in political terms they went sour as a result of the British public outcry against the Darlan deal. Public anger was directed (with some encouragement from the government) against the Americans; and the State Department, with Cordell Hull in the van, grew exasperated with the British public and the failure of the government to curb its outbursts. This was not the prime cause of the long and deep Anglo-American estrangement over France which ensued; but it was certainly the case that relations between the two countries on French affairs had been comparatively good until November 1942. They then got off on the wrong foot and never recovered; and a major cause of this first difficulty was the British public reaction to the Darlan deal. The deal itself was unlikely to cause a rift (the tacit agreement between Roosevelt and Churchill would have seen to that); but the public outcry did.

Other consequences followed, though growing less distinct, like ripples when a stone falls into a pool. That there should be no more Darlan deals, no more compromises with quislings or collaborators, was a cry raised at the end of 1942 and echoed many times later – when Italy changed sides, and during the liberation of western Europe. A warning had been given which could not be ignored; and the ripples persisted for a long time.

The main points of comparison between this examination of public opinion and the Darlan deal and our discussion of the Katyn affair lie in the reactions of public opinion and of government. Public opinion was much

---

[28] Harvey, *War Diaries*, pp. 260–1, entry for 21 May 1943; *Cadogan Diaries*, p. 537, entry for 18 June 1943.

more obviously stirred by the Darlan deal than it was to be by Katyn a few months later. There was open trouble in the House of Commons, though only on the part of a few critical MPs. The press was much more active, and more generally critical of government policy. Very noticeably, the basis of this criticism was moral. The Darlan deal was treated as a betrayal of the allied cause by coming to terms with a quisling. The arguments of power politics and strategic advantage tended to be brushed aside as of little importance in comparison with the moral damage being sustained. As we have noted before, this stands in marked contrast to the attitude of the majority of the press during the Katyn affair in April and May 1943, when the keynote was one of *realpolitik*. The main reason for this was presumably the overwhelming nature of the need for the Soviet alliance compared to the limited advantages conveyed by the Darlan deal, some of which were in any case not known to the press at the time. This aspect was certainly real; but it is also tempting to speculate as to whether most of the press allowed a greater moral latitude in dealings with the Soviet Union than in those with Darlan – or even with the United States.

When we turn from public opinion to government policy, the similarities with the Katyn affair (and also with the Warsaw Rising) are much stronger than the differences. The disturbance of public opinion over the Darlan deal was strong – much more so than over Katyn – but it was not allowed to deflect the course of government policy on the major issue. The Darlan deal was maintained as long as the admiral lived, although the government was pressed into a number of minor shifts and expedients in the pursuit of its main policy. This tends to reinforce the main argument of the book: that when the government's mind was made up on a major issue, public opinion was very unlikely to change it, though the government would probably adopt measures to damp down or divert public opinion. It is of some interest that, in the affair of Admiral Darlan, the government (including Churchill) was more willing to deflect public hostility against the United States than they ever were to do so against the Soviet Union. If this were generally true, it would raise some intriguing questions.

Bibliography

I **Primary Sources**

1 *Archive material*

Public Record Office, Kew
    War Cabinet: CAB 65, War Cabinet Minutes
                CAB 66, War Cabinet Papers
    Prime Ministers' Papers: PREM 3
    Foreign Office: FO 371, General diplomatic correspondence
              FO 800, Private Office papers
              FO 954, Avon papers
    Ministry of Information: INF 1 series
BBC Written Archives, Caversham Park, Reading
    Especially files on:
    Censorship
    Talks Policy
    Talks: Russia
    European News Directives and Special Directives
    Listener Research Reports.
Gallup Poll papers, Gallup Poll offices, 202 Finchley Road, London NW3
House of Lords Record Office
    Beaverbrook Papers
Mass-Observation Archive, University of Sussex
Polish Institute Archives, 20 Princes Gate, London, SW7 1PT
The Times Archive, *Times* Newspapers, 1 Virginia Street, London, E1 9XN

2 Published documentary collections

GENERAL SIKORSKI HISTORICAL INSTITUTE, *Documents on Polish–Soviet Relations, 1939–1945*, vol. I (London, 1961); vol. II (London, 1967)

KIMBALL, WARREN F. ed., *Churchill and Roosevelt: the complete correspondence* (3 vols., Princeton, 1984)

POLONSKY, ANTHONY, ed., *The Great Powers and the Polish Question* (London, 1976)

ROSS, GRAHAM, ed., *The Foreign office and the Kremlin: British Documents on Anglo-Soviet Relations, 1941–45* (Cambridge, 1984)

3 Newspapers and periodicals

Catholic Herald
Catholic Times
Daily Express
Daily Herald
Daily Mail
Daily Mirror
Daily Telegraph
Daily Worker
The Economist
Glasgow Herald
The Listener
Manchester Guardian
New Statesman and Nation
News Chronicle
The Nineteenth Century and After
The Observer
The Scotsman
Soviet War News
The Spectator
Sunday Express
Sunday Times
The Tablet
The Times
Tribune

4 Diaries And Memoirs

ARMSTRONG, WILLIAM, ed., *With Malice Toward None. A War Diary by Cecil H. King* (London, 1970).

BARMAN, THOMAS, *Diplomatic Correspondent* (London, 1968).

CHANNON, HENRY, *Chips: The Diaries of Sir Henry Channon* (London, 1967).

CHURCHILL, WINSTON S., *The Second World War* (6 volumes, London, 1948–1954).

COLVILLE, JOHN, *The Fringes of Power: Downing Street Diaries 1939–1955* (London, 1985).

COOPER, ALFRED DUFF (Lord Norwich), *Old Men Forget* (London, 1957).
DILKS, DAVID, ed., *The Diaries of Sir Alexander Cadogan, 1938–1945* (London, 1971).
HARVEY, JOHN, ed., *The War Diaries of Oliver Harvey, 1941–1945* (London, 1978).
McDONALD, IVERACH, *A Man of the Times* (London, 1976).
MAISKY, IVAN, *Memoirs of a Soviet Ambassador: The War, 1939–43* (London, 1967).
NICOLSON, NIGEL, ed., *Harold Nicolson: Diaries and Letters, 1939–1945* (London, 1970).
RACZYNSKI, EDWARD, *In Allied London* (London, 1962).
STUART, CAMPBELL, *Secrets of Crewe House: The Story of a Famous Campaign* (London, 1920).
THOMSON, GEORGE P., *Blue Pencil Admiral. The Inside Story of the Press Censorship* (London, 1947).
WILLIAMS, FRANCIS, *Nothing so Strange: An Autobiography* (London, 1970).

5 *Interviews*

The late Lord Taylor of Harlow
The late Mr Philip Zec
M. Josef Czapski

6 *Parliamentary debates*

HANSARD, *House of Commons Debates*, 5th series

II. Secondary sources

1 *Books*

ADDISON, PAUL, *The Road to 1945* (London, 1977).
ALDGATE, A., *Cinema and History: British Newsreels and the Spanish Civil War* (London, 1979).
ATTLEE, C. R., GREENWOOD, ARTHUR, and others, *Labour's Aims in War and Peace* (London, 1940).
BALFOUR, MICHAEL, *Propaganda in War 1939–1945* (London, 1979).
BARKER, ELISABETH, *Churchill and Eden at War* (London, 1978).
BARNETT, CORELLI, *The Collapse of British Power* (London, 1972).
BEAUMONT, JOAN, *Comrades in Arms: British Aid to Russia, 1941–1945* (London, 1980).
BELL, P. M. H. and WHITE, RALPH, *Images of the Soviet Union at War* (Inter-University History Film Consortium, Studies in Film No. 8, London, 1990: film with accompanying booklet).
BOYLE, ANDREW, *Poor Dear Brendan* (London, 1975) [Brendan Bracken].
BRIGGS, ASA, *History of Broadcasting in the United Kingdom*, vol. III, *The War of Words* (London, 1970).

BULLOCK, ALAN (Lord Bullock), *Ernest Bevin*, vol. I, *Trade Union Leader* (London, 1960), vol. II, *Minister of Labour* (London, 1967).

CALDER, ANGUS, *The People's War: Britain 1939–1945* (London, second ed., 1971).

CANTRIL, HADLEY, *Public Opinion, 1935–1946* (Princeton, 1951).

CAUTE, DAVID, *The Fellow-Travellers* (London, 1973).

CIECHANOWSKI, JAN, *The Warsaw Rising of 1944* (London, 1974).

COCKETT, R., *Chamberlain, Appeasement and the Manipulation of the Press* (London, 1989).

COOKE, COLIN, *The Life of Sir Richard Stafford Cripps* (London, 1957).

CRAVEN, W. F., and CATE, J. L., *The Army Air Forces in World War II*, vol. III (Chicago, 1951).

CRUICKSHANK, CHARLES, *The Fourth Arm: Psychological Warfare 1938–1946* (London, 1977).

DAVIES, NORMAN, *God's Playground: A History of Poland*, vol. II (London, 1981).

ERICKSON, JOHN, *The Road to Stalingrad* (London, 1975); *The Road to Berlin* (London, 1983).

ESTORICK, ERIC, *Stafford Cripps* (London, 1949).

FITZGIBBON, LOUIS, *Katyn Massacre* (London, 1977).

FOOT, M. R. D., *SOE: An Outline History of the Special Operations Executive* (London, 1984).

GANNON, F. R., *The British Press and Germany, 1936–1939* (Oxford, 1971).

GARLINSKI, JOZEF, *Poland in the Second World War* (London, 1985).

GILBERT, MARTIN, *Winston S. Churchill*, vol. V, *1922–1939* (London, 1976); vol. VI, *Finest Hour, 1939–1941* (London, 1983); vol. VII, *The Road to Victory* (London, 1986).

GORODETSKY, GABRIEL, *Stafford Cripps' Mission to Moscow, 1940–42* (Cambridge, 1984).

GRIFFITHS, RICHARD, *Fellow Travellers of the Right: British Enthusiasts for Nazi Germany, 1933–1939* (Oxford, 1983).

HARRISSON, TOM, *Living through the Blitz* (London, 1978).

HYAMS, EDWARD, *The New Statesman. The History of the First Fifty Years, 1913–1963* (London, 1963).

JONES, BILL, *The Russia Complex: The British Labour Party and the Soviet Union* (Manchester, 1977).

KECEWICZ, GEORG V., *Great Britain, the Soviet Union and the Polish Government in Exile* (The Hague, 1979).

KERSHAW, IAN, *Popular Opinion and Political Dissent in the Third Reich: Bavaria, 1933–1945* (Oxford, 1983).

KITCHEN, MARTIN, *British Policy towards the Soviet Union during the Second World War* (London, 1986).

LUKACS, JOHN, *The Last European War, September 1939–December 1941* (London, 1977).

McDONALD, IVERACH, *The History of The Times*, vol. V, *Struggles in War and Peace 1939–1966* (London, 1984).

McLACHLAN, DONALD, *In the Chair: Barrington-Ward of The Times* (London, 1971).

McLAINE, IAN, *Ministry of Morale: Home Front Morale and the Ministry of Information in World War II* (London, 1979).

MASTNY, VOJTECH, *Russia's Road to the Cold War: Diplomacy, Warfare and the Politics of Communism, 1941–1945* (New York, 1979).

MINISTRY OF INFORMATION, *The Press in Wartime* (London, 1944).

NORTHEDGE, F. S. and WELLS, A., *Britain and Soviet Communism: The Impact of a Revolution* (London, 1982).

PRONAY, NICHOLAS, and SPRING, D. W., eds., *Propaganda, Politics and Film, 1918–1945* (London, 1982).

ROLL, CHARLES W. and CANTRILL, ALBERT H. *Polls: Their Use and Misuse in Politics* (Cabin John, Maryland, 1980).

SEYMOUR–URE, COLIN, *The Press, Politics and the Public* (London, 1961).

SILVEY, ROBERT, *Who's Listening? The Story of BBC Audience Research* (London, 1974).

TAYLOR, A. J. P. *Beaverbrook* (London, 1972).

TAYLOR, PHILIP M., *The Projection of Britain: British Overseas Publicity and Propaganda, 1919–1939* (Cambridge, 1981).

TOLSTOY, NICOLAI, *Stalin's Secret War* (London, 1981).

ULAM, ADAM B. *Stalin* (London, 1974).

WALEY, DANIEL, *British Public Opinion and the Abyssinian War* (London, 1975).

WEST, W. J., ed., *Orwell: The War Broadcasts* (London, 1985).

WOOD, NEAL, *Communism and British Intellectuals* (London, 1959).

YOUNG, KENNETH, *Churchill and Beaverbrook. A Study in Friendship and Politics* (London, 1966).

ZAWODNY, J. K. *Death in the Forest: The Story of the Katyn Forest Massacre* (London, 1971).

ZAWODNY, J. K., *Nothing but Honour: The Story of the Warsaw Uprising, 1944* (London, 1978).

2 Articles

FOSTER, ALAN, 'The Times and Appeasement: The Second Phase'. In LAQUEUR, WALTER, ed., *The Second World War: Essays in Military and Political History* (London, 1982).

GORODETSKY, GABRIEL, 'The Origins of the Cold War: Stalin, Churchill and the Formation of the Grand Alliance', *Russian Review*, vol. 47, 1988.

HARRISSON, TOM, 'What is Public Opinion?', *Political Quarterly*, vol. XI, 1940.

HOWARD, MICHAEL, 'Total War in the Twentieth Century: Participation and Consensus in the Second World War' in BOND, BRIAN, and ROY, IAN, eds., *War and Society: A Yearbook of Military History* (London, 1975).

LABEDZ, LEOPOLD, 'Alexander Werth', in *Survey*, vol. 30, Nos. 1–2, March 1988.

LANGER, J. D., 'The Harriman–Beaverbrook Mission and the Debate over Unconditional Aid for the Soviet Union, 1941', In LAQUEUR, WALTER, ed., *The Second World War* (London, 1982).

PRONAY, NICHOLAS, 'The News Media at War', in PRONAY, NICHOLAS, and

SPRING, D. W., ed., *Propaganda, Politics and Film, 1918–1945* (London, 1982).

REYNOLDS, DAVID, 'The Churchill Government and the Black American Troops in Britain during World War II', *Transactions of the Royal Historical Society*, 5th series, 35, 1985.

SPRING, DEREK, 'Soviet Newsreel and the Great Patriotic War', in PRONAY, NICHOLAS, and SPRING, D. W., eds., *Propaganda, Politics and Film, 1918–1945* (London, 1982).

STRANG, LORD, 'Foreign Policy in Wartime', in DILKS, DAVID, ed., *Retreat from Power*, vol. II (London, 1981).

TAYLOR, PHILIP, 'Censorship in Britain in the Second World War: An Overview', in *Too Mighty to be Free: Censorship and the Press in Britain and the Netherlands* (Zutphen, 1988).

Index

209